W9-AWW-939

The Star Dressing Room

The Star Dressing Room

Portrait of an Actor

Alan Shayne

Rand-Smith Books

Copyright © 2023 by Alan Shayne

All rights reserved. No part of this book may be reproduced in any manner whatsoever without written permission except in the case of brief quotations embodied in critical articles and reviews.

First Printing, 2023

Print ISBN: 978-1-950544-38-7
Digital ISBN: 978-1-950544-39-4

Registered with the Library of Congress

Some names and identifying details have been changed to protect the privacy of individuals. no part of this book may be copied or duplicated except with the prior written permission of the author or publisher. Small excerpts may be used for review or media purposes with proper credit given.

All attempts have been made to provide accurate information. The publisher is not liable for typographical errors, content mistakes, inaccuracies, or omissions related to the information in this book.

Cover design and artwork courtesy of Norman Sunshine

Rand-Smith Publishing
www.Rand-Smith.com
USA

CONTENTS

1   1

2   13

3   27

4   35

5   47

6   54

7   66

8   73

9   82

10   89

11   93

12   97

13   102

CONTENTS

14 ▎ 106

15 ▎ 115

16 ▎ 120

17 ▎ 124

18 ▎ 132

19 ▎ 137

20 ▎ 142

21 ▎ 147

22 ▎ 153

23 ▎ 157

24 ▎ 163

25 ▎ 168

26 ▎ 173

27 ▎ 181

28 ▎ 186

29 ▎ 191

30 ▎ 199

CONTENTS

31 | 204

32 | 211

33 | 215

34 | 219

35 | 223

36 | 231

37 | 237

38 | 242

39 | 250

40 | 256

41 | 261

42 | 268

43 | 273

44 | 278

45 | 287

46 | 290

47 | 294

CONTENTS

48 ┃ 298

49 ┃ 307

50 ┃ 312

51 ┃ 318

52 ┃ 324

53 ┃ 329

54 ┃ 335

55 ┃ 338

56 ┃ 342

Epilogue 350

Alan

Whatever possessed me to think that I was going to be a star on Broadway? I was 17 years old, I had no money, no training, my parents were dead set against my being in show business, and I had just been fired from my first acting job in a touring company of *Junior Miss*. Yet here I was on my way to New York.

I had just given my last performance in Philadelphia, packed up my makeup kit, grabbed my suitcase, and headed for the train. An actor in the company, Louis, who'd become my good friend, had taken me into the city a few days before to show me how to make the rounds of agent's offices, and help me find a furnished room I could afford. I had managed to save a few dollars from my salary in the play, but I knew that wouldn't last very long. It was Louis who had assured me that since so many actors were being drafted into the army, I could get a job immediately. And I was now a member of Actor's Equity, a requirement to get into a Broadway play.

I wanted to believe Louis, but in the back of my head I kept remembering what Guerita, an actress who was in the same play, had said to me: "If you insist on going to New York, have enough money saved up, because it'll take you five years to get a Broadway show." I wonder if I'd known what was going to happen, would I have stayed on the train, not gotten off at New York and just gone home to Boston? But, of course, I couldn't go home and let everyone know that I was a failure.

***

It was all such a miracle the way things had happened, that is except for the end when I got fired. Right after graduating high school, I saw an ad in *The Boston Globe* for actors in a summer theater in nearby Rockport. It was a few months after Pearl Harbor and most men who were old enough were either enlisting or they were being drafted. I was barely 16, but I managed to get a job at the theater playing middle-aged men with the help of dark makeup under my eyes and gray streaks in my hair. It taught me a lot and I even got good reviews. I had persuaded my parents to let me have a year off before college.

I had skipped a grade so I was younger than all the other kids I knew. I did some Shakespeare plays with local theater groups, got some more good reviews, and made up my mind to be an actor. I heard that radio stations were also having trouble losing their announcers to the war effort, so I auditioned and got a job at WMEX, reading the news and spinning records on the music shows. It was there that the real miracle happened. I had a show where I interviewed actors who were appearing in touring plays in Boston. Two actors from *Junior Miss*, an older woman Guerita, who played the maid and Louis, who played the romantic interest, turned up on my schedule. They were open, charming, and even stayed after my show to chat. I confessed I wanted to go to New York to be an actor, and they sympathized but told me how difficult it would be.

Then, a few days later, Louis called to say an actor was leaving the show and he and Guerita had gotten me an audition with the stage manager. There was a pass for me for the play that night and I went to see it. I was horrified. The role I was to read for was a loud, boorish football player who had to be totally disgusting. I was thin as a rail with a high pompadour and looked like I could only play a sensitive poet or a love sick teenager. I didn't see how I could possibly get the job, but Guerita stole the costume that the actor wore from the wardrobe room, dressed me up in the camel-hair coat and bright yellow scarf and told me to yell since the stage manager was hard of hearing. He also turned out to be a bit of a drunk so when he saw me on the dark stage In the costume, I looked like the character in the play. He also was able to hear me (you could have heard me in Hoboken). I got the job.

There was a week's hiatus for the company, and I was to open on Christmas Day in Hartford. Getting my parents to allow me to go into the show was another matter. They had to sign the contract because of my age. All I heard was "those people do nothing but smoke and drink and worse." Another miracle happened. I was so upset that I became ill. My father, who was a hypochondriac vegetarian, finally gave in, afraid that I would get even sicker if they didn't allow me to go. I opened in *Junior Miss* with a 101 temperature, not really sure what I was doing, but I yelled loudly and the audience applauded when I exited. I spent the next weeks either in bed or in a doctor's office having my throat painted. The day came when someone from the New York office saw the play and was appalled at how wrong I was for the role. My days as a football player were over.

Guerita had left the show suddenly to have an operation, but Louis was great. He had suggested that we room together to save money and was so solicitous of my health. I wouldn't have been able to get through it all without him. But the night before I left the show, he surprised me by saying that he wanted to tell me something he had held back because I was so ill. He was in love with me. I was totally surprised. We had never discussed our personal lives, and I was still suffering from my first and only relationship with an older man that had ended miserably. I didn't know how to react. The last thing on my mind was a love affair with Louis. I just stared at him trying to think of what to say. He'd been such a good friend and taken care of me, but I didn't love him. However, Louis saved what could have been an unpleasant moment.

"I know you don't love me," he said, "but hopefully one day you will. I've got to tour with the play for six more months. If we could just write to each other and speak on the phone now and them, maybe we could grow together and when I get back to New York, even live together."

"Oh Louis," I replied, "You know how much I like you. It's just hard for me to feel anything at this point. All I can think about is New York and what's going to happen there. But if I cared for anyone, it would be you. You're my best friend so let's just wait and see." I was off the hook.

The furnished room on a depressing block in Greenwich Village turned out to be unbearable and as cold as the winter outside. The furnace gave off the smell of heat without its warmth. Through a fluke, I read an ad in *Show Business* (a weekly paper that told actors where to go to look for work) that there was an inexpensive room for rent uptown in an elevator building, and I went to check it out. A pianist, who lived next door to it, owned what looked like a large storage room with a tiny bath and kitchen. Since he practiced all day, he had trouble getting anyone to take the place. No one could stand the noise. I didn't care. It was warm and away from the Village where I'd been so depressed.

Looking for acting jobs was only uptown so I got back downtown just to sleep and it was dark and cold. I got the room for $35 a month, much more than the $16 that I was paying, but I had to have it. Besides, I was sure it was a matter of time before I'd get a role in a play. With the help of Madeline and Marie, two friends of Louis' he had introduced me to, I got some of their stored furniture and fixed the place up. It even had a narrow balcony and I could walk out onto it in the freezing weather and look at the tall apartment buildings. For a moment I was living in the penthouse of my dreams and was a success in New York. Then I would rush back inside to the warmth of my tiny room. At least it was mine and an oasis from the misery of looking for work. The pianist had told me that the great Gertrude Lawrence lived in an apartment across the way. I couldn't wait to tell Louis if he called one of these nights. She was his favorite musical-comedy star.

Finding work was not as easy as Louis had said it was going to be. Although many men were being drafted in 1943, theater jobs were hard to come by. There was no television that would one day create myriad opportunities for actors, and not even off-Broadway. The only possibilities were in plays, usually with small casts chosen by directors who already knew the actors they wanted. Musicals did have big casts, but I couldn't sing or dance. I had even been asked not to sing at my high school graduation because I was so off key, and I dragged some of the other singers with me. Nevertheless, I set off each day to make the rounds of agents and producers' offices.

February in New York is bitter cold, windy, and often snowy. My coat was a thin tweed suitable for spring that my mother had bought at the yearly Filene's sale where everything was marked down to $11. Louis had told me to always dress my best since, in those days, jeans were looked down on and actors were supposed to be elegant. I had some decent dress shoes, but they had thin soles and rubbers, I was afraid, would make me look like a vagrant. So I spent the days getting colder and colder and wetter and wetter, The only relief was when I got to the warmth of an office, but I had to leave as soon as the girl at her window in the wall looked up from her phone or stenographer's pad and said, "Nothing today."

Sometimes, someone would greet me with, "You're too old for what they're looking for," or "The role calls for someone much younger than you." My only contact with the world came from *Show Business*, which I read religiously to check out the places I had planned to go. But very soon I discovered that the jobs listed in the paper were either incorrect or just old news of roles that had already been filled. I spent days without anyone speaking to me. There were actors in the offices looking for work, as I was, but they were all competitive and only spoke to people they knew. I was sure they would never give me a tip on where I could go to get a job.

One day, going through my list of agents, I went to one office where the secretary cut me off before I even opened my mouth. "I'm too busy now," she said. "Wait until I'm free." I was so excited that she hadn't said the usual, "Nothing today," that I rushed over and sat on a bench and waited expectantly for her to finish what she was doing. Actors kept coming in and she sent them away, but she said nothing to me. I didn't want to annoy her so I just sat quietly and waited for what she was going to tell me about work.

After several hours, I finally went up to the window. "I don't want to disturb you," I said, "but you told me to wait."

The girl looked up at me as if she'd never seen me before. "There's nothing for you," she said.

"But you told me to wait," I said sounding like the little boy I'd been when my father took back the train that he'd gotten me for Christmas.

"Nothing today," she said as she closed the opening in the glass window and went back to her work.

I did actually get a job. Well, not a part in a play but a walk-on in *Janie*. At the end of the second act, dozens of soldiers walked into Janie's home for a party she'd invited them to. They didn't have to do anything, just walk in laughing and making noise as the curtain fell. I can't even say that it was my talent that got me paid $1 for each performance. I happened to fit the costume of a boy who had just been drafted. Several of the boys did actually speak to me, and I began to see more of Louis' two friends, Madeline and Marie, so I didn't feel so isolated.

The girls had just graduated Smith College so I felt nervous about my lack of education, but they quickly put me at my ease. Madeline was tall and awkward with a small head for such a big frame. She had a plain face made even less attractive by old-fashioned steel-rimmed glasses. Marie had enormous China blue eyes, beautiful skin, and incisors that slightly crossed each other. Her thin brown hair was gathered in a style that seemed to be copied from the print above the sofa. She was effusive while Madeline was withdrawn. Sometimes a girl named Jacqueline ("Jackie") would be with them. She had also gone to Smith. She always made me uncomfortable, staring at me with her piercing eyes. She was great-looking, but she made me feel she was about to stick a pin in me and add me to her butterfly collection.

I listened as the three talked of their college days and their plans for the future. Madeline wanted to be a writer, Marie an actress, and Jackie just wanted to "make it big" as she said several times. The girls served dinner every night for some of their actor and writer friends. You just had to chip in whatever the food amounted to when it was divided by the number of people who were there. I could only go when I could afford to splurge. My budget allowed me 10 cents for a Nedicks breakfast of a glass of orange drink, a whole-wheat doughnut, and a cup of coffee. For dinner, 20 cents got me a small ramekin dish with frankfurters and beans at the Automat. I had to keep part of my $8 a week from the play for rent and my mother mailed me a $10 bill every once in a while.

It was so cold that I began to dream of owning a heavy coat with a fur collar and sometimes I stood in front of Saks Fifth Avenue and looked at one in the window. In addition to being cold and often wet, I had no idea how to find work. I couldn't go on living on practically nothing, but I was getting nowhere making the rounds of agents and producers' offices. It just seemed to pass the time and make me feel that I was doing something, but at the end of every day, I had nothing to show for all the walking and waiting that I did. I thought that there had to be a key to unlock the mystery of getting work as an actor, but I wasn't finding it.

The only relief was getting back to my rented "penthouse," being greeted by the doorman and going up in the elevator as if I were on my way to a grand apartment. Then I would spend the hours before bed sitting in my only chair under a rickety floor lamp reading Stanislavsky's *My Life In Art* that Louis had given me as a closing night present. I tried desperately to understand "The Method" that the actor-director talked about in the book, but it was way over my head. I would go to sleep thinking of the next day and hearing over and over "we're not looking for anyone in your age category" or "no casting."

One of the actors who I walked on with in *Janie* told me I could volunteer at The Stage Door Canteen and get to meet important actors and producers, so I went there and was immediately given a job as a bus boy. I felt as if I didn't belong and any minute, they'd find out I'd been fired from a play and tell me to get out. But they didn't so I began working there before going to the theater. I was so shy that I just kept my head down and went about my work. I never saw any important people, but I wouldn't have recognized them if they were there. The best thing about the experience was that I was around music and laughter, and I did get to eat leftover food that made up for a lot of what was missing from my meager diet.

One day I walked into the office of Jane Broder, one of the most important agents in the business. I never expected to see her, but I figured I might as well put my name on her list, if she had one. It was lunchtime and there was no one at her secretary's desk. The door was open to an inner office, and I heard a voice calling out, "Who's there?"

I felt like I'd been caught doing something wrong and I replied furtively, "Oh, it's just an actor. I wanted to register with you. But I'm leaving."

A woman's deep voice replied, "Well come in here so I can have a look at you!"

I couldn't believe my luck to have an interview with such an important person. Maybe there was some point to making the rounds after all. I walked into a cozy, paneled room with many old-fashioned windows facing Times Square. Behind a huge desk was a stout woman with a weathered face and grayish hair who looked like one of my mother's mahjongg partners.

"What's your name?" she said in a warm down to earth way. I told her and she peered at me as if she were examining an insect. "I know you," she said. "Have we ever met?"

"No, Miss Broder, I've been on the road in a play."

"Wait a minute," she said. "What was the play?"

"*Junior Miss,*" I replied.

"Oh my god," she shouted, "I saw you. You were the football player."

"Yes," I said getting excited.

"You were terrible!" she said and all the warmth had gone from her voice. "How could you give such an awful performance? You were so wrong for the part, but you made it even worse by yelling all the time. No wonder you were fired."

I was devastated. I didn't know what to say. I blurted out something about knowing I was wrong but wanting to be an actor.

"I don't care what you wanted," she said. "You didn't show one iota of talent. I certainly would never recommend you for anything. Now please leave. Go back where you came from or learn how to act. And don't come here again."

I mumbled an automatic thank you and turned and left. I went back to my room. I couldn't take anymore that day. I lay on the narrow studio couch and tried to sleep, but all I could think of was the woman saying I had no talent. I kept going over and over what people had said about my acting. It had always been so positive, but maybe they were just making me feel good.

Yet Elliot Norton, the Drama Critic of the *Boston Globe* had said I should be an actor when I won Prize Speaking, and he was considered one of the most important critics in the country. And the critic in Rockport who singled me out said I'd have a great career. Why would they say those things? I knew I hadn't been right for the part in *Junior Miss,* but the kids in the show kept saying how good I was getting and that I was better than the boy who left. But he was a hunk and at least looked like a football player. I didn't.

I thought of what I was reading in *My Life In Art*. Stanislavsky said you had to find something of yourself in a part and as hard as I tried, I just couldn't. I wasn't gross and blustering and I never would have smeared a partially eaten chocolate candy on my spanking-clean camel-hair coat, like the character did. I was a polite, nice boy from Brookline who would never smack a man on the back and almost knock him over to say hello, another thing the character had to do.

But maybe, if I did have talent, I would have found a way to make it work. I felt sick, almost like I did when I was caught stealing at the 5 and 10 when I was a kid. It had taken me almost a year before I could walk down the street without thinking that the whole town knew I was a crook. Now, I kept wondering if the agent would tell everyone I had no talent and whatever office I went into, they would look at me and know I was no good.

Finally, I got up and put on my bathrobe. Maybe if I read some of the Stanislavsky, I'd get sleepy. I walked over to the little table Marie and Madeline had lent me where I kept the few books that I had brought with me. Lying on top was a note that I'd been too upset to see when I walked in. It was from my landlord. I had an extension of his phone and he was kind enough to take messages for me knowing I was looking for work. The call had been from Louis and he had left a number to phone him collect after his show. He knew he couldn't call me or it would disturb the landlord. I looked at my watch. It wasn't too late so I called long distance. The hotel connected me to Louis' room and he accepted the call.

"Hello," he said. "I'd given up waiting for you."

"I'm sorry, I just found the note that you called."

Louis replied, "I was just dropping off to sleep so I'm a little groggy."

"Is something wrong?" I asked.

"No," Louis replied, "as a matter of fact everything is better than it's ever been."

I wanted to tell him the good news about getting the penthouse, but I waited to see if he would say something first. There was silence for a moment and I thought we were cut off. "Hello," I said.

"I'm here," Louis answered. I heard him take a deep breath and then he said, "I gave my notice tonight. I'm leaving the show."

"Louis!" I said.

"I can't be away from you any longer." He sounded as if he were almost crying. "I'm not going on tour for six months without seeing you unless you tell me that you don't want me to come back."

I felt embarrassed to talk this way on the phone. I was sure someone was listening in. "Can't you come into New York on the weekend so we can discuss it?" I asked.

"If you don't want me," Louis said, "just say so."

"No, of course I do," I answered, "but your career."

"I'll get a job in New York," Louis said. "There may even be a replacement in the company there of *Junior Miss*."

I didn't know what to say and then I blurted out, "I just hope you won't blame me if you don't get anything."

"Don't be silly," he said, "we'll be together and that's the important thing,"

I felt I had to say something, but all I could manage was "Yes."

"I had to give them four weeks' notice," he said, "but it's not forever."

After I hung up, I walked around the room looking at it as if I were Louis seeing it for the first time. It wasn't much, but the drapes and furniture that Madeline and Marie had lent me made it seem cozy and warm. It looked so much better than when I had first seen it. I wondered what Louis would think of it. In just a short time it had become my home, the first place in my whole life that was all my own. But now, with Louis, I would be sharing a space again as I had with my brother and once even with my grandmother. *At least for a while*, I thought, *this will still be mine.*

In the weeks before Louis arrived, I went back and forth in my mind trying to decide what to do. I owed so much to Louis, but I just didn't love him. I knew what real love was. I'd experienced it with an older man, but he went into the army and stopped contacting me. He always said that the age difference made it impossible for us to have a lasting relationship, but I know I could have been with him forever. All I wanted was to be with one person and even though Louis was handsome and bright and funny, he just wasn't the one. What should I do? If I refused to live with him, would he do something terrible to himself? He had given up his job for me. That was a pretty strong indication of what his feelings were.

Would he want me to have sex with him? I'm sure he would, but for me sex was about love. I'd refused to have sex with an actor at the summer stock theater because I didn't love him. Actually, I didn't like him at all and I do like Louis. He's my best friend. How can I hurt him by refusing to live with him? And then, of course, there's the money. We'd be sharing everything and my life would be so much easier. I'd been so lonely. Now I'd have someone to be with.

I decided to make a list of the good and the bad of our living together. I always wrote down everything when I was trying to come to a decision. When I finished, I studied it for a short time. One column was so much longer than the other.

There was no question of what I would decide.

2

Louis

In the four weeks of March while Louis was finishing off his commitment to *Junior Miss*, I wrote two letters to my mother. The first was at the beginning of the month.

I had the most amazing luck, I wrote. *A very important agent gave me a reading today and said I have real talent and I'm a fine actor. He thinks he can put me up for three parts and out of that number, there ought to be one that is just right. I also have a chance to be in* The Eve of St. Mark. *It's a hit show...so you see things are turning out just the way we hoped they would. I know you want me to come home to Brookline for a while but now that I've got my irons in the fire, I couldn't possibly. I've never felt better and I know I'll succeed. Keep your faith in me. I'm going to get something and I won't come home until I do.*

Toward the end of the month, all my leads had fizzled. I'd also had a bad toothache that led to my losing a tooth on the side of my mouth. I had to learn how to smile by practicing in the mirror so I wouldn't show the gap. I had nowhere near the money to have it replaced. I didn't mention it when I wrote to my mother again:

I've put off writing this letter hoping that something would turn up and I could write to tell you of a beautiful gift I was sending you for your anniversary, but no such luck! For the first time since I was a little boy, March 23rd is here and I can't even afford to send you an anniversary card. However, I was able to buy a three-cent stamp and so this letter will have to do. I hoped I could get a job so that I could come up to Brookline tomorrow, but you can't do much on practically nothing a week.

Now I suppose that you want to know all that's happened; the best news has nothing to do with the stage. Today I finally decided after six weeks in New York that I would see if I could get an announcing job. I went to about 20 radio stations and they all will arrange auditions for me. One man at WOV said I had a beautiful voice and made an appointment with me for next week. This is quite amazing as they usually keep you waiting two or three months. It sounds good but I've been disappointed so many times, I can't get excited about anything anymore...There's hope anyway.

Saturday morning, I read for the authors of Life With Father *for the part of Clarence. They liked me very much but said I was 23 or 24 on stage and the part calls for a boy 17. I guess it's almost hopeless. I'm either too old or too young for everything. But don't think I've given up!!! Please send me $10 or cash one of the war bonds I sent you from my* Junior Miss *salary and my new ration book – I need it to get into restaurants. Hope you have the happiest of anniversaries.*

When Louis arrived and moved in with me, the penthouse suddenly seemed very small. We couldn't afford to buy a larger bed and the pianist was not about to get one for us. He wasn't too happy having somebody else in the room, but he put up with it. We squeezed into the studio couch and were very uncomfortable. For the first time in my life, I had felt that I had my own place, but now I was back to sharing it with someone. The good part was that since Louis found humor in everything – mimicking agents, secretaries, other actors – making the rounds together became fun. We did have to pretend not to know each other too well. Louis used his parents address in New Jersey so that no one in the offices would know we lived together. The stigma of homo-sexuality could keep us from getting a role so we had to be careful. Our relationship became a comfort to both of us. I was no longer alone and Louis was with the person he thought he loved.

We spent free time with Madeline and Marie. I was still walking on in *Janie* so evenings were out. The girls adored Louis and never stopped ruffling his magnificent hair, patting his back or his shoulders and hugging him endlessly. Madeline, a budding writer, was working on her first novel. She was very tall, towering over Louis and me. She had an ungainly body that made her movements awkward. She was rather remote. She spoke perfect French and the bookshelves in their apartment were filled with French titles I couldn't decipher. Marie, on the other hand, was outgoing and warm. I wondered about her being an actress since her teeth seemed too big for her mouth.

The apartment was on the second floor of a reconverted brownstone on 12th Street in the Village. Bookcases lined every inch of wall space in the living room except for a section above the sofa that held a large picture of people in period clothes having lunch by a river. The girls told me it was by an artist named Renoir and that it was just a print. It had a very elaborate frame and it looked like it was in a museum. There was also a grand piano that took up a great deal of room, and Marie always got Louis to play some of the Noel Coward songs that he loved. He had a charming voice and Marie often sang along with him. Madeline sometimes left us to go to the theater where Eve LeGallienne was starring in *Uncle Harry*. Madeline was a part-time secretary to Miss LeGallienne and dropped everything when she was summoned. Both of the girls worshipped LeGallienne and never stopped talking about her and how great of an actress she was.

Louis and I got along very well. With the disappointment of not finding work and the shock of being fired from *Junior Miss* that still hung over me, I had begun to lose any confidence in myself. But Louis' constant admiration and his insistence of how talented I was, little by little, brought me back. Everything seemed possible. I secretly thought of him as if he were my college roommate, though I had never been to college. He was my buddy, and I learned a great deal from him. I began to know things about the theater and people I'd never heard of before like Bea Lillie, Tallulah Bankhead, all the Algonquin habitues like Dorothy Parker. Louis had anecdotes about them all and never stopped entertaining us. I remember one about Tallulah Bankhead that's stayed in my head all these years. Louis loved imitating her deep, husky, raucous voice.

"Tallulah was a huge star on Broadway," Louis would begin, "and though she was rumored to be a lesbian, she had married the actor John Emory. Some friends, to celebrate, took the couple to a sex show in Harlem. They walked into a room as big as a basketball court that had nothing in it but two wooden kitchen chairs. Tallulah and John sat down while their friends stood in the back. A man and a young girl came in, bowed to Tallulah, and took off their clothes which they piled on the floor. When they were nude, they bowed again. Obviously, they had never performed for such a big star before and they seemed visibly nervous. The girl proceeded to go down on the man who was enormous. She had a lot of trouble getting him into her mouth. Finally, she managed it but after a few moments he slipped out. In a panic, she turned to Tallulah, bowed and said, 'Excuse me, Miss Bankhead!'"

Louis, as he told it, made the girl sound like Butterfly McQueen and his audience always roared with laughter. I wondered if this was the closest that I would ever get to the theater, just sitting with Louis and his friends, listening to stories about the stars.

Louis continued to profess his love for me, but I tried to put it aside without hurting him. We did begin a sexual relationship, but on my part, it was without emotion or caring. I'd come to rely on Louis so much that it didn't seem wrong to me. I began to wonder if there was such a thing as love for me anyway. Maybe art would take its place and I so wanted to be an artist. But it was not yet in the cards. Instead, I got a job as an announcer at WNYC. Louis was hired to play his old role in the Broadway company of *Junior Miss*. It wasn't a perfect solution to what either of us wanted, but at least we both had work.

***

Every day of the summer seemed the same. The heat was intolerable yet the sun was nowhere to be seen in the white blanket of the sky. Madeline and Marie had decided to spend the sweltering months in Nantucket so Louis jumped at the chance for us to sublet their apartment. He had been miserable in my penthouse with the tiny bed and the constant din of the pianist practicing next door. I didn't mention it, but I was sad to leave uptown and all it symbolized for me. The first time I had ever come to New York was on a stultifying day in the summer when I was 12. My parents were taking me and my brother to the World's Fair. The trip from Boston was hot and endless. I was irritable and I scrunched down in the back seat of the car refusing to look at anything.

"I won't open my eyes until we get there," I said in a whining, babyish voice. My family ignored me as I said every few minutes, "Are we there yet?"

As we entered what I later learned was the Bronx, my father said, "You can open your eyes – we're here."

I sat up and looked out the window. All I could see were filthy, rundown buildings jammed into city blocks, interrupted only by gas stations, warehouses or vacant lots. The dust and heat seemed to emanate from the sidewalks. On the porch of a rundown bungalow, I saw an old man open his pants and show another man his penis as if a doctor were examining him.

"I want to go home," I wailed. "I hate New York!"

But when we arrived in Manhattan at 57th Street and went up in the elevator at the Parc Vendome to my father's uncle's penthouse, I saw the skyline with the lights coming on and I fell in love. I spent every moment when I could be alone on the terrace looking at the Hudson River where the Normandie and the Queen Mary were docked. *Someday*, I thought, *I'll have a penthouse like this*. And then I had a penthouse which didn't have a view and was just a bare room, but still it was uptown. I had felt I was on my way to my dream. But now I was back in the Village.

Louis and I sat in our undershorts with the living room windows open to 12th Street. They were high enough up so that no one could see us but low enough down to catch any breath of air as well as the sounds of the trucks and cars going east to the river. Noel Coward was singing "Wild Thyme" on the record player and Louis was singing along. I got up from the sofa and carried the cut glass pitcher over to him and poured the reddish liquid into his glass. Several ice cubes spilled out and some drops fell onto his bare leg. He sopped them up with his finger and licked it.

"What is this?" he asked. "It's delicious."

"I don't know," I said articulating my words more than I usually did. "I just put in rum and all the fruit juices we had in the fridge. It's mostly cranberry."

"Delicious," Louis repeated and he drank half his glass in one gulp.

I sat back down. I felt I was on the set of a play. The grand piano, all the books, the print above my head that I now knew was by Renoir – this was the way I'd always wanted to live, surrounded by books and art. But all my hopes of the first few months in New York had vanished. I was back radio announcing for $37.50 a week. It was still barely enough to live on. I had to send some money to my parents since my father was out of work, so I still had to walk-on in *Janie* eight times a week. I got up at 6:00 every morning and took the subway to the Municipal Building in lower Manhattan. I worked until 3:00 in the afternoon. It was then too late to make the rounds for acting jobs so I went back to the apartment. I sat around with Louis who was still not dressed. It was so hot and there was no air-conditioner or fan so we sipped iced drinks to keep cool.

One day Louis had suggested we put some rum in our drinks for flavor and now every day we got a little drunk. We slept it off until it was time for us both to go to our theaters. Since I was through at 10:00, I rushed home to get some sleep before getting up at dawn but there was never enough time. I felt I was in a rut and I didn't know how to get out of it. All I could think of was how to make more money. Acting seemed far away.

Louis had gone to the piano and was singing in a voice halfway between Noel Coward's and Gertrude Lawrence's that we heard over and over on the records: "Someday I'll find you, moonlight behind you, true of the dream I am dreaming." He sounded as if he'd come from London. There was not a trace of Jersey City where he'd grown up, gone to school, and finally fled as I had from Boston. I watched him. *He's very handsome*, I thought. *He has wonderful chestnut hair – I wish mine was as good – and hazel eyes and a short straight nose. I can see why he gets modeling jobs and I don't. And he's a wonderful actor and I'm not – I'm a stiff. I just can't fall in love with him. But he's a terrific friend and I'd be lost without him.* I poured myself another drink.

The monotony was beginning to wear me down, I was in the 12-by-12 square foot room for almost eight hours a day announcing and putting records on and off the spinning turntables. I couldn't even read for fear I'd miss a cue so I just sat and thought about my life. I got so depressed at the hopelessness of it. There wasn't any time to hunt for acting jobs, but even if there were, where would I look? Making the rounds hadn't gotten me anything and I was afraid that walking on in *Janie* had relegated me to being an extra in everyone's eyes. My 18th birthday was imminent and I knew I would be drafted soon. My brother was in the Coast Guard and had advised me to join the Air Force and get a V course at a college, but all I wanted was to be an actor, so I just waited to see what would happen.

I was resigned to going to war but I didn't look forward to it. I had always hated fighting from the time my brother had made me fight an older boy when I was in the second grade. I still remember the neighborhood kids standing around in a circle on a chilly fall day cheering us on. I was knocked down immediately and lay stunned on a pile of leaves. Everyone ran away and my brother helped me up. He didn't say a word and I could see how ashamed he was of me. I tried to make it up by practicing fighting at school. But I just wasn't coordinated enough. "You run like an old lady," they yelled at me when I tried out for baseball. The first day of basketball practice I got hit in the groin and lay in agony on the gymnasium floor. I began to be ashamed of my body and did anything I could to avoid taking showers with the other boys. I was sure they were making fun of me behind my back. The gym teacher, Mr. Bemis, would always catch me trying to slip away.

"You take a shower," he would yell so everyone would stop and look at me. "How come you never take a shower?" There would always be a ripple of laughter.

The voice of the engineer took me out of my reverie. "It's time to change your record," he said over the speaker.

I jumped up and slapped a disk on the second turntable. I turned down the sound knob on the first and turned it up on the second. The music continued with no interruption. "Thanks Al," I said into the intercom, "I was a million miles away."

I picked up my schedule. After the Sunrise Symphony, I had The News, the Police Glee Club, Ration Recipes and Nutrition, and the Masterwork Hour. I alternated with Tommy, an announcer in his 60s who'd been with the station for years but whose voice had become thin and unpleasant. Since our jobs were with the civil service, no one could be fired so the old man was only given short spots in between my shows. It meant that I talked almost nonstop, but I liked Tommy and didn't resent having to do all the work.

The light flashed on the telephone and I picked it up. The operator said there was a call for me and she was putting it through.

"Are you the announcer doing the program that's on now?" A woman's accented voice asked.

"Yes," I replied. I did sometimes get people calling admiring my voice or a program I was doing.

"This is Dame Myra Hess," the woman continued.

"Oh," I said, recognizing the name of the famous pianist from the album covers, "I'm so pleased you were listening."

"Don't be," the woman snapped. "I'm very annoyed. You've just put music from the third movement in the middle of the second. Now, pay more attention, young man."

She slammed the phone down in my ear and I felt terrible. I was beginning to make mistakes and I didn't know what to do about it. It was the working at night and getting up at 6:00 in the morning. A few days before I'd made a terrible blunder. Every day at noon, a record was played on the air with the sound of chimes and the announcer who was on duty said, "Twelve o'clock noon by the century-old chimes in historic city hall in New York City where seven and a half million people enjoy the benefits of democracy."

It was my turn and I was exhausted as usual. The chimes were ringing and I repeated the sentence by rote. but when I got near the end, I said, "Where seven and a half people enjoy the benefits of democracy." I didn't even know I'd left out "million" until a few minutes later Mayor LaGuardia telephoned. He happened to be tuned in and he was furious. I realized I had to give up walking on in *Janie*. It was the only way I'd ever get some sleep.

Later in the morning, while Tommy was doing a five-minute marketing program, I walked out in the hall to get some air. Sitting on a sofa was a little old man with hennaed hair and a white face that looked like it was caked with powder.

He looked at me and said in a coy voice, "I bet I know who you are. Tommy has told me all about you." He pursed his mouth with annoyance. "How long is Tommy going to be?" he asked.

"He'll be out in a minute," I replied, not knowing what to make of this man.

He crossed his legs coquettishly and said, "I get all dressed up for him to take me to lunch and he always keeps me waiting."

I said I'd tell Tommy he was there and went back into the studio. "There's someone waiting for you," I told him after I'd put on a record and we could speak.

I looked at Tommy gathering up his papers. He was a plump, ordinary-looking man with gray frizzy hair and glasses. He went to all the baseball games like a jock. I never would have guessed that he lived with another man. He seemed so masculine, but his friend acted like his wife. Was this what happened in a long relationship? Did two men living together take on the roles of a man and a woman? Would that happen to Louis and me? If so, which one of us would be the woman?

Louis and I moved again. The girls were back from Nantucket and we had to get out of 12th Street. In some ways I didn't mind. The bedroom there was tiny – only big enough for bunkbeds. Louis had insisted I have the bottom one since I was bigger and it would be easier for me to get in and out. I was startled the first night I slept there once I got settled on the narrow bed. I looked up and pasted on the beam supporting the upper bed were pictures of the actress Eva LeGallienne who Madeline worked for. LeGallienne was in costumes of what were obviously her many roles. I thought it was weird. Why would anyone want to see these pictures before they went to sleep? But now, I was the one who had to look at them every night. At least since we were moving, I wouldn't have to see them anymore. I wondered whether it was Marie or Madeline looking at the pictures. I wanted to ask them whose bed it was, but I was afraid they might figure out why I wanted to know.

We found a furnished room in an old brick building near Abington Square. The owner, Mr. Dorn, was German, in his forties. He had worked hard to turn an old ruin into a charming house like the ones he remembered from his childhood village. Our room overlooked his garden that was shut off to the tenants. Dorn had a thick accent and was pleasant-looking but prissy. He was very private and kept far away from us. We figured that he was afraid we'd ask for something. We never did. The room was quite large with two windows, draperies with a pattern of leaves that went to the floor but with not enough material to keep them closed, a fireplace that didn't work and a print of Van Gogh's young man in a bright yellow jacket and a hat. Van Gogh was an artist I knew and admired and as soon as I saw the picture.

I felt that this was the place for us. In addition to a king-sized bed, there was a studio couch that doubled as a sofa so we could sleep separately if one of us was restless. A red desk sat below empty shelves that we would fill with books. Louis and I sometimes spent free time in the old bookstores off Union Square where we could find bargains. I had developed a passion for Thomas Hardy and his novels about the Dorset countryside. I found many of them for almost nothing. Both of us had Sundays off so we wandered around the Village or went to the Modern Museum to see an old movie. Garbo was my favorite actress and we always tried to see one of her early silents. Most of our dinners were at the Beatrice Inn a block away where we could get a full meal for $1. I would read in the evening while Louis was at the theater. Sometimes I saw Louis when he got home from the theater, but usually I was asleep on the studio couch so he wouldn't wake me.

Some weeks after we moved in, there was a knock on our door. I opened it to find Mr. Dorn standing next to a tall, rather plain girl around 20. "This is Carolyn Baker," he said. "She's studying dance and has taken the room next door so I thought you should meet."

We said "hello" and "welcome" and "if there's anything we can do." As the days passed, we'd bump into Carolyn in the hall leading to our shared bathroom, but we never exchanged more than a few words. We went back to the house one night after dinner and ran into Carolyn outside the door adjoining our room.

"Oh," she said, "I was just going to see if you were home. I got this wonderful bottle of wine and I thought you might want to share it with me."

Louis and I looked at each other. I didn't have to go into the station until the afternoon the next day when I was pinch hitting for a sick announcer and Louis didn't work until the evening performance.

"Great," said Louis and Carolyn went and got the wine.

We drank and talked and laughed until 2:00 in the morning. We were quite drunk when Carolyn said she'd better be going. I offered, in my most gentlemanly way, to see her home. Since she only lived 15 feet away, we all found this hilarious. After she'd gone, Louis and I undressed and got into bed. There was a knock on the door. I opened it to Carolyn who was standing there in her nightgown.

"Can I stay with you for a while?" she asked with a little girl's voice. "I'm so lonely."

She got into bed between us and nothing else was said. The three of us lay in the bed trying not to touch each other. We pretended to be asleep, but I could tell from the tension in Carolyn's body that she was wide awake. I felt quite giddy from all the wine I had drunk and began to smile to myself. I'd never slept next to a woman before. I stole a look at her out of the corner of my eye. Her long straight brown hair extended almost to her waist and her dancer's body was outlined by the white shift she was wearing.

I'd always thought she was plain with no makeup and her hair braided around her head, but in the filtered light that seeped in at the bottom of the shades from the lamp in the garden, she looked fresh and young. I could imagine her in one of her modern dances in a contraction with her arms held out from her sides and her hair flying forward, like pictures Louis had shown me of Martha Graham. I wondered if Louis was awake, but her body blocked him out so I couldn't tell. I was feeling mischievous. I reached over and pulled Carolyn's nightgown above her knees. I waited a moment, but nothing happened, so I put my hand under the material and moved it along her leg until I reached her pubic hair. I held my breath but Carolyn seemed to be asleep, so after a time I began to play with the hair, running my fingers through the curls. I was enjoying myself immensely and thought I would just experiment a little longer. I pushed one of my fingers into Carolyn and began to slide it in and out.

Suddenly I felt Louis' hand grasp mine and push it away back to my side. I lay quietly smiling. I had enjoyed it and I wanted to do it again. After all, Carolyn hadn't seemed to mind. When I thought Louis was asleep, I cautiously moved my hand over again and pressed my finger into the opening. As it began to part for me, Louis grabbed my hand and flung it back to my side. Carolyn got up without saying anything and left the room. When we saw her the next morning, she acted as if it had never happened. She moved out of the house a short time later.

I turned 18 and was drafted. I'd been waiting for the notice to come so I was prepared. I had made up my mind to do my time in the service and then study when I came out with the help of the GI Bill. That would give me the money for the classes that I couldn't afford now. I realized I had to learn The Method and the technique of acting or I'd never be a great actor. Everything I had done so far was instinctive. Louis had taken me to some acting classes run by Phoebe Brand who had been with the Group Theater. She was a very pretty woman in her forties married to the great character actor Morris Carnovsky. She sat on a folding wooden chair and chain smoked while she watched about ten boys and girls in their twenties follow her instructions. It was all about improvisation that I had never done. We were all supposed to be in a concentration camp. I watched the actors assume various attitudes of what I thought was fear or sickness or hunger. They seemed to be staring at the barriers that imprisoned them. I looked around. All I could see was a bare rehearsal room and as hard as I tried, I couldn't feel anything.

I quit the radio station as soon as I got my draft notice. I had grown to hate the boredom. I felt that I was a monkey on a string who had been trained to talk which I did for eight hours a day. I had learned to ad lib about anything and all I did was fill the air with words that took up the necessary time but were meaningless. I was afraid that I was getting to be just a mellifluous voice. How could I play characters that were real if they all sounded like I was selling toothpaste?

When the day came for the physical, I said goodbye to Louis and told him I would call as soon as I could. I had been told they would take us right to an army camp in New Jersey or New York State and I could telephone from there. I went through the routine like a robot, distancing myself from the hundreds of young men who stood self-consciously in their underwear, by putting my mind somewhere else. I was sure, by doing that, I could somehow get through the war. Everyone was saying that it would soon be over, anyway. One of the doctors took a long time examining my ears.

"Did you have mastoids as a child?" he asked.

I came out of my cocoon. I did remember something about being in my parents' bed and a doctor standing over me, putting a strong-smelling handkerchief over my nose. Then it was like a phonograph record as the faces of my parents and the doctor kept going round and round. And after a while, I felt a terrible pain. I think it was something about cutting open my ears. I know after that I was in the hospital for a long time with pneumonia.

"I do know," I answered the doctor, "that I had a lot of ear trouble."

I was outside the draft board shivering in the cold. I had felt as if I were a dead person all through the exam, as if I were just an automaton going through the motions of being alive.

"Perforated eardrums," the doctor had said. I guess they were the reason I had hearing problems when I was older. But they had given me back my freedom. I would keep my promise to study and learn to be a really good actor.

3

It was almost as if fate had planned the next step in my life. I got a scholarship for The New School of Social Research that was right across from Madeline and Marie's apartment. There was a prestigious drama department there, and I was thrilled when the judges applauded my audition of a Shakespeare monologue. They also, to make my life easier, got me a job as a waiter in the cafeteria so I'd have my meals paid for and get tip money as well. Louis and the girls were excited for me. I was confident, at last, that I would learn the technique of acting rather than just waiting for inspiration to hit me when I worked on a character.

My first day at school the registrar, Miss Van Bynam, gave me my schedule of classes: Drama Technique, Fundamental Acting, History of Theater, Fencing, Modern Dance, and Makeup. Since we had spent time in the morning as I signed all the papers, she took me to where my group was already in session. She opened a door and I saw, seated at small tables in front of standing mirrors, ten students applying cosmetics to their faces. They all stopped and looked at me as I walked in. Miss Van Bynam introduced me as if I were an honored guest at a party.

"He's joining your class and I hope you'll make him feel at home."

Several boys got up to shake my hand and the girls said hello. One extremely handsome boy, who had drawn a line from the center of his forehead down to his chin, and only made-up half of his face, stood up and walked over to me. He stared at me antagonistically. I thought he looked like an American Indian in warpaint. I put out my hand but the boy glared at me and walked out the door.

Everyone giggled and Miss Van Bynam said, "Don't mind him. That's just Marlon trying to get attention." But somehow the boy had put a pall on my good feelings about being a student again.

One of the boys lent me some makeup until I could bring my own kit and I sat applying it, looking in the mirror. *I hope I don't make a mistake*, I thought. *After all, I am a professional actor with an Equity card. I've been in a Broadway touring company* (I put out of my head that I was fired). *I've been in summer stock and here I am learning how to put on makeup that I've done many times. No, I've got to study or I'll never be a great actor. I think that crazy boy with the warpaint just brought me down.* I didn't know the half of it.

The next few weeks I was as busy as I had been when I was doing both WNYC and *Janie*. There were classes all day and then in the evening I ran to the cafeteria to wait on the older people who came to the school for lectures. They were an unpleasant lot, incredibly demanding, making me run back and forth to the kitchen – vegetables overcooked or not cooked enough, salmon raw or too well done. It was as if they were playing a game to see how far they could push me before I would break. Many of them, I was told, had come from Europe to escape the Nazis and they seemed resentful of everything. I just kept smiling even when they didn't leave me a tip.

I was always cheered up, though, seeing the Orozco murals on all four walls of the room. They were stunning and another lesson in my desire to appreciate art. The colors were brooding browns and blacks and the figures were of workers and oppressed people. One of the other waiters told me the artist was a Communist. The people I served were often bent over, huddled together, talking politics, and I wondered if they were Communists too.

The classes were interesting but not enough about the technique of acting that had brought me there. It amused me when the fencing master told us how useful fencing would be for us.

"When you take the Queen Mary to Europe," he said, "hand your case with your foils to the steward and say in a loud voice, 'Take these to the fencing room.' You'll see that you'll be approached by the creme de la creme to fence with them. Often, you'll be invited to their homes. It's the best way to meet the right people." It sounded like the plot of an old movie and, as I looked around at the other gawky boys, I knew this was something that was never going to happen.

Theater history class was fascinating. I worshipped the theater. I couldn't get enough of it – the stories of the great actors, the pictures of sets by scenic designers like Robert Edmond Jones, and the costumes. To think that there was a time, before the movies, when theater was the public's most important form of entertainment. I loved reading about Fanny Kemble, Sarah Bernhardt, Ben Greet, Henry Irving. We would listen to the old recordings of 19th century actors who sounded as if they were singing the words rather than speaking them. My favorite was Ben Greet who did Macbeth's soliloquy as if he were running up and down the scale.

"Is this a dagger that I see before me?" was like *do, ra, me, fa, so, la, ti, do.* Then Greet came crashing down again when he reached the end of the line "Come let me clutch thee." I did a rather good imitation for Louis and I also did one of the speech teachers who was a double for Leslie Howard in *Pygmalion* that we'd seen at the museum.

But what about learning acting technique? When was that going to happen? At last Stella Adler, the most important acting teacher in the country, was coming to do a class. I was terribly excited. She had not only been with the Group Theater, but she had also actually studied with Stanislavsky. I was still reading his book *My Life In Art* over and over as if it were the *Bible*. Still, I couldn't make sense of The Method and how to do it. I was sure Stella Adler would teach me how.

She was a half hour late but no one seemed surprised. Everyone had been talking, sprawled on the folding chairs or perched on the edge of the raised platform with the makeshift curtains. Suddenly it was quiet. The class shifted their positions and looked toward the double doors, almost as if they were animals sensing the approach of another. There was a waft of expensive perfume and Miss Adler appeared. Hands rushed to take her umbrella, her bag, her fur coat.

"Darlings," she said as she kissed and hugged the students closest to her. They guided her into the one armchair in the room and she reached her hands above her head to remove a hat pin. "What do you think of my chapeau?" she asked to no one in particular. It was a frothy black cap from which feathers danced whenever she moved.

A girl said unctuously, "It's beautiful, Miss Adler."

She was ignored as Miss Adler shed a suit jacket that revealed a filmy satin blouse and deep cleavage. She suddenly looked at me. "You must be the new boy," she said.

I felt her eyes peel back the layers of my clothes. "Yes, Miss Adler," I said.

She reached out her hand and I stumbled over to take it. "I hope you're very talented," she said in a sexy and surprisingly British accented voice. I knew that when she was with the Group Theater, she was acclaimed for playing old Jewish mothers so I was quite surprised by this apparition. I stood awkwardly above her as she looked me over. "Sit down, darling," she said and I staggered back to my seat.

For half an hour, she discussed her clothes with the class. "Do you really think this suit is more becoming than the one I wore last week?" Then she listened to their comments about whether she was better in green with her Gibson girl red hair or in blue. Finally, she said, as if we had delayed her, "Let's get to work. Marlon, you lazy boy, get in that chair," she said imperiously to the actor who had been so rude to me in the makeup class.

He hadn't turned up in any of my other classes, but I had seen him sitting on the floor in the hall playing bongo drums. He was surrounded by a coterie of admirers. He made a point of not looking at me. One of the students, who I had become friendly with, told me that Marlon's last name was Brando and the rumor was that he was being kept by a rich, older man and also had a girlfriend named Blossom Plum. The whole class watched as Marlon slumped across the room and fell into the folding metal chair Miss Adler had indicated. He acted as if he had crossed the desert without water and only had enough breath left to sink down next to the oasis.

"Now, Marlon," suddenly Miss Adler was all business, "peel an apple." Marlon began to pantomime the knife slipping under the skin and he started to peel it. He did it so convincingly that it seemed to be in one piece that was reaching to the floor. "Now, Marlon" Miss Adler said, "I'm going to say some words to you and I want you to react accordingly. Cold... Hot... Hungry... Tired... Depressed..."

I couldn't believe my eyes. Marlon continued to peel the imaginary apple but each time he heard a word, he seemed to change. The metamorphosis was almost imperceptible, but he actually became cold or hot or hungry. I thought, *My god, I'll never be able to do that. Here I am believing I'm so talented. What if I'm not? Maybe this whole New School scholarship is a waste of time.* My thoughts were interrupted by the class applauding as Marlon staggered back to his chair as if he couldn't care less.

"Ooh," Miss Adler sighed, "our time is up. Now listen, I believe that every actor should be able to do something in addition to acting. Like singing or telling a story or dancing. After all, if you have to get up at a benefit, you don't want to stand there with egg on your face. So next time, I want you all to come in with a story or a poem or whatever and perform it as if you were in a cabaret. Is that clear?"

There were murmurs of agreement and a shuffle of chairs as the actors bumped into each other rushing to help Miss Adler with her coat. I sat for a moment in my seat. I knew what I would do: my rendition of *The Devil and Daniel Webster* for which I'd won Prize Speaking senior year in high school. I'd show them Marlon was not the only talented one in the class.

When the day came for the next class with Miss Adler, everyone was as excited as if we were getting ready for an opening night. No one would tell anyone else what they were going to do. It was all to be a surprise. A guitar was being tuned, props were being arranged on a table, a girl paced back and forth mumbling to herself and then, as if two hands had been clapped together, everything stopped. The perfume, the fur coat, the hat, the "darlings" and Miss Adler had arrived turning a plain basement room into a salon.

As soon as she had settled into her comfortable chair and been helped out of her coat, she announced, "Today I'm just going to be an audience and you're all going to amaze me." There was a ripple of laughter which her voice cut through. "Stuart," she said, "begin."

A studious looking boy with glasses and a big nose got up and stood in the open space in front of all the chairs that had been arranged in a semi-circle. "I really can't sing –"

Miss Adler stopped him. "Don't explain and don't complain," she said. "We're not here to judge each other's performances. We're here to learn."

Stuart walked over and stood in front of the raised platform. He closed his eyes for a moment as if he were trying to control himself; then he opened them, clasped his hands together and said in a voice throbbing with emotion, "Without a song," he paused and looked up to the heavens, "the day would never end." He spoke the entire song walking about the room as if he were going down a country lane. He even found a spot to point out "that field of corn," When he finished, the class was absolutely still, waiting to hear Miss Adler's opinion before they reacted.

"Very good, Stuart," she said decisively and then everyone applauded.

After a show of hands, Miss Adler chose a lanky blonde girl to go next. I had learned her name was Elaine Stritch and that she was connected to someone high up in the Catholic church in Chicago. She was wearing a trainman's overalls and her hair was pulled back as if she just wanted to keep it out of her face. She sat down on the floor and strummed her guitar.

She sang in a haunting simple voice, "I wonder as I wander out under the sky, how Jesus the Savior did come for to die?" When she finished the song there was no question that she was a talented singer as well as an actress. The class didn't wait to gauge Miss Adler's response. They applauded loudly.

I was afraid that the class would end before I had a chance to show what I could do so I waved my hand in front of Miss Adler's face. "The new boy seems very eager," she said. "All right darling, you go next."

I stepped up onto the platform. I had decided I wanted to be above the class instead of on the same level. I looked at the other students sitting on either side of Miss Adler. I was relieved to see that Marlon had left the room. I felt as if I were performing in front of the queen and her courtiers. It had been two years since I had won Prize Speaking, but I remembered every word of the Stephen Vincent Benet story. I was nervous in the beginning, but I felt a new authority that acting in *Junior Miss* must have given me. I played about 20 different parts all with different accents or characters. I told the story of the Devil's battle with Daniel Webster to possess a man's soul. I grew more impassioned. I felt transported to the New England farm where it was taking place and I got very moved when Daniel Webster finally won at the end.

I had hardly finished when Miss Adler's theatrical voice trumpeted "Excellent" and the class applauded. I went to my seat feeling a camaraderie with the others for the first time. As soon as I sat down, Miss Adler gestured in my direction. "Now," she said, let's not be confused that what he did was acting. He told a story and put on voices for the different characters. That's all right for cabaret, which was the assignment, but we mustn't mix it up with real acting." Everyone agreed. I didn't see why it was necessary for Miss Adler to diminish my performance that way.

There was a sudden flurry of activity. The curtains on the platform were drawn and the lights went out. I could make out one of the actors at a record player putting the arm on a record. As the music began, he rushed over to the side of the platform and pulled the curtains. Standing in the center of the makeshift stage in a pool of light was a gorgeous woman in a velvet evening dress wearing long white gloves. The class gasped! It was Marlon in a blond wig. As Judy Garland began to sing "Zing go the strings of my heart," Marlon lip synced her. I realized he had had the record put on at twice the speed so that the sound of Garland's voice was comic. It was as if Betty Boop's voice was coming from a large woman. The effect was hilarious and the class went to pieces. The students screamed and applauded. Several of them slid off their chairs and rocked with laughter on the floor. Through it all, Marlon went right on as if nothing were happening which only fanned the flames of laughter more. Miss Adler collapsed in her chair.

I realized that my *Devil and Daniel Webster* had been completely forgotten.

4

"Twelfth Night"

The cabaret incident was the last time I saw Stella Adler. She had taken a role in a play called *Pretty Little Parlor* that was to try out for weeks on the road and then come into New York. She wouldn't be able to teach her class for some time. The show played Boston and my parents went to see it and then went backstage, explaining that their son was studying with Miss Adler. According to my mother, Miss Adler told them I was extremely talented, but she hoped they would have a nice little business for me to go into when I returned to Boston. That made me remember her put down by saying what I had done at the cabaret was not acting. I wasn't sad for her when her play came into New York and closed after five performances.

Many years later, I would run into her in Positano. She said she had seen me play the lead in an off-Broadway production of Jean Cocteau's *The Infernal Machine* several seasons before and "I was brilliant." I didn't ask her why she hadn't come backstage to tell me when it would have been so helpful. It was now too late. I just thanked her and left her with her group of admirers.

Miss Adler had gotten her brother, Luther, to take over the class. He had also been in the Group Theater and was a renowned actor having appeared many times on Broadway. We were all excited that he would teach us. He was in his forties, stocky and short, although he wore lifts so he seemed taller. He was all business, but also very warm and help-ful. I was finally going to learn The Method that was beginning to be regarded as the basis of all good acting.

Mr. Adler gave us an improvisation his first day: we were all to be chickens in a barnyard. We heard on the radio that war was declared. We had to react as chickens, but we had to decide whether we were married and had to leave our families to go off to war, or single awaiting the draft, etc. Were we cowards or heroes? Each of us had to be one or the other. I looked around. The whole class started clucking as they moved on their knees toward each other. Some of the girls grabbed boys and acted as if they were their husbands. I felt uncomfortable as I still did with improvisation. I just couldn't react to the others so I decided I was a loner and didn't like any of the other chickens. I sat and sulked and managed to get through the ordeal.

In the next class we were given partners and told to choose a scene to work on. We would rehearse our scenes on our own and then act them in front of the class. I was assigned Phyllis who we all knew was the heir to a pickle fortune, but she never mentioned it. She didn't put on airs or act like she was better than any of us. She and I decided we would do a scene from a short play by Noel Coward called *Still Life*. We would meet at my furnished room because she still lived with her parents and they were usually home.

Louis had gone to the movies that night – his show had finally closed – so I could have the room all to myself. I straightened up the books and put the newspapers out of sight. I thought it looked rather good for a furnished room. The shelves above the red lacquered desk that was between the two windows were now filled with books. The studio couch had diamond patterned pillows that matched the dust ruffle. There was a screen blocking the sink, the double bed was half concealed by a mountain of more pillows, and the green draperies with the leaf pattern along with the Van Gogh print of the man in the hat and the yellow coat had been arranged tastefully by the owner. We hadn't added a thing. I thought Phyllis would be impressed even if she was so rich. She knew I was waiting on tables in the school dining room and had no money. I figured we would just read through the scene and then maybe try an improvisation based on it. That way we'd get to know each other and then start the serious work at our next session.

The doorbell rang and I jumped up. I didn't know why I was so edgy. When I let Phyllis in, she said how nice the room was as she took off her coat. I thought she seemed awfully sure of herself, but I figured that was because she had so much money. After we read the scene from *Still Life*, we talked about the play. We agreed that when the doctor told the married woman about his practice, he was not really talking about his passion for preventive medicine, he was telling her that he loved her. We decided to improvise on that theme. I, as myself, would tell Phyllis about my passion for acting, but what I was really doing was telling her how much I loved her.

We both sat down on the bed. I stared at her trying to get the inspiration to begin. She reached out and took my hands. She had a pretty heart-shaped face with plump cheeks and knowing brown eyes. Her bleached blond hair had a dark streak where she parted it. She had pushed off her shoes and her legs were folded under her. I thought of what I'd learned in acting class. Luther Adler had said everything must be specific. "Don't just look at someone and say, 'I love you'," he said. "Find something in them, their eyes, their hair, that you really think is beautiful and love that." I looked closely at Phyllis. She was slightly overweight and her breasts were bursting out of her blouse. I had the wildest urge to touch them. I began to talk about my love of acting, but all I could think about were her breasts.

She encouraged me to talk more and before I knew it, I had my arm around her and was gently working on the buttons close to her neck. She didn't stop me so I opened her blouse all the way. Underneath, I was confronted with a brassiere, but since I'd never coped with one before, I kissed her deeply while I fumbled in the back. I hoped she thought that I knew what I was doing. I couldn't figure out how to relieve the tension of the elastic, but suddenly she reached around and undid it herself. I began to fondle her breasts while I kissed her passionately. Neither of us pretended we were working on the scene any longer. Phyllis responded to my kisses by working her tongue around in my mouth. I thought I would burst unless I undid her skirt. When I got the clasp open, Phyllis slid the skirt down over her legs and took off her stockings. She lay up against the pillows with a Cheshire Cat smile. I pulled down her panties and began to probe through her pubic hair with my fingers. Her girdle was bunched up around her waist and I saw a fluid start to ooze down her leg.

"Please let me put it in," I begged.

"Do you have anything?" she asked.

I had never had any reason to buy condoms, but I didn't want her to know that. "Not at the moment," I said, "but I'll just put it in and take it right out. I promise."

Phyllis began to straighten her clothes. "Accidents can happen," she said. "Some other time."

My penis was beginning to hurt. I hoped she'd make another suggestion, but she was busy putting herself together. "I've got to get home," she said.

I felt like a child being punished but I didn't quite know what for. "What night shall we meet next week?" I asked.

"I've got a lot of family coming in," she answered. "Maybe we should just work at school before class." She suddenly seemed much older than me and totally in control of the situation.

"Okay," I said, "I'm sorry you're going so soon."

"I think it's better," she said as she put on her beaver coat and swept out the door, looking more like a young matron than an acting student.

I sat on the bed, my groin aching. *I wonder if she somehow knew about Louis. I'm glad he didn't walk in.* I didn't feel any guilt because I wasn't cheating on Louis with another man. Besides, one day when Louis finally accepted that I didn't love him and he wasn't hurt by it any longer, I would leave him. We both knew our relationship wasn't permanent. But I sure would have liked to have put it in.

Auditions began for the big play of the year. It was Shakespeare's *Twelfth Night,* and I got terribly excited. I'd acted in *Much Ado About Nothing* in Boston and had, at least, the rudiments of doing Shakespeare, and I'd gotten my scholarship by reciting one of his soliloquies. I went to the audition feeling confident and discovered that all the boys were trying out for Duke Orsino, the part that I wanted. Everyone had to read for the director, Erwin Piscator, who was also the head of the school. He was a slight man around 50, beautifully dressed with meticulously combed silver hair. He had been famous in Germany for doing Epic Theater and had come to New York to escape the Nazis. He sat hunched in a seat toward the front of the auditorium while we came out on the stage one by one.

I was startled to see Marlon who hadn't been around much for a while. I'd heard about him from one of the actors who'd said he was raving about John Barrymore's antics in *Good Night Sweet Prince* that had just come out and that all of us were reading. Evidently, Marlon thought the best parts of the book were when Barrymore did something really disgusting like pee on the floor of his dressing room in front of people who came backstage to praise his performance. I thought how sad it was that a great actor had to resort to such low tricks to get attention. But I wasn't surprised that Marlon was taken in by them. It was so much in his character to always show off.

As usual, he looked right through me as we all waited in the wings for our turn. I couldn't understand what it was about me that annoyed him so, but I put it out of my head. As I waited, I could hear the boys who went before me and none of them seemed exciting. Marlon was the worst. He mumbled his way through, making no sense of the words or the iambic pentameter. I did consider that he might get the part since he was such a favorite of the faculty. But when it came to my turn, I forgot about Marlon and the others and just gave in to the thrill of being on the stage and the pleasure of reading such beautiful words. Piscator never said anything but "thank you" and we all left with no idea of who had won the role. A few days later, a cast list was posted. I was to be the Duke Orsino.

The first day of rehearsal we were all a little nervous. Piscator had directed and worked with the greats of Europe and we were just kids trying to find our way. He settled in the front row and looked up at the stage. "Alright, begin," he said. I started to speak the opening lines of the play and Piscator jumped out of his seat. "No, no, no," he shouted. "You Americans are zo afraid of the poetry." He came up onto the stage where we all stood around self-consciously. He walked over to me. "You have one of zee most beautiful speeches in Shakespeare," he said with his German accent. "It begins zee play and it must be like a rhapsody. Your voice should zound like a cello. Now begin again."

I sat on the chair that was the rehearsal equivalent of the Duke's throne and looked toward the wings where I imagined the musicians were. "If music be the food of love, play on," I said as if I were giving the orchestra the cue to begin.

"Young man," Piscator bounded onto the stage again. "Listen to zee way I do it." He stood with his face toward the empty auditorium. He held his hands out as if he were expecting a benediction from heaven. "Eef moosic be zee foood uv luv, play on." He elongated every vowel.

"Give me excess uv eet zat surfeiting zee appetite may zicken un zo die."
He broke his pose and turned back to me. "You understand?" he asked.

"Of course," I said, "thank you." All I could think of was I had
wanted this part so badly and I wasn't going to lose it. Piscator had
chosen me but I still had to prove myself. I decided to mimic him without the accent. I took a deep breath. "Ifff muusic bee the foood of lovve,
play onnn." I almost sang it.

"Zats it," the director clapped his hands, "now you've got it. Go on."
I continued the speech copying the old recording of the 19th-century
actor Ben Greet that we'd heard in class. I began to vary the tempo and
melody of the lines. It was as if I were doing an aria in an opera and
when I finished Piscator applauded. "Perfect," he said. "Now you have
to do zat with zee whole part." *If I did*, I thought, *I'd be the biggest ham
that ever stood on a stage.*

After weeks of rehearsal, I sat putting on makeup for the first of
two performances. I had let my hair grow long and my costume was
stunning: a red doublet with a diamond pattern, red tights, a navy-
blue blouse with puffed sleeves and a silver cape. There was to be one
performance in the afternoon for the whole school, friends and agents,
and in the evening the official opening. I was just finishing combing my
hair when the director walked into the communal dressing room.

"Good afternoon Mr. Piscator," everyone said heartily.

"Good afternoon," he said. "I just came to zay merde."

We all knew the French word for "shit" was traditional in the
theater for wishing someone luck and it made us feel very professional.
Piscator walked over and stood beside my chair. "There's been a bit of a
problem," he said tentatively, "but I zinc we've zolved it very well."

"What is it, Mr. Piscator," I asked.

"You zee," he continued apologetically, "Stuart's mother is ill zo he
had to go to Washington last night and he can't get back in time for ze
performance. He'll be here tonight, but we had to get someone to take
his part this afternoon. Of course it's only eight lines zo it's not that
difficult."

I thought, *Oh my god, that's the Priest, the hardest moment in the play for me.* It was the scene when the Duke finds out that the woman he loves has just married his man servant, who seems to be in love with him. All hell breaks loose and the Priest is called in to confirm the ceremony. "Who's going to play it?" I asked.

"Marlon has been good enough to help us out even though it's zuch a small role." The director beamed. "It's very nice of him."

"Can we rehearse before the curtain?" I asked.

"Zere's no time unfortunately," was the answer. "He's in ze costume department now, but he knows ze spot on the stage he has to go to and I'm sure he will be fine."

Of all the actors they could have gotten... I put it out of my head. There was a whole play to act before I got to the scene with the Priest.

I sat on the throne onstage listening to the music, enjoying the excitement of the moment before the curtain goes up. After the applause for the set, I said in a voice exhausted with yearning, "If music be the food of love, play on." I went through the opening scene with just the right balance of the truth of the emotion and the beauty of the poetry. As I made my exit saying the words "Away before me to sweet beds of flowers, love thoughts lie rich when canopied with bowers." There was a tremendous sound of applause.

The rest of the play went splendidly. When we were almost at the end, and I discovered that Olivia, my love, had married Cesario, my servant, the Priest was sent for. I was in the midst of acting the conflict between my desire to kill my boy servant and my suspicion that he was in love with me, when I heard the audience start to laugh. I couldn't imagine what had happened until I turned to see the Priest.

There was Marlon in a pair of tights into which he had stuffed a small drum that made him look pregnant. As the audience began to recognize the joke, Marlon beat out a rhythm on the drum as he mumbled the lines that no one could hear. The audience went wild. They laughed. They applauded. They egged him on until his hands were doing an African drum solo. The other actors on stage broke up laughing, but I was furious. It was as if everyone were laughing at me and the play was totally forgotten. When Marlon finally finished, he left the stage to an ovation. I had the next speech, but I had to wait until everyone quieted down. As I spoke, the audience started to laugh again, but soon controlled themselves and somehow, we finished the play.

I walked to the dressing room in a fury. I went through in my head the past year that I had been in New York – never having enough food, losing a tooth because I couldn't afford a dentist so now I had to be conscious of my smile, never being warm enough in my thin coat, having to be an ignominious walk-on, and waiting on tables for people who always treated me as an inferior and seldom even gave me a tip – all this to be in the theater that I loved. But this wasn't the theater I had read and dreamed about.

When I walked into the dressing room, Marlon was sprawled on a chair with cold cream all over his face. I went up to him. "How dare you," I said. "How dare you ruin this play?" Marlon said nothing. "Aren't you even going to say you're sorry?" I went on, but Marlon looked away. My frustration was building. "I'll do everything in my power to keep you off Broadway," I said and walked over to my dressing table with a sinking feeling of defeat. Mr. Piscator walked in.

"Vunderful, vunderful," he said.

I got up and walked over to him. I asked very calmly, "Are you going to say anything to Marlon?"

"My dear," the director said, acting very suave and European, "it was wrong, but it was just high spirits. Tonight is the most important performance, and Stuart will be here for it."

I looked at him. He no longer seemed like a great international director. "If you don't reprimand him for his unprofessional behavior," I said with my heart pounding against my chest, "I'm going to leave the school." Piscator raised his hand with a deprecating gesture and left the room.

I did the evening performance and never went there again. Marlon Brando was on Broadway within a few months.

One good thing did come out of my time at the New School. Madeline had gone off to a writer's colony to put the finishing touches on her first novel, *The Small Rain*. Marie had become friendly with actress-director Miranda d'Ancona. Miranda's mother was a former opera singer with connections to wealthy people and she helped Miranda raise enough money to back a summer theater in Nantucket. Marie would star in the plays that Miranda would direct. Marie brought Miranda to see me in *Twelfth Night* and they asked me to join the company. Needless to say, I was thrilled. Louis had already signed a contract so we would be together. In several months, I would be acting again. Meanwhile I would make the rounds, but the pressure was off. My summer was taken care of.

The registrar at the New School sent me a note saying how sorry she was that I had left the school. She knew I had no money so she mentioned that a plastic surgeon friend of hers needed someone to help out in his office and asked if I was interested. I jumped at the chance, went to his office high up in the Squibb Building on Fifth Avenue with an amazing view of Central Park. The doctor was in his fifties but looked younger. He was extremely handsome with tiny streaks of gray just beginning in his full head of black hair. He greeted me in his sumptuous office above the park. I told him that I couldn't take dictation or do other secretarial work, and I had a summer stock job starting in May. He didn't seem to mind any of it. He just wanted someone around to run some errands and be available. He offered me $35 a week. It would take care of my expenses until I went to Nantucket. I thanked him and got up to go.

"What time is it?" he asked.

"I'm sorry I don't have a watch," I replied.

He looked at me for a minute and then pushed up the sleeve of his white doctor's jacket. On his wrist were two watches. He undid one and handed it to me. "Here," he said, "take this. I don't need two watches." I didn't know what to say. I felt funny about accepting it, but he put it in my hand and said, "Be here at 10:00 tomorrow. We'll find things for you to do."

When I told Louis about the watch, he asked me if the doctor had come on to me. I said absolutely not but we both thought it was a bit strange. Louis said, "Just be careful."

The job turned out to be easy and the doctor paid almost no attention to me. There was no question of his having any personal interest and the watch must have been just a whim. I went every day and sat in a small cubical. Occasionally the doctor dictated a letter to me, but he spoke very slowly so I could write it in longhand. Then I would type it, usually spending most of the day as I made mistakes and had to do it over several times. The doctor didn't seem to care.

Several times he took me with him to lunch. We would sit in the elegance of the nearby Hotel Pierre or the Sherry and he would insist I have a complete meal. We didn't talk much since he was busy greeting people who'd come over to our table to say hello. He seemed to know everybody and always introduced me as his assistant. I had the feeling I was there because he didn't want to be seen eating alone. Once in a while, he would send me with a little gift to the Sherry-Netherland where he kept an apartment for his mistress. I always gave it to her maid so I never saw her. Rose, the doctor's nurse, told me she was a beauty.

The nurse and I had become friends during the times she wasn't busy assisting the doctor. She was a tall middle-aged woman with a weathered face and dark hair pulled back in a bun. She looked like she could have been crossing the prairie in a covered wagon, but her looks belied a raucous, party girl with a stevedore's vocabulary. Rose told me harrowing stories of being drunk and assisting on operations with coffee grounds in her mask so no one would smell the liquor. The coffee grounds made her sick and she would sometimes throw up. She had other anecdotes of working in hospitals, and she always sought me out when she was free. I usually had little to do so I was glad to talk to someone. However, her stories didn't give me much confidence in the medical profession.

The months went by and I watched Central Park change from being white with snow to the green of spring. Louis and I went often to his parents' home in New Jersey. His mother, a little bird of a woman, chirped away happily when we were there and loaded us with food that would last for days. Louis and his parents told amusing stories about their Irish relatives. How they would take grandma for a ride and only slow the car down outside her apartment house and say, "We don't have time to stop, Grandma. You'll have to jump out now." The old lady would be terrified, but they just thought it was good fun. Then there was an Uncle Paddy who was a panhandler on Communipaw Avenue. I listened as if I were hearing about people from another world.

One night, Louis' parents got tickets to an ANTA benefit as a surprise. It was an evening to celebrate the theater. I got to see some of our greatest stars do scenes from their successes: Jane Cowl, now an old lady, did *Smilin' Through* that had made her a star 25 years earlier. Judith Anderson revived a scene from *Come of Age*, not a success on Broadway but one of her favorite roles.

My mouth must have open with wonder for the whole evening as I watched famous actors and musical stars bring down the house time after time until long after midnight. It gave me back my love of the theater that Marlon had almost destroyed. Here were the real actors who didn't stoop to stunts to win an audience. They relied on their talent and their love of performing. *That's the way I would do it*, I thought.

At the end of the evening, I felt reborn.

5

Alan, Sylvia, and Louis in Nantucket

The Reuban Joy house was at the head of Nantucket's Main Street, only a ten-minute walk from the Straight Wharf Theater. Although it was built in the 18th century, it had none of the beauty of the Starbuck houses nearby. There were many inconveniences in the old house: the staircases were narrow, the windows didn't close properly, and the floors creaked. Louis and I shared a room that was hot, had no screens to keep out the mosquitoes, and no closets, so we lived out of suitcases.

I loved it and thought the whole experience was beautiful. It was as if my dream had come true. After all the scraping and scrounging, the menial jobs, the disappointments, I was part of a repertory company of actors all working together to create art with no feelings of jealously or competitiveness. We each received $10 a week and our room and board. All the roles had been assigned in the beginning so there were no rivalries. We would all work for the same ideal. I was sure we would be happy in our feeling of mutual love and the comfort of that love. It's what I had always believed a family should be and at last I was part of one. We were all going to have our meals together in the dining room where the tables had been pushed together for the group. I had found a sentence in Stanislavsky's *My Life In Art*. I copied it on a shirt cardboard and put it in a cheap black frame. I hung it in the dining room. It said, "The artists are eating; the artists are getting ready for the performance."

Louis' friends, Madeline and Marie, had both worshipped the great actress Eva LeGallienne and had inherited her dream of repertory theater where actors played a small role one night and a lead the next. Every effort, as a result, would go into the artistic whole rather than into the individual egos of the actors. Miranda had taken Madeline's place when she left to write and was equally enthusiastic about repertory. The two decided to turn what had been a typical summer theater with old Broadway comedies into an art house. The program for the summer included Ibsen, Chekhov, and Oscar Wilde. The hope was that the tourists would trade their popcorn and salt water taffy for culture. It remained to be seen.

Louis and I waited outside the house to walk Marie and Miranda to the theater. The cobblestones were dappled by the morning sun striking the ancient trees. There was the usual faint smell of the sea in the air. Miranda, slim as a teenage boy, appeared first. She was wearing corduroy pants the color of her straight, shoulder-length copper hair, and a man's white shirt. She carried a long-stemmed carnation. Marie came soon after her in a full skirt of many colors, a blouse with a lace stock, and a slouch felt hat with the brim low on her forehead. She was smoking a cigarette from a long ivory holder. She kissed both Louis and me and looked straight into our eyes.

"Good morning, darlings," she said.

We began our promenade to the theater. I was aware of people watching us as we walked past the shops. I was in a pair of old dungarees and an orange and black sweatshirt. My hair was a mass of curls which I hadn't bothered to comb after my shower. Louis was the most conservative of the group in a pair of slacks and a summer shirt. The girls walked ahead and we followed. I heard the owner of the greengrocer's say to his wife, "The stock actors are here. I guess the summer's begun."

The theater was on the straight wharf at the very end of the main street. The building had originally been a huge loft for making sails for the many boats that clogged the harbor. Nantucket had been a tourist mecca from the whaling days and an art center since the 1920s. The theater was small, charming, and in the heart of all the shops that drew the tourists. There was a small garden in the back where we would gather for line rehearsals or notes. There were eight of us in the cast: the two girls; Louis and me; Sylvie, a plump woman from Canada who I suspected had given money to the theater; Bob, a dark, tall, leading man; James, thirties, balding, already a character actor; Isabella, 20, pretty, fantastic long blond hair that she was either always combing or drying in the sun. We all gathered in the garden and Miranda outlined the summer and our goal as artists to do great plays. I was ecstatic. It was everything I dreamed the theater could be.

Unfortunately, it turned out to be a dream that wasn't to last. As the summer progressed, the camaraderie disappeared. Marie and Miranda were starring in and directing all the plays. When they weren't rehearsing or performing, they kept to their room which made them seem distant and mysterious. The other actors thought they were just being grand. Since Louis and I were the girls' friends, suspicion was also leveled at us. The others thought we were privileged, and they resented us. It became a summer of them against us. We worked together, did our jobs together, but I gave up my feeling of belonging to a loving family. My sign in the dining room was ignored as was the word "artist." The actors had little to say to each other off the stage and gobbled their food as quickly as possible.

Marie's mother, a matronly woman who did the cooking, provided some inadvertent humor to the meals. She had a cat she had brought with her as well as a husband, Dave, who came up from New York on the weekends. In the middle of dinner, she would announce to the table, "I bet Dave can't wait to see his pussy tomorrow." Later she would announce, "Dave just loves his pussy." The shrieks of laughter, which she never understood, brought the actors together for a moment, but there was just too much enmity for it to last.

I felt I was really learning to act at last. On the opening night of Ibsen's *The Master Builder*, something happened that I had been hoping for. The play is about a successful contractor who is no longer in his prime. A girl, Hilda, seeks him out and stirs him up until he believes he is vital and young again. Hilda tells him that a builder, when he has finished a building, must be able to go to its highest point and hang a wreath. He felt too infirm to do so, but Hilda goads him on and he attempts the climb. I played a young man in his office who worshipped him and watches as he climbs.

When he falls to his death, Hilda cries out ecstatically, "My master builder!" and the curtain comes down. I, for the first time in my acting career, felt so completely in my character that I burst into tears. I stood in the curtain calls sobbing. When they were over, I was almost hysterical and the actors comforted me. They were forced to give me all the attention that should have gone to the leading man. I'm sure they resented my behavior and thought it was a great ploy for attention, but I knew I'd become a true actor. I didn't care what they thought.

Something else happened that turned the other actors against me. We were performing *Lady Windermere's Fan* by Oscar Wilde. I was playing an attractive, witty young man, so I could look my best unlike the way I had to look in several other plays. At the end of the show, a movie scout came back and asked to see me. He talked about a stock contract at Universal and would I think about it and come to his office in New York when the season was over. He also said I was the only one of the group who could make it in movies. One of the local kids helping with scenery must have heard it and told everyone because I was met with more coldness than usual.

My life seemed to change with *The Animal Kingdom*, a play by Phillip Barry. It was my first chance to be the lead in a show and see if I had the talent to carry it. It was about a man who loved both his wife and his mistress and finally had to choose between them. Marie was my wife and Miranda my mistress. They were both wonderfully supportive and praised me constantly. Opening night was a success. The audience that supported the theater was a little tired of the heavy drama we'd been forcing them to sit through, so they were delighted with a contemporary work. Even though the girls were older than I, at 19 I seemed to be in my mid-twenties so it all worked well. Marie was an elegant woman who loved her house more than her husband, and Miranda, with her slight accent and odd demeanor was perfect as a Greenwich Village artist. Whenever the play came up in the repertory, a lot more people came than usual.

One performance was a little strange. As soon as we came offstage from the curtain calls, I walked over to Marie, "What was going on?" I asked.

"Didn't you realize?" she responded.

"No, I just saw you getting up and walking upstage to the fireplace," I said. "I thought I was going crazy."

Marie said, "The gel that was wrapped around the bulb in the fireplace started to catch on fire. Didn't you smell it?"

"I was so concentrated on trying to tell you that I was leaving you, that I couldn't think of anything else."

Marie laughed. "I finally decided to pull out the plug."

"You were both very good," a voice said coming out of the darkness in the wings. We turned to see Jackie, the girl who had often been at Marie and Madeline's.

"I didn't know you were in Nantucket," Marie said.

When I saw Jackie, I had the same feeling of apprehension I always had when I saw her. Something about her put me on my guard, as if she was a danger. "Why did you have to be here tonight?" I said to her. "We had technical trouble in the last scene. Every time I looked at Marie she was gone. Just when I was telling her I was leaving her, she walked offstage."

"It didn't make any difference," Jackie assured me. "You were excellent. Why don't you get ready and I'll buy you all a drink."

As we walked to the bar, Jackie joined me while Louis and the two girls went on ahead. Jackie told me that she had gone to work for a theatrical agent and would introduce me when I returned to New York. I thought how lucky I was that she had seen *The Animal Kingdom* where I had the lead instead of the other plays where I had small roles. I always felt uncomfortable with Jackie, as if I weren't smart enough to keep up with her. She was so attractive and filled with such energy that she excited me.

"I have a theory," she said between drags on her cigarette, "that an actor has to have a face that you can do a caricature of. That's why I know you will be successful. It's not that you're not handsome, but with your scoop nose and high forehead, I can see you on the wall in Sardi's."

I was flattered. When we were seated in the smoky bar, dimly lit by ship lanterns, Jackie ordered a martini on the rocks with both olives and onions. She smoked incessantly, as we all did, with a short cigarette holder held between her fingers. I noticed her huge diamond ring and remembered that Miranda had said Jackie's parents were rich.

Jackie asked how the season was going and Marie told her that although they were selling out on the weekends, there weren't enough people during the week for them to do more than break even. Miranda said she would go back to New York with little to show for their hard work except the knowledge that they had done Wilde, Chekhov, and Ibsen, as well as two modern playwrights and gotten the summer tourists to see them.

Louis laughed. "A lot of them hate *The Sea Gull*," he said, "but there's nowhere else to go at night."

Miranda was strangely quiet but Marie talked enough for both of them. We said goodnight to Jackie and the four of us walked back to the house on a deserted Main Street lit by old street lamps. Miranda managed to walk alone with me while Louis and Marie were up ahead.

"What do you think of Jackie?" Miranda asked in her rich contralto voice with its trace of an Italian accent.

"I like her," I said, "but she makes me uneasy. She's so sure of herself."

"Don't ever say anything about what I'm going to tell you," Miranda whispered.

"Of course," I promised.

"Someday," she said with almost religious fervor, "Jackie and I will be together."

"Does she know that?" I asked.

"It doesn't matter," she replied, "it will be in time."

She seemed to withdraw into her own thoughts and I walked quietly beside her. If I'd only had a crystal ball, I would have been amazed to see who Jackie really did end up with.

6

All the actors had to help shift the scenery since, in repertory, the sets had to be changed every night. Marie and Miranda couldn't possibly afford enough stagehands, so after we took off our makeup, we'd all go to the stage and pitch in. The worst thing about doing it was having to be around Laura. She was the scenic designer in charge of taking down and putting up the sets. We all hated Laura who treated us as underlings and we called her "the white rat." She was enormously fat and looked like an albino with her white skin and bleached blond hair. She was particularly officious and snide with me. As the summer wore on, she began to aggravate me even more.

One night, after a performance of my lead in *The Animal Kingdom*, I was waiting for another actor to help me move some furniture onstage. Suddenly I heard Laura's sarcastic voice, "Come on, dead ass! Are you going to stand around while everyone else does your work?" I'd been up since early in the morning. I'd done two performances and had one more of the many fights I'd had with Louis about my inability to return his feelings, and I just couldn't take anymore. I saw Laura standing on the floor of the theater just below the stage. She was wearing what looked like a white tent and in the darkness, I thought she resembled a huge plate of vanilla ice cream. She was doing no work herself but criticizing everyone.

She looked at me with her little rat's eyes sparkling. "You're almost as good a stagehand as you are an actor," she said. I ran over to the edge of the stage, leaped into the air and landed on top of her. The two of us went rolling about on the floor and had to be separated by the other actors. I didn't stop to think that she was a woman. She was just a monster with no gender. She had baited me for the last time.

She cried softly and I said, "Don't ever talk like that to me again." The other actors applauded and several cheered.

That night I was almost asleep when the light went on. "I think we have to talk about this," Louis said.

I rubbed my eyes. "What is there to discuss?" I asked.

"Well, I don't know about you," he said, "but I can't go on this way."

I sat up in the bed and hugged my knees. There was a mosquito in the room buzzing, but I couldn't see it. There had been so many discussions and confrontations, but they always ended up the same way. We both knew we had to separate, but it was so much easier to just drift along. With all the problems of trying to get work and pay the rent, why face the turmoil of breaking up, dividing the few possessions we'd accumulated and splitting our friends into two camps?

But something had happened during the summer. I had begun to feel confident about my acting and had stopped depending so much on Louis' approval. I had always thought that my relationship with him was symbolized by an etching I had bought at a second-hand bookstore near Union Square. It showed the two littler princes in the Tower of London clutching each other before they were killed. I had held onto Louis for dear life, afraid I wasn't any good as an actor, afraid I wouldn't have enough money to eat, afraid I'd have to admit failure and go home. Part of me still hedged my bets, but the other part longed to be out on my own.

"Maybe we should think of living apart when we get back to New York," I said.

"Maybe we should," Louis replied.

It was the first time in the endless discussions of our relationship that he hadn't quickly said, "I don't know what I'll do without you." I felt a slight wave of panic go through me. One step further and I knew I'd be on a road I'd never traveled before. I thought *I'm not ready, just a little longer*.

"I don't think we should do anything rash," I said. "Let's just see how we feel when we get back to the city."

"No," Louis said firmly, "we're not going to live together any longer. I'm moving in with Sam."

I was stunned. Sam was an actor we knew slightly. "You don't have to do that," I said.

"You don't understand," Louis interrupted, "I want to live with Sam. He's everything you've never been for me."

I felt as if I'd been slapped, as if it had all been my fault. What had I done wrong? I couldn't help not loving Louis but I suddenly did feel guilty for using him. "I'm sorry," I said.

"Don't be," Louis smiled. "I'm very happy. It's a relief to have it out in the open."

"We'll still be friends," I said as a half question.

"Of course," Louis replied. "After all, Miranda and Marie are going to try to raise money for a winter repertory and we'll both be in it."

"Yes," I said, but I worried that Sam might take my place in the company. And now, how could I pay the rent for the room on my own? I lay awake thinking of going back to New York, no further along as an actor than when I'd first arrived a little over a year ago. What would I do with no money and all by myself?

It was my third cold winter in New York, and I was barely getting by. The plastic surgeon had told me I could have my job back after the summer, so I returned to the office with its view of Central Park and listened again to Rose's horrific tales of operations and hospital life. The money was still not enough to get by so I got an evening job as an usher at the Alvin Theatre. Without Louis paying half, I couldn't afford the room we'd had, but Mr. Dorn kindly gave me one for $4 a week. It was only big enough for a single bed squeezed between two walls and enough space to change clothes. Maybe being squashed in a small room kept me from feeling lonely. Still, I didn't have any time to feel sorry for myself, rushing to make the rounds in the hours between the office and the theater at night.

The first play I ushered at was Margaret Webster's production of Shakespeare's *The Tempest*. It took place on a tropical isle and Norman Bel Geddes had designed a fantastic island that took up the whole stage and revolved to show different locations. One of the ushers told me that the producer, Cheryl Crawford, in an interview describing a difficult time in rehearsal had said, "The director Margaret Webster was so upset, she climbed up on the stage, sat on Mr. Bel Geddes' beautiful erection and wept." It became part of theater lore.

It was always fun going to the theater and talking to the other ushers who were almost all out of work actors. Each one had stories they'd heard, true or not, and it was like a party. One night I held the door open for Greta Garbo and I've never forgotten the way she said, "Thank you" with the same voice that had asked for whiskey in the movie *Anna Christie* and then called out, "Don't be stingy, baby." I couldn't believe my luck at actually seeing her in the flesh, and she was as beautiful as she was in the movies.

The Tempest itself was a different kettle of fish. Though the cast included the first Black actor, Canada Lee, to play Caliban and the great dancer Vera Zorina to play Ariel, it was rather ponderous. One night at the end of the play when Arnold Moss, as Prospero, said in his mellifluous voice, "We are such stuff as dreams are made on and our little lives are rounded with a sleep." I heard a loud snore from someone in the audience.

Following *The Tempest* into the Alvin was *The Firebrand of Florence*. Kurt Weill had done the music and Ira Gershwin the lyrics so I couldn't wait for it to open. Unfortunately, as an usher, I had to see every one of the 43 performances. The show was a flop. It wasn't helped by Mr. Weill's wife, Lotte Lenya, playing the sexpot Duchess. She was anything but a beauty and she was getting along in age. She did have the best song, but her odd voice (which must have been great for Pirate Jenny in *The Threepenny Opera*, Kurt Weill's masterpiece) was quite wrong for a femme fatale. I was learning more about the theater and even starting to criticize what I thought was wrong.

I finally got a role in a play, still not on Broadway, so the actress in *Junior Miss* who'd predicted I wouldn't get there for five years, was turning out to be right. Actor's Equity was trying to help actors be seen by agents and producers so they started Equity Library Theater where plays could be done at little cost in the New York libraries. The actors weren't paid and there were minimal sets and costumes on a low budget. I got the leading role of Kostya in Chekhov's *The Sea Gull*.

We had done the play in Nantucket with Louis playing the part. There, I had the small role of Medvedenko and my *bette noir* was having to be on stage through all of the long second act and only having one line to say. I searched through my new Method knowledge and came up with the idea that every minute of the interminable act, I started to say something but somebody else spoke first and I had to be quiet. I'm sure the audience didn't get what I was doing, but it kept me busy and concentrated. Now I had the great role of a young, sensitive, would-be writer who is dependent on his mother, a flamboyant, selfish actress, and finally kills himself. One of the jokes about the play is the boy is called Kostya all the time, but the last line of the play is "Konstantin Gavrilovich has shot himself." That brings the curtain down and often many in the audience, having had their surfeit of long Russian names, would say to each other, "Which one was Konstantin Gavrilovich?" But that's Chekhov.

The rehearsals were in the afternoon so I could go right after I finished at the doctor's office. The library was way uptown, off the beaten track, but I had learned enough about the subway system to find it easily. The director was Iza Itkin, whose father had been a member of the Moscow Art Theater, so she had grown up in The Method. She was about my age, short, pudgy but already sure of herself and her ability to dominate a cast of actors.

The other actors were excellent, several of them had been in plays on Broadway and I finally felt that I was working with all professionals.

The woman who played my mother was extremely handsome with a pronounced, squarish chin line and a broad forehead. Iza told me she had been a studio standby for Garbo in case the star became too difficult to handle. Now she was married and had put up money for the production so New York could see her talent.

I related to my role completely. Kostya was an aspiring writer as I was an aspiring actor. He was distraught that the successful writers were getting all the opportunities and I felt the same way about actors. His mother wouldn't give him any money so he was as penniless as I was. My only problem was that I was exhausted. Between the doctor's office, rehearsals, learning my role and ushering, I just wasn't getting enough sleep. I would stretch out on the floor of the library and fall fast asleep and the stage manager would wake me when it was time for my scene. Looking back, I think the only mistake I made was in letting the costume woman dress me in a stunning dark blue Russian blouse. Everyone said how gorgeous it looked so I'm afraid I let my vanity take over and ignore the fact that my mother in the play wouldn't even give me money for clothes so I should have been in rags. But no matter. No one came to see us and we played to just a few friends. Either we were too far uptown or agents and producers just didn't want to sit through Chekhov.

I was back to making the rounds again and looking for tips in *Show Business* on what shows were casting. Marie and Miranda had not been able to raise enough money for a winter repertory let alone a summer one so they were concentrating on the following summer and starting to solicit for that. I saw them whenever I had some free time. Louis was busy starting his new life with Sam so I seldom saw him, but that was probably best for both of us.

As spring was beckoning, I noticed an ad for the USO. I had always felt guilty about not doing anything for the war effort so I went over to their headquarters to see if there was a play they were sending out that I could be right for. It was almost a joke: a company of *Junior Miss* was being put together to go overseas and the director thought I was perfect for the football player, the role that got me fired in Philadelphia. Of course, I now was two years older, heavier from exercising and my Byronic look was pretty much gone, so after the shock, I agreed to join the company. We would be gone for six months to somewhere in Europe. The war was still going on, but it looked like it was almost over.

The next weeks were spent rehearsing and fitting the heavy uniforms for the cold weather that would also identify us as performers. I notified Mr. Dorn that I'd be leaving and he was so impressed that I was going to entertain the soldiers who were risking their lives in the war, that he moved me back into Louis and my old room at no extra cost. I was being paid a salary and I was given additional money when I agreed to be the stage manager as well. I decided to have one third of my money sent to my parents who were still struggling, and one third sent to Marie and Miranda for the summer theater they were planning. I would keep one third for additional expenses I would have, though they wouldn't be much so I could save the rest.

The days rushed by like a whirlwind with a quick trip to see my parents in Boston that I paid for out of a two-week salary advance. Jackie wanted to celebrate and wish me bon voyage so she asked me to meet her at Tony's, a supper club in the basement of a brownstone building on 52nd Street. It had been a speakeasy during Prohibition and still retained the intimate, adventurous atmosphere that came with being clandestine. It was always hard to get a table, but Jackie was a favorite of the star attraction Mabel Mercer and the maître d' would squeeze us in. Jackie and I had become good friends since the day she had taken me to meet the agent she worked for and raved about my performance. She was seeing a woman who was married so many of her evenings were free and since I was alone, we went out together. Jackie paid the bill which embarrassed me, but she insisted the money meant nothing to her and that she loved my company.

Tony was standing on his head singing an aria from an Italian opera as Jackie arrived and we were seated. As we slid behind the table onto the banquette, we joined in the snickering laughter that accompanied him. The sophisticated crowd thought he was ridiculous, but he did own the place so they had to indulge him. I looked around. I always felt excited being there. The people were so beautiful and successful. The women dressed expensively and the men in tailored suits seemed protected from the smoke-filled air by their own aura of perfume or cologne. I thought Jackie fit in perfectly. She was wearing a pale brown silk dress with a pattern of flowers. The bottom was pleated and swirled around when she walked, A heavy gold chain encircled her neck and the diamond ring she always wore caught the light of her cigarette. She had told me that her perfume was Chanel's Russia Leather, but she used it sparingly and there was just a hint of the mysterious scent. She smoked constantly, and once a night, went through the ritual of changing the filter on her short holder that was black from the nicotine. She loved blowing huge smoke rings that she did like a man. With her long hair and dimpled, knowing smile, I thought she resembled Lauren Bacall, even down to the husky voice.

As our martinis were served – Jackie's was always in an old-fashioned glass on the rocks with both olives and onions – Mabel Mercer was introduced to wild applause. She spotted Jackie and walked over to our table and sat down. In a simple black dress with a red chiffon scarf against her light brown skin, she sang trilling her R's: "Remind me not to find you so attractive. Remind me that the world is full of men." As the piano accompaniment supported her faltering voice, the room was absolutely still. She had a cult following and she reigned like a queen in the club. I felt everyone watching Jackie and me and wondering why Mabel had sat at our table. I felt suddenly important in Mabel's reflected glory. How I would love to be a member of this special group who never had to worry about money or getting a job. To be rich and handsome and not have to worry if there were a hole in my stocking or that someone would notice my frayed collar. "I had a feeling when I met you, you'd drive me crazy if I let you," Mabel sang. "Now all my efforts to forget you, remind me I'm in love again."

Mabel had moved to another table and was singing "Just one of those things" when I noticed a man at the bar. He was the only person there except for Billie Holiday who was seated a few stools away listening intently to Mabel. She was wearing her signature gardenias and a pair of rimless glasses that looked out of place with her evening dress. She worked at a club across the street and often came in between sets. My eyes connected with the man who seemed to be staring at me and we both quickly looked away. Mabel had gotten to the line in the song her audience always waited for: "We'd have been aware that our love affair was too." She paused for a fraction of a second and hit the next word with her full voice: "HOT, not to cool down." The elegant men and women screamed and applauded like children at a little league game.

I turned back toward the bar trying to look disinterested. The man was still looking at me. I thought he was incredibly handsome. He had thick black hair parted in the middle and pushed up on both sides so that locks of it fell onto his forehead. His eyes looked as dark as his hair, and his olive skin was set off by a perfectly fitted gray pin stripe suit with wide lapels. He was smoking, and as his hand raised a cigarette to his mouth, I could see an expensive gold bracelet hugging the cuff of his shirt. He smiled at me and I half smiled back before turning to Jackie.

"You've been looking at him a lot," she said.

"Oh, I'm sorry," I said, "I didn't mean to be rude."

"Don't be silly," she replied. "He's great-looking. Do you want me to ask him to join us?" I felt dizzy.

"Are you crazy?" I protested. "You can't do that."

"Why not?" Jackie said in her most practical voice. "You don't have many nights left so why overlook an opportunity?"

I hated myself for acting so coy and helpless, but I felt totally out of control, as if I were a feather blowing in the wind. I was warm from the drinks and the proximity of the people jammed into the small tables around me. There was a moment of the most delicious anticipation as everything stood still. *Whatever happens, this moment is perfect* I thought. I felt attractive, secure, even rich and as if I were on the brink of a great adventure. "You are too beautiful for one man alone," Mabel sang as I watched Jackie talking to the man at the bar. He looked toward me, smiled, and walked with Jackie to our table.

The only one at our table who was awkward, after Jackie had said, "This is Cass Stevens," was me. I hardly said a word as Cass answered Jackie's rapid-fire questions. She always grilled a person she was meeting for the first time as if she were interviewing them for a newspaper. She found out that Cass, who had the slightest Southern accent, was from Texas and in publishing. He was extremely charming and well-mannered and the two of them got on famously. I began to think that I was being left out until Cass said coolly, "Can we take you home, Jackie?"

Jackie replied with a matching lack of expression, "There are two friends over there who've asked me to join them so I'll just say good night." She insisted on paying the check.

When we were outside the club, breathing the cold air, Cass told me he was staying with a friend and we could go there to have a drink, but he wished we could be alone. I said with some hesitation, "I have a room in the Village. It's not very much."

"I don't care what it is," he said romantically, "as long as we can be together." Neither of us spoke in the cab going downtown, but Cass held my hand below the seat so that the driver couldn't see it.

As we walked in, I saw my room as if for the first time. It looked shabby with the double bed taking up most of the space and my Valpak and the ditty bag leaning against the wall. It was as if the light pouring from Cass's perfection shone into the corners and exposed the dirt. As soon as the door was closed, Cass kissed me, and the rest was like a skein of wool coming unwound, at times slowly and at other times as if someone were running with it off into the distance, but always with an inevitability that it would go on unraveling until it was done.

I had never felt so natural making love before. Acts that had always had names in my mind became simply signposts on the road to my destination. The bed was underneath a barred window, and when we finally lay still, the moon shone down on us. Cass raised himself up on one elbow and looked at me.

"You're so handsome," he said. "I love you and I want to live with you forever." I suddenly thought of the magic potion in *Midsummers Night Dream* when a few drops of a flower made the characters fall in love with each other. Had Cass sprinkled the drops in my eyes? I felt totally without artifice and the most honest I'd ever been with a lover.

"I love you too" I said, "but I'm going overseas in a day or two."

"No," Cass said, "it can't be."

"I signed up with the USO for six months and we leave any minute. That's what Jackie and I were celebrating."

Cass sat up in bed with his head against the window sill. "Can you get out of it?" he asked.

"Of course not," I replied. We both lit cigarettes and stared into the darkness away from the moon.

"It's all right," Cass said, "I'll just have to wait till you come back."

The next few days were frantic. I had to be packed and ready to leave at a moment's notice. Since I was stage-managing as well as acting in the *Junior Miss* tour, I had to be in the USO offices going over technical plans for the set and the lighting. The minute I was done, I flew to Cass's apartment. He seemed to be between jobs and had been given a room by a friend who was a composer. In return, Cass said he helped him by writing some lyrics. I couldn't quite figure out what Cass did, but it didn't matter. The important thing was that we be together every minute before I shipped out.

With my two-week salary advance, I got tickets for *Carousel* and *On The Town*. When Nancy Walker sang "Some Other Time," all I could think of was the day I would return and Cass and I would live together. We talked of it constantly. And when we weren't planning the kind of apartment we would have, we told each other about our lives before we met. Cass didn't know his real parents, but he did have a sister he was close to. We realized that I would not be able to write freely with censorship, so we decided I would address my letters to Cass's sister. That way, we could write all the things we wanted to. I told Cass about giving one third of my salary to the girls for the theater. I said I would tell them to give some of it to Cass if he needed it, at least till he got a job. I had a momentary question in my mind as to where Cass got the beautiful clothes and jewelry that he wore, but it disappeared like leaf smoke on a fall day. Everything had to be settled before I went.

I rushed around packing and repacking, seeing Jackie and Marie and Miranda, storing my few possessions, racing to meet Cass, and going to Tony's with him for a last farewell. And then I was on the train for Seattle feeling as if I were in a war movie.

7

USO

I sat next to the window trying to write to Cass. The train was bouncing around so badly that I had trouble controlling the pen, but I was determined to have a letter ready to mail in Chicago.

Good morning –

Tried to write you last night as I lay in my berth, but the train was shaking so that I couldn't. It's bad enough now, but I think you'll be able to read this.

I am so thankful for the extra time we had together last night and yesterday. It was so nice just having dinner with your friends and then walking so casually through Central Park as if we could go there whenever we wanted to. The whole evening gave me a feeling of peace. All day something had been welling up inside me, growing and growing, until after dinner I thought I'd burst into a million pieces and then it was all over. For the first time since I met you, I started to breathe again. It was at that moment I realized how much I love you. Then I knew I could leave you for six months, or any length of time, and be able to bear it. Not that the physical need of you would be gone – that will last until I die. But now I know I'll always love you and you'll be with me every minute I'm away. I've found you, and distance and time can't take you away from me.

We've been traveling through beautiful country, Pennsylvania and Ohio. It reminds me of New England except that it hasn't the gnarled, wizened age that my wonderful New England has. But it's pretty as a picture, miles and miles of perfectly tilled fields and neat farmhouses. I love farms and sometimes wonder if a farm life wouldn't be a truly happy one. There's something so clean and wholesome and good about any life that's built around rain and sun and heat and cold. Nature should be much more important than it usually is in people's lives.

Every time I pass a beautiful spot, I want to jump off the train and bring you there to see it. There are so many lovely brooks shaded by more weeping willows than I've ever seen. And the hills, they are so round and look like they'd fit into the palm of your hand.

It's so difficult to write on the train – my pen keeps jiggling. What can I write besides "I love you?" It must sound so flat. I want to say such beautiful things to you but I'm an actor, not a writer. Too many words that other people have written come into my mind and my own seem inadequate – no way good enough to tell you how I feel. It's 2:30 now and we'll be in Chicago at 4:30y. I may call you if it's not too expensive. I've got to stretch my money through to Seattle.

I must close this now. I'm getting dizzy watching my pen skip around. I haven't said half the things I've wanted to. Looking back, all I've said sounds a little silly, but I hope you'll understand. All I know is that I love you so have faith in me and love me. If you can't, never be afraid to tell me. You've given me so much that you could never destroy, even by your not loving me. If you can't love me, don't be sorry. You must be sure of anyone you give your love to. When you love someone, you give them your brains, your body, your talent, your whole essence of being. That's a lot to give away thoughtlessly. So, if you have a change of heart, please write me.

All my love,

Yours,

A

The lights of Milwaukee streaked by as I lay in the lower berth and thought about Cass. I had spent all my time during the train stop in Chicago trying to reach him on the telephone, but there was no answer. After dinner with a wealthy aunt who lived on Lake Shore Drive, a taxi driver took me to the train, pointing out the sights with great pride: the Palmolive Building, the Art Institute, Soldier's Field, the Loop. But all I could think of was I had to reach Cass before the train left. I wanted to shout at the driver to go faster, but I couldn't hurt his feelings when he was being such a generous guide. At last, I reached the station, rushed to a phone booth and this time Cass was home. I didn't want him to know how desperate I had been to reach him, so I tried to be chatty and light, but Cass was the serious one and said how much he missed me. After I hung up, I walked to the train smiling at everyone. I was loved. It wasn't long before the euphoria wore off. I felt as if I had been having a brief respite from a toothache, now that it was back, the pain was twice as bad.

The clicking of the train passing over the railroad ties lulled me into a half sleep. I left the curtains of the berth open so I could watch the lonely lights of the farmhouses, and I thought about love. *How was I so sure this time?* I wondered. I had obviously made such a mistake about Roger. I had never faced my feelings after Roger rejected me. It had happened so gradually that when I finally realized it was over, there was hardly any pain. Besides, Roger had been twice my age and Cass was only a couple of years older than me. We have so much more in common. I thought about Jackie and how she had cautioned me at lunch only a few days before. "He's very attractive," she said, "but you're going to be away six months. You'll meet so many people. What do you want to be tied down for?" She couldn't understand that all I wanted was the love of one person.

As a child, I had felt so secure in my mother's love. As I grew older, I couldn't always find it. She was away at her bridge games or parties and I had begun to feel lonely. One night, as my brother and I lay awake talking, he told me that everyone in the world was selfish and only thought about themselves.

"I don't believe it," I had replied in a frightened childish voice. "Mother isn't selfish. She'd do anything for us."

"Don't be an idiot," he replied. "She thinks of herself first, everybody does."

I was shattered. I began to test my mother to see if it were true and each time, she failed me. I realized my brother was right. I couldn't count on her love. Eventually, I had to get away from the oppressive affection that she offered as a substitute. As for my father, I knew as a baby that he couldn't give me love. I have never forgotten being ill when I was five years old and we were living in Florida. My father had brought me a little cardboard trunk with leather straps. It was the first present he had ever given me. I was so excited. I reached out my arms to kiss him. He pushed me away and left the room. I kept the trunk for years as a reminder of what my father's love really was. The trunk finally wore out.

How wonderful it would be if two people could love each other equally so there would be no doubts, no misunderstandings, no jealousies. That's what I wanted with Cass. I looked at my watch. It was 4:00 in the morning. I closed the curtains and tried to sleep.

A few hours later, I sat with a writing pad in my lap at work on another letter:

Dear Cass:

Have managed to get through this morning eating and talking and looking at some of the most beautiful scenery in the world, the Rockies. But now that the day is really starting, the only thing I want to do is talk to you. I posted your letter yesterday in a little town called Ortonville, South

Dakota, which was so friendly to us. We only stopped for ten minutes, but the women of the town run a USO lunch counter so every minute of the ten, they pushed more wonderful things at us: thick, creamy, fresh country milk; doughnuts; jelly; fruit; and the best homemade cake I've ever tasted. The biggest surprise was heavy pheasant sandwiches. There are thousands of pheasants running all over the countryside. People here in the small towns of the West are so warm, and they try so hard to be nice. I have no way of describing these glorious mountains to you. I sit here writing, looking out the window, and I keep wanting to say, "Look! Look at that tall, snow-capped mountain that seems to reach right up to heaven. Look!" But you're not here and so I write, completely unable to express how I feel. The valley that stretches for miles with trees and lakes and maybe a farm or two, a couple of horses, some sheep, a cow, and then the hills. Oh god, greens, browns, blacks, blues, purples – pastel colors and great, dramatic, bold tones mixed.

What really impresses me most about the West, I suppose, is what impresses everyone, the vastness. But more than that, it's the colors, great blobs of color. In my part of the East, colors are jumbled, millions of shades all combined, mingled to form an insane patchwork quilt. But here, the artist has put whole tubes of one color in a great space, and then a huge quantity of another color beside it. The effect is startling, bold, dramatic, and so big. I suppose I can't help loving my subtle New England more. (Though what could be more brilliant and less subtle than autumn in New Hampshire or Vermont?) I guess that I just love it all: the lush tropical beauty of Florida, the Shenandoah, the Mohawk Valley, the boat trip up the Hudson, Cape Cod, miles and miles of wheat and alfalfa and rye in Missouri and Kansas, Niagara Falls, and Canada, the trees with their Spanish moss hairpieces in the Carolinas – everything I've seen so far and everything I plan to see in the rest of my life. But now I will love it all more because I will see it all with you.

Actually, the trip has been interesting. There are a couple of soldiers who have been very friendly. They talked with us, played cards with us, and ate with us. There's a guy called Chuck from Oregon with a good, clean, strong face and a warm personality. His hair is gray before its time because he handles the movements of prisoners of war and is one of the guys who goes out alone to a live bomb and renders it harmless. He's a swell guy, easy-going, tough with everybody, but he talked to me about his mother and how much he loves her. Then there's Tex from somewhere in the West. He's handsome, young but mature because of many bombing missions over Germany. Tex is a great animal. Life, to him, is a series of women in Seattle, San Francisco, Casablanca, Teheran, etc. plus the money he can make selling GI things to the Arabs. Tex's proudest boast is being one of the few white men to ever rip a veil from a Muslim woman's face. And so, like most animals, Tex spends most of his day resting, storing up energy for new and greater conquests as soon as our trip is over.

Chuck is resting up too. He has a bad cold he caught from a woman he had in an alley in Chicago. She stole his money as well. There are several others in our car but they're all pretty much the same. Duke, a lieutenant, has been in the Navy for 16 years. He has a wife and kids but is looking around, and so on ad nauseam. Part of our job for the USO is to listen to these men and make them feel less lonely. I'm trying and I suppose in time I'll be able to talk brightly to all of them, but now I can think of no one else but you.

I go over and over in my mind every minute of the four days that we were together: seeing you, wanting to meet you, wonder of wonders meeting you, our first night together with dawn coming up over your face, seeing On The Town *and relating it to our imminent separation, our last night together as I watched you sleep, the awful frustration of being told our departure was delayed and only being able to find you in a room full of people. Then, the opening of a taxi door, your face and "I'll see you in six months."*

We've gone through the Continental Divide now, Montana, the Piedmont Valley, and just over the mountain there is Yellowstone. Somehow the only miracle of nature I want to see is you. I look out the window at the thousands of trees climbing up to the peak of a mountain and see you sitting in a chair, reading or writing, while I study a role doing brilliant work because you're near me. I see the life we'll lead together, the happiness we can have and the curve of a mountain is the curve of your back, the foothills, your knees as you sit, the arrangements of branches in a tree, your fingers. Everything is You and I realize that only three days of the six months have gone by.

I'll be in Seattle tomorrow and will call you as soon as I get there. Smile and be happy. My love is always with you.

A

8

Everyone went up on deck right after breakfast to lay down in the sun. We were satiated from the fruit, cereal, griddle cakes, bacon and eggs, jams and jellies, and endless cups of coffee. Except for the zigzagging of the ship to avoid submarines, and the yells if anyone appeared without his lifebelt, it was hard to remember that a war was going on all around us. The sea was an opiate, and it made us forget where we were going and what we would have to do. All the USO troupe were first-class passengers so we were allowed to share the top deck – the men were below in an open space. The only activity was applying suntan oil since there was no pool. Occasionally someone would try to read a book, but they'd give up after a few pages. We were at a point farther away from land than any place on earth and the sea had turned a pure, dense blue. The sky, in contrast, was transparent – its usual pale blue had turned almost pink.

The other actors surrounded me. There were 14 in all: five of them, including me, were the young men in the play; three were the young girls; and the other six were adults. We had rehearsed for a month in New York and already I had formed a strong impression of each one. I had shared a room with Bill, one of the boys, in Seattle. He had been a model in New York and was handsome, likable, blond, 21, and desperate about beginning to lose his hair. He asked me to take a walk whenever he brought a soldier or sailor back to the hotel. I was happy to get out rather than hear the noise from the next bed. I knew the other boys were homosexual as well. One of them, Eric, looked like a typical college cheerleader; another, Merrill, was what I considered a swish with effeminate gestures and affected speech; and the last, Johnny, was a prissy boy from the mid-West who seemed shocked and titillated by the others.

The three girls were totally different. Peggy, who played the teenage lead, was wide-eyed and innocent, but when I found out she was 22, I thought there must be more there than met the eye. The girl who played her sister, Dana, was a farm girl who tried to be very sophisticated but whose lack of polish was obvious. The lead's best friend, also playing a teenager, Dodie, was jazzy and full of fun. Two of the adults were married to each other. The man playing the father, Brandon, was a typically vain, failed leading man who was also the company manager; and his wife, Alice, who played the maid, was younger and constantly coddling her much older husband. Nancy played the mother, very elegant with upswept hair. There was a character man in his sixties who was fat and hard of hearing and the two grown up lovers were played by Liz, an attractive woman in her late twenties and Paul, a new father in his fifties. We all got on well together with the exception of the swish who had made a scene in Grand Central Station when we were about to leave New York. He brandished a bottle of perfume he was afraid to pack and shrieked that he would not sleep in an upper berth. I was surprised, with all the investigating that we had been put through by the FBI, that the boy had still been allowed to go overseas. Everyone tried to keep away from him.

I had begun to question whether I was right to have taken this tour. It wasn't only because of Cass that I thought I'd made a mistake. I'd been so convinced that I ought to do something about the war. I had felt so far away from it. Everyone I knew had friends, husbands, brothers, and lovers in danger and they hung on each word in the newspapers and on the radio. My father was an air raid warden and my brother was in the Coast Guard, but he was never sent overseas. I was untouched by the war and although I prayed for it to end as everyone did, there was no urgency, no immediacy in my prayers. I knew that the war would be over and won, but although I thought of the dying, the dead, and the ones who were to die, I didn't have an emotional response in my gut that I felt I should have. I decided I had to be a part of it in some way, for my growth as a human being as well as an actor. The USO had seemed a perfect opportunity. Now, as I lay in the sun listening to the waves hit the side of the troop ship, I doubted that I had anything to give these men who were being shipped out to fight. What would a little comedy about a coming-of-age teenage girl do for anybody facing death? In time, I would find out the answer.

The lazy hum of the ship's engines must have put me to sleep, for when I opened my eyes, some of the cast had wandered off to play shuffleboard. It was the only activity besides cards that there was room for. There was no lounge or dance floor since space was so limited. The advantage was that everyone came to know each other, if only to say hello – at least the officers and the USO people. The men were huddled below as if they were on a slave ship. I went down to the cabin to wash up before lunch. Five of us slept on triple decker bunks in an eight-by-ten-foot room with a wash stand. It was empty for the moment and I was grateful to be alone. My only problem was always having to be with people and make conversation, so I took advantage of the quiet and lay on my bed.

I thought I should write to Cass, but I couldn't mail the letter until the ship reached land, so I kept putting it off. I wanted to tell him about the days in Seattle before we left: all the cholera and tetanus shots, the photographs for new identification cards, the luggage searches for liquor and drugs, the doling out of summer uniforms (we had thought we were going to Europe so all our clothes were too heavy) and the endless physical and medical exams. I knew Cass would be amused at the "short arm" inspection. I thought back over it so I wouldn't forget what happened.

I had been ushered into a small room, filled with soldiers, where a doctor said, "Take it out and milk it down." I couldn't believe what I was hearing so I asked him to explain. When I realized what he meant by "it," I was horrified. How could he expect me to masturbate in front of all the men standing around. By the time the doctor had made a few gestures in the air, I realized what was required of me, but by then the room was reverberating with laughter.

Seattle was mainly about the suspense of wondering where we would go and when. I had wandered through the Farmers Market in my spare time and gone into a record store. I wanted to hear the Warsaw Concerto that I'd listened to on the radio one night with Cass. We had decided it was to be our music, and as I heard it again in a small, padded booth, I thought about the prospect of eternity and how I must learn patience. There must be a reason Cass and I had found each other and then were separated. Then it came to me.

Of course, now I understand: True happiness can't be achieved unless it's struggled for, fought for – if it comes too easily, it's not appreciated, and people lose it because they never even realize that they have it. Cass and I have been given a test and if we get all the answers right, we'll have a lifetime of glorious living and love.

Lunch was announced on the loud speaker and I was jolted out of my reverie to find myself staring at the empty bunk above me. I sat up, ducking my head and slid over the side to the floor. I felt happy and ravenously hungry.

The grotesque, volcanic mountains of Oahu seemed to leap right out of the sea. I had expected the island to be flat with lush vegetation, but all I could see were palisades with distorted peaks brown and blue, purple and green. Nerves were just beginning to fray from the week on the water so the excitement of seeing land was almost orgiastic. There was a loud speaker on deck playing recordings made especially for the Armed Forces. As we approached Honolulu, I heard Dinah Shore pretending to be in a taxi in New York, stopping at the theaters and singing songs from shows that were playing there. When she got to "If I Loved You" from *Carousel*, which Cass and I had seen together, I felt a moment of yearning but I pushed it away. When we were close enough to see the Aloha Tower and the huge pineapple atop the Dole factory, people began to say goodbye. The night before the ship's crew had given a huge party. The members of the USO concert and variety units had performed arias from *Rigoletto* and *Carmen*. Then they led all of us in songs like "My Old Kentucky Home" and "Home On The Range." As we sat on deck, under the stars that were so crowded together you could barely see any sky, we joined hands and sang "Should auld acquaintance be forgot." There were tears in many eyes as we thought of our loved ones far away and also, of the future. As long as we were on the ship, despite the danger of submarines, we had felt protected, but now our war was a about to begin. An army band on shore cut through all the other noise and dominated it with "Lay That Pistol Down, Babe." I had hoped for "Aloha Oe."

The actors and I waited on the top deck until the troops disembarked. I thought how young the soldiers were, even younger than I, but I could no longer see their faces. They were covered from head to foot with equipment and looked like so many matches in a matchbox or holes in a window screen. They were no longer individuals, just part of a horde. As they went trudging down the gangplank, there was a flurry of applause which was cut short as handkerchiefs were dug out of pockets.

All the USO personnel were herded into army trucks and driven 35 miles to Camp Schofield. We passed the outskirts of Honolulu and I was disappointed to find it exactly like the States with hot dog stands, gas stations, bowling alleys, and bungalows. I only saw a few palm trees. The island seemed to be covered with army and navy installations: barracks, office buildings, parking lots and airfields. When we got into the country, however, there were acres and acres of sugar cane and pineapple fields. The soil was so red, it almost hurt my eyes. The clouds over the jagged hills looked as if an artist had used a palette knife to give them their density. From a distance we could see Pearl Harbor with its many locks cut into the earth, looking like fingers on a hand.

We were billeted at a group of cottages opposite the camp. I was put in one with Paul, the older actor who was the romantic lead in the play.

As soon as I'd thrown my bags into my room, I was taken out to a Jeep and introduced to a stern-looking Captain with jet black hair and movie star looks. He was to be the Special Service officer in charge of our unit. The Captain informed me that we had to immediately set dates for the performances and take care of the sets and costumes. Within minutes I was on my way back to Honolulu.

Overlooking the bustling city, the University of Hawaii was an oasis of calm sheltered, as it was, by a ring of volcanic mountains. The Captain took me inside the institutional-looking buildings that were the headquarters for the Special Services to an office where we discussed a schedule of dates and service bases the company would play. The plan was for us to stay on Oahu until the end of August, before going to the Forward Area or "Down Under" as it was called. The army would build us a set that would be much more substantial than the canvas backgrounds we were carrying with us. I gave the Captain a list of furniture and props I would require and he then gave me a tour of the section. I was amazed.

Maurice Evans, who I knew was a famous Shakespearean actor, had been in charge before he returned to the States. He had created a theater workshop that toured plays throughout the Pacific. There were rooms for makeup, costumes, furniture, an electrical shop, even a dye room. It was more professional than anything I had ever seen. When I saw pictures of the productions they had done, I thought *Junior Miss* would seem like a summer stock show in comparison. The Captain, who now encouraged me to call him Carl, showed me photographs of the *GI Hamlet* that had been a great success. Standing next to Maurice Evans, looking barely recognizable, was Carl with blond hair. When I said how well he looked, he was very pleased.

"I was Horatio," he said.

I suddenly realized why his hair was so black now – he must have dyed it back. I couldn't imagine how a Captain in the army would have bleached hair, but I couldn't very well ask him about it. I guessed that everyone accepted the fact that he was an actor and *Hamlet* took place in Denmark where the men were blond. On our way back to Schofield, Carl talked about his wife and children so any suspicions I had about him were dispelled. At my door, Carl asked if I would like to go to the theater that night. I was delighted to be away from the other actors so I quickly said yes.

I hadn't asked what the play was and I was amazed when I saw the poster in front of the theater: Gertrude Lawrence and Mildred Natwick in *Blithe Spirit*. I couldn't believe they were here in the middle of the Pacific. Carl told me they were doing a special production for service men and the theater was jammed. Carl had excellent seats, and I felt like I was back in New York. I thought of when I waited in the freezing cold in Boston, I was just a kid, for Gertrude Lawrence to come out of the theater after *Lady In The Dark*. I had thought her performance was so wonderful. At last, she came out surrounded by people. I shyly asked for her autograph. She seemed so tired, but she said of course she would sign my program if she could just sit down out of the wind. She settled herself in the limousine like a queen and took the pen I handed her through the open door.

"What is your name?" she asked in her musical voice.

I still have the paper with *Best wishes, Gertrude Lawrence*. And now, years later, here she was, just a few feet away from me in Honolulu. I was thrilled – until she started to act. I couldn't believe how exaggerated and unreal her performance was. She had evidently decided to give the men what she thought they wanted, so she tried to put a sexual double entendre into every line. When she said to the leading man "Your hair is so curly," the audience guffawed. It was clear she was not referring to the hair on his head. She also elongated every one of her words. I began to hold my breath, out of empathy, as if I were helping her get to the end of the line.

Afterwards, Carl took me backstage and introduced me to the star. She was surrounded by as chi chi a group of people as I had ever seen. She flitted about glamorously, kissing everyone and chatting in the most superficial way. There was an older Hawaiian man – Carl said he was of royal birth – who seemed very effeminate to me as he held court with a group that would have been more at home at Tony's. They all hugged each other and screamed at the new arrivals. I felt so strange. I had thought I was going to a war zone and it had turned out to be just like Shubert Alley.

The curfew, which had been at 10:00 in the evening, had just been lifted, but the bars still closed at 6:00. Carl took me to a place where he said, "You can't get a drink but you can see everyone on the island." It looked like a California drive-in with a huge painted sign on the roof – "Kau Kau" that means "eat" in Hawaiian. It was in a section heralded as "The Crossroads of the Pacific." There were arrows pointing in different directions with the names of major cities in the world and the distance to them. I felt so far away from Cass and my friends. Once inside, it was like any large hamburger stand, brightly lit and crowded with tables. The people, milling about, looked like dancers choreographed for an exotic musical. There were sailors with rings in their ears, mixtures of Polynesians and Chinese, Japanese, and Black people, prostitutes and homosexuals. The natives had jet black, thick straight hair with dark skin and black eyes. The women had beautiful bodies, and the men were barefoot and dressed in red or blue slacks with flowered shirts open to the waist to show their muscular bodies. They all seemed to exude sex and a sensual pleasure in their own beauty.

On the way back to my bungalow, Carl was quiet. The top of the Jeep was open and the myriad stars seemed closer than I'd ever seen them. The air was cool and fresh with just a hint of the warm trade wind.

As we drove along the sea, Carl said, "Let's go in for a swim; it's very calm right here."

The black mountains were etched faintly against the sky and the smell of the pineapple and sugar cane fields almost made me dizzy. Carl stopped the vehicle on the sand. We both undressed and dashed into the water. I felt a sharp chill, but as I swam, it disappeared. I began to feel as if I were in a warm bath. My movements stirred up the phosphorescence in the water. I savored the thousands of lights in the sky and the sea enveloped me. *This is the Pacific I've always dreamed about*, I thought. Carl was floating nearby making gestures with his hands as if he were scooping up the air and sending it in the direction of his face.

"It's so glorious," he said, "can you smell it?"

"What?" I asked.

"My cologne," Carl replied. "It's Jean Patou's Moment Supreme."

I swam away from him. Was he waiting for me to make some kind of move on him? Fortunately, he didn't seem to be aggressive at all. I thought, *I've been here one day and I feel as if I've been set down in the middle of a lunatic asylum*. I saw Carl getting towels from the Jeep and after a short ride, I was in my bed wondering again if the whole trip had been a terrible mistake.

9

Celebrating the end of the war

I was sitting in the dining room of the Moana Hotel with the older actors of the company when Carl appeared. We had been moved from Schofield Barracks to Waikiki, and we were all so much happier to be in Honolulu than way out in the country. We had been watching the activity on the beach with the native boys standing up on their precarious surfboards in the breaking waves, the rowers battling to keep right side up in the out-rigger canoes, and the hundreds of bathers in their scant, flower-patterned suits running into the surf or basking in the sun.

I had at first been disappointed in the narrow strip of dirty sand covered with too many people, and the ocean floor made up of rough coral and sharp rock. Now, as I saw the pale green water turn to deep blue at the horizon, and the mountain emerging from the sea to form, with a line of palm trees, the outer rim of the beach, I thought it was one of the most beautiful sights in the world.

Carl sat down with us and talked about the show and how pleased all the brass were with the way it was going. The theater at Schofield only had 800 seats, but there had not been an empty one all week. Paul, my roommate, said that I deserved a lot of the credit and the others agreed. I said everyone should get the credit, but I was pleased.

When the rehearsal for the opening performance had gone badly, I had stepped in and started to direct the show. The actors were startled, but they did what I told them to and by the time the curtain went up, the production was the best it had been. The audience was filled with generals and colonels and the applause was like a Broadway opening night. As I watched the actors taking their bows – I was too busy with my stage-managing chores to take a curtain call for my own role – I thought *maybe there's more to this business than just acting*.

Carl drove his Jeep up into the mountains. Since it was Sunday and my day off, he was taking me to dinner at a friend's house. He had helped get everything I needed for the show and been a good companion. There was nothing close about our relationship, but we got on well and I was grateful to have a friend outside of the company. From the top of the hill, we saw a lovely small valley. "It's called Manoa," Carl said in response to my praising its beauty. We drove through it and onto a precarious dirt road high up on a ridge. Deep into the lush vegetation, we came to a small, unimpressive one-story house. As Carl pulled up the brake, a bald man in his early seventies came out of the house with a dog. I thought I had never seen such a kind face. It reminded me of H.B. Warner who I had admired playing Christ in the film *King of Kings* at the Modern Museum.

"This is Doc Wyman," Carl said and I jumped down and we shook hands. Doc took us into his house and I was overwhelmed. Here was the Hawaii I had imagined. Through one enormous room that led into a lanai, I could see the whole valley framed by mountains and, in the distance, the sun sparkling on the surf at Waikiki.

After we had taken off our shoes and stockings and traded our uniforms for blue jeans and brightly colored Hawaiian shirts that Doc gave us, we went into the lanai that was a huge, screened porch with built-in sofas overlooking the view. We were given an old fashioned and Carl put a record on the phonograph. Beatrice Lillie sang "I Hate The Spring" and we laughed and talked. Louis had played me all the Beatrice Lillie records so I knew them well and even sang along with some of the verses. Several other men appeared and we all sat at an oval table in the living room eating avocado pears, pork, and Hawaiian salad. It had grown dark, but there were candles on the table and a mound of gardenias giving off an exotic smell.

Doc had been a professor at the university for years and had directed some of the shows for Maurice Evans before the actor returned to the mainland. The walls were lined with bookshelves filled with theater books and plays. I couldn't resist taking some down and riffling through them.

"You can borrow as many books as you want," Doc said, "but you must bring them back."

"Thank you," I replied, "I'll take you up on that."

The conversation drifted from the petty intrigues and jealousies in the service, to the overbearing attitude the officers had with the men, the gay bar at the Alexander Young Hotel in Honolulu where servicemen were lined up a block away waiting to get in, and a lot of anecdotes about the theater. When it was time to go, I thanked Doc by saying it was the happiest time I'd had since I arrived on the island.

"Do you have to work in the morning?" Doc asked.

"No," I replied, "we're not moving to another theater so I don't go to work till four."

"Why don't you stay overnight then?" Doc said. "You can sleep on the lanai and see the sunrise over the Manoa Valley."

After the others had left, I sat with Doc looking out at the twinkling lights of Honolulu and the mountains bathed in the warmth of a full moon. Doc asked me about my life and I found it perfectly natural to talk about Cass and my hopes for the future. The old man told me he had once been in love but had not been able to be with just one person, so they had broken up. We began to share our experiences as if we both were the same age. I said I was worried about Cass meeting someone else and that we had promised each other not to feel guilty if we were unable to resist "temptation" as I called it. I was afraid Cass would let his guilt feelings turn something purely physical into an important issue, so

I had encouraged him to be with someone rather than keep everything pent-up inside. I was going to remain faithful, but I realized at our ages that six months was a long time.

Later, when I was lying on my mattress that was arranged Japanese-style flat on the floor of the veranda with a sheet pulled up over my chest, Doc padded in. He had put on his bathrobe and slippers.

"I was thinking about what you were telling me," Doc said and his bald head shone in the moonlight. "You're going to need some physical relief," he paused for a moment, "I would be glad to help you."

I lay still. It had been said in such an off-hand way that I couldn't take offense, but it was awkward to know just how to respond. I measured my words. "I'll be all right," I said making it clear that the subject was closed.

Doc walked back into the living room and from the darkness I heard him say, "I'll take my teeth out."

I was too stunned to reply. After a moment, I heard Doc go into his room and close the door. I lay awake with the sound of the cicadas drumming in my ears. I wasn't angry or disgusted. I just felt sorry for Doc. How sad it was to be old and alone. If Doc had been able to be with only one person... I knew it wasn't all that simple, but I determined my life would be different. *There must be a way*, I thought, *for two people to love each other and spend their lives together. I have to do everything I can to make that happen.* I fell asleep planning the long letter I would write to Cass in the morning.

The pounding on the door seemed to be in a dream, but it persisted so I finally opened my eyes. For a moment I thought I was still in Camp Schofield, but in the darkness, I could make out the other bed a few feet away and then I remembered I was in the Moana Hotel. We had moved there a few days before but where was Paul? His bed was empty. The knocking didn't stop so I got out of bed and opened the door. Paul and Carl stood there grinning at me.

"Get dressed," Paul said. "The war is over." I stood half asleep on my feet and tried not to wake up completely so I could go right back to bed. They were obviously drunk.

"What time is it?" I asked.

"Four in the morning," Carl replied. "Now put your clothes on. We're going to wake up the section and tell them the news."

"Are you serious?" I asked.

"The war with Japan is over," Paul said as if I were hard of hearing, "now come on."

In the lobby of the hotel a few Navy men were huddled around a radio listening to the latest bulletins. As we drove down the boulevard past the Hali Kulani and the Royal Hawaiian hotels, a few cars raced by and the people waved at us. When we got to the university, it was pitch dark and we went to each one of the shed-like barracks and banged on the doors. The men came tumbling out naked, or with towels wrapped around them, scratching their heads or rubbing their eyes. When they heard the news, they shouted, yelled, swore and cracked jokes. We all began to surge together and move toward the Hambs Club which was a beer bar named by the actors as a tribute to the Lambs Club in New York.

Once inside, the radio was turned on and we listened to the news. It was still not official but promising enough for us all to have a beer and talk about going home. One of the men sat down at the piano and we all sang. Several of the men danced together. It was 5:00 in the morning and we were all groggy, but we were afraid if we went back to sleep, it would all turn out to be a dream.

I barely had time to go back to the hotel and shower before I got a call that my driver was waiting. We drove out to Bellows Field where I supervised the loading of the set, costumes, and props. I counted off the three large canvas cases, the nine smaller cases and the furniture as it was placed in a truck. When we arrived at the submarine base at Pearl Harbor, a detail of six men waited and I taught them how to put up the set. We were moving to a new base every day now so each time, I worked with a different crew. They had to be instructed on how to bolt the structure together from which the backdrops would be hung.

When everything was in place, I began my search for the furniture that we couldn't carry with us. First, I'd go to the Officer's Club and if I didn't find it there, I'd go to the elegant offices of some of the brass. By early afternoon I was done. The lights and props I'd take care of when I returned several hours before the show. On my way back to the hotel, I marveled at the enormity of Pearl Harbor. It was a group of many harbors that were connected and a multitude of ships from small airplane carriers to battleships, transports and huge carriers. My driver chatted away, boasting about the $9,000 he had made in just three months in crap games. He told me as soon as he was discharged, he was going to buy a custom-built Packard.

At 4:00, the company was picked up and driven to the theater. The actors had begun to bicker and divide up into groups. They complained about their dressing rooms as well as the food. They looked on me now as someone who worked for them since I was either putting up the set or assigning their dressing rooms or telling them when it was time to go onstage. Each night, after the performance, I had to take the set down and pack it away. That estranged me even more since I always seemed to be busy. When we arrived at the theater, I went to work with the men setting the lights. That night, the others went to the Commander's cocktail party. When I joined them, I saw white-coated Black butlers serving hors d'oeuvres to all the executives of Pearl Harbor. The women were given silver pins with the submarine insignia and Chanel Number Five perfume. The men got Moroccan wallets. I had gotten used to the elegance of the officers' clubs, but this one seemed like it was out of a movie. There was a wave of excitement in the room as everyone talked of the rumors that the war was finally over.

When we were in the middle of the second act, the sirens sounded. That had been the agreed upon signal for the end of the war since there had already been so many false rumors. Paul, my roommate, was on stage when the Commander of the base walked down to the footlights and told him to announce that Japan had accepted the peace terms. When he did, a sound came from the 2,000 sailors in the audience that was like a train going into a tunnel. It was a roar that seemed to come from just one throat magnified many times. The cheering lasted for five minutes and the actors forgot their differences as they stood with tears in their eyes. Guns fired in the distance and flares turned the sky into a checkerboard above our heads in the outdoor theater.

I thought of the beginning of the war when Roger, the man I was having an affair with, was at my house having dinner. A neighbor had burst in with the news that Pearl Harbor had been bombed. It was so long ago. And now I was at Pearl Harbor for the peace. Though I had never heard from Roger during the war, I said a silent prayer that he was all right. The emotion was broken by the audience insisting we go on with the play. At last, there would be plenty of time to think about the future.

10

At 1:30 in the morning, we piled into a carry-all and drove to the airport. Since the plane didn't leave until 3:00, we spent the time getting our custom slips signed and weighing in. The women had brought everything they thought they couldn't get down under. When the total was added up, we were 100 pounds over. The company manager appealed to us all and piece by piece shoes, books, slacks were piled up on the scale until we were passed through.

A soldier who had attached himself to one of the girls had come to see us off. He had spent three years overseas in the thick of the fighting and was resting on Oahu before returning to Saipan. He started to talk about intolerance. He was very tired and still not legally out of the hospital. His limp was more noticeable in the early morning. His eyes seemed pained as he talked of traveling all over the world, in all the theaters of war, and finding so much prejudice. As the rain poured down outside, I listened as he said, "What's wrong with men who go through all this and still hate?" The loudspeaker crackled announcing plane 2974 and we all stood up and gathered our belongings. The moment had passed with no answer for the soldier but I knew there wasn't one. He insisted on hiding a bottle of rum in my musette bag and we all promised to meet on Saipan.

As we ran out through the rain, the soldier yelled after us, "Get as far forward as you can! The tail gets knocked around quite a bit."

I climbed up the stairs and entered the plane. After the luxury of the airport buildings and the sleek, newly painted exterior, the cabin was a shock. I had walked into a room, about 32 feet long and 12 feet wide, that looked like a small submarine. In the dim light, I could see that most of the space was taken up by luggage piled to the ceiling and roped to the floor. There was a single row of canvas benches along the one wall that was free of luggage. As soon as we were seated, a sergeant told us to put on our Mae Wests. I took mine, that I thought looked like a yellow oversized version of a bomb used to put into a siphon bottle to make seltzer, and tied it around my waist, over my back, and through my legs. I heard the motors warming up and the propellers churning the air fiercely. It seemed like an eternity waiting for the plane to stop taxiing. Suddenly the sound of the motors pitched higher and seemed more frenzied. The plane throbbed as if it were anxious to leave the ground and before I knew it, I was looking down at the lights of Honolulu, as bright as in the amusement park at Coney Island, even though the city was still asleep.

Once we were in the air, we all realized how tired we were. We removed our Mae Wests – they only had to be worn at takeoff and landing. The netting was tightened behind the bucket seats and several soldiers who were flying with us lay blankets on the floor to sleep. I managed to crawl in between a snoring soldier and the escape hatch and hugged myself to keep warm. There was a draft from a crack in the door and the cabin was freezing cold. I couldn't sleep so I got up and walked toward the cockpit. I found a stack of in-flight lunches and opened one. I ate a sandwich and a carton of canned apricots.

The sergeant looked up sleepily and said, "You better save that for the long flight from Johnston to Kwajalein. You only get one."

Through the round window in the side of the plane I could see the sun coming up. I pressed my face as close as I could and looked at the thousands of puffs of clouds below, cloud banks, mists of clouds and layers of clouds above. I thought it looked like the earth with valleys, lakes and mountains in the background. Nancy, who was the mother in the play, caught my eye. She had been looking out as well.

"You see how easy it is to get into heaven?" she whispered. I smiled.

The rain slashed through the screen door and almost reached the army cot where I lay, trying to get up the energy to go out into it with some soap to wash myself. I never felt clean from the saltwater showers. The coral dust seemed to embed itself in every pore of my body. I thought I should send Cass a letter, but now that we were away from civilization, I felt almost unrelated to anything at home. Since we had passed the International Dateline, it wasn't even the same day as it was in New York. I had begun to wonder why Cass never told me what he was doing when he wrote. I had to read between the lines to realize that Cass wasn't working and he didn't seem to have any income. I had told him to get in touch with Marie and Miranda and they would give him money from the account I had opened for them. But it was over two months since I had left New York and Cass had never contacted them. In the last letter that I had received, Cass said he'd had an argument over me with the composer whose apartment he shared and had left to go back to visit his family in Texas.

Why over me? I had thought, *unless there was something between them*. It was just so difficult to be thousands of miles away and not be able to discuss things that came up. All sorts of suspicions were aroused by every letter. I had to fight against believing that Cass was no longer interested in me. But there was nothing I could do anyway. If I wrote asking Cass if there was something wrong, it would be a month before I would get an answer. By then, there'd only be a few months before we went home, so it seemed better to just write love letters and wait.

I was enjoying myself for the first time on the tour. Oahu had been like a country club and, although I had worked very hard, I felt the men didn't really need the show. There were plenty of diversions and they could get into Honolulu for movies and bars. But Kwajalein was a coral island a mile long and a half mile wide with nothing to do. There was no vegetation except for four palm trees. In the daytime, the sun beat down on the rock so fiercely that the heat and the glare were almost unbearable. There wasn't even anything to see except for army and navy installations, Quonset huts, and an occasional plot of ground where

200 or 300 Japanese soldiers had been dumped in a hole and a sign estimating their number had been pushed in to mark the spot.

Hard to believe that men had been on the island for as long as 20 months. I didn't know how they stood it, but I felt that at least the show was a break in the monotony for them. Although the plot was simple, there was no question that the play gave the men a taste of home, their parents, girlfriends, and even the memory of sharing Christmas with their families. I went out of my way to talk to the men who helped me put up the scenery. I asked about their wives, girlfriends, their families. They seemed so glad to talk to someone new who hadn't heard all their stories. I was fascinated by their exploits. I listened spellbound to a sailor who had been on the first submarine to enter Tokyo Bay, in September of 1942, when they went to take pictures that would guide Doolittle for his raid that was to take place in Tokyo months later.

I still had to put the set up in the daytime so I only saw the actors during the show. Then, I was so busy ringing doorbells and telephones, and rewrapping Christmas presents for props, I didn't have time to talk to them. The women, except for Alice, the company manager's wife, seemed to latch on to an officer in every new place we went to. Since there was a party after the show each night and there was an endless supply of liquor, the women were usually drunk by midnight.

Bill, the model I had roomed with in Seattle, kept me abreast of the boys' activities. They found interested men everywhere they went, even on tiny Kwajalein. Bill was having an affair with a married soldier who had been a football player. I couldn't believe that there was a place on the barren rock where they could go and not be seen, but Bill assured me they had found one.

I looked at my watch. "One o'clock in the afternoon on Tuesday," I said aloud. "That means in New York it's 10:00 in the evening on Monday." I stripped off my clothes, grabbed a bar of soap and went out into the rain.

11

The air pressure in the huge B54 Army Transport was making my pen overflow, so there were ink blots all over the pages as I struggled to write to my parents:

Dear Mother and Dad:

Here we are flying from Saipan to a place that not so long ago made great history: Iwo Jima. I certainly never thought a few months ago, when I saw the magnificent picture of the flag raising at Iwo, that I'd be seeing the place where it was taken.

We left Kwajalein last Sunday night and had a wonderful seven-hour plane trip arriving at Saipan at 3:00 in the morning (two-hour time change}. The trip was the roughest we've had yet – we hit a pretty bad storm and, for a while, bobbed up and down like the little boat I used to float in the bathtub when I was a baby. I loved the storm, though – I have become completely crazy about flying. It will seem funny to be back in the States and not go for a hop once a week, as we do now.

Saipan looked beautiful under a full moon. Unlike the other islands we've seen, it has many hills and lush, Kelly-green vegetation. It's about 14x4 miles and, except for the complete lack of civilization, is reminiscent of Oahu. After an hour's ride to our quarters, past such bloody landmarks as Hill 500, we had coffee. We were high on a hill overlooking a mirror-like bay lit up by hundreds of ships. After a good night's sleep, I was up early for breakfast. I sat watching the activity far below in the harbor and eating delicious hot cakes drowned in thick rich honey that I hadn't had in so long.

All morning we sat in a group awaiting the officer who was bringing our mail (no mail for over two weeks). You should have seen us devour the stacks all of us got. You couldn't get a word out of us until we'd read every letter at least several times. I got three wonderful letters from you.

Monday afternoon the Navy briefed us here in Saipan and got our itinerary for the next three months. We should be home the day after Christmas. Seems like it won't be very long now – last Saturday was the halfway mark of the tour.

We moved into new quarters after the briefing and really became aware of overseas living. Our showers are a steel helmet that we fill with brackish water and spill over us. I live in a room with three USO people from a Sports Unit that is here. They're pretty horrible, rowdy, drunken, but they'll be gone by the time we get back from Iwo, which is only 750 miles from Tokyo.... There are millions of lizards, bugs, snails the size of your fist, and frogs on Saipan. At times you can hardly see out the screen door, it's so covered with animal life.... I am still pretty healthy except for a slight case of ringworm that most everyone gets. It's a fungus caused by the heat and perspiration, but the doctor almost has it annihilated.

Monday night I sat with the rest of the cast in a huge amphitheater set in the hills and saw Saratoga Trunk *with Gary Cooper and Ingrid Bergman, I liked it tremendously and thought she was wonderful. Tuesday, the girls from the show, a couple of sailors, some American prisoners of war just here from Japan, and I toured the island. We saw the remnants of some of the bloodiest battles of the war. Strewn everywhere are destroyed guns, tanks and Japanese bodies that are still rotting in the caves.... Outside my door is a pole with a Japanese skull on the end of it.... In caves up in the hills, there are still many Japanese snipers who won't surrender, so parts of the island are pretty dangerous. Our women must be accompanied by two armed guards after sundown and believe me, there's nothing dramatic about it. Last night snipers shot two naval officers. But where we are, there is no danger unless you go where you're not supposed to. The only people hurt are souvenir hunters and I don't want any souvenirs. The fellows I work with, putting up the set, have been marvelous to me.*

They want to do everything they can to help me. I never will get over how many wonderful people there are in the world. Though I'll only be able to remember first names like Frenchy, Bud, Mike, Gordon – the people themselves I'll never forget.

In my last letter, I left off just as we were landing at Majuro – what a beautiful place covered with palm trees glowing under a three-quarter moon. We were quartered in a building the Japanese had used as a rest home for pilots. When Jack Benny was on Majuro some time ago, he named the building the Biltmore Hotel. After everyone had turned in, I walked along the beach alone: it was the most beautiful night I've ever seen – on my left was the lagoon, clear, calm, silvery from the moon; on my right, a jungle of palm trees. I had the feeling for the first time of living in a strange, uncivilized land, primitive and untouched. It was like being under a mystical spell. I walked for hours thinking about my life.

The next day (Sunday) I worked on the set and spent the afternoon clomping over the coral reef in army boots looking for shells. How fantastic to see the millions of different animals that make their home in the reef. You know every tiny shell houses a strange creature and I saw many different ones – even saw baby octopi swimming around, trapping tiny animals. It was unbelievable. That evening the show went beautifully and the applause was tremendous.

Monday was unforgettable. We sailed in a tiny crash boat to Laura Island where the natives were living in small huts as tall as I am. They sleep four and five in a space that would make me double up. The island was primitive and exactly as you would picture it from descriptions and the movies. Of course, there's nothing glamorous about it – the natives are filthy, the heat is unbearable and the life is not worthy of pigs. It was interesting walking around and watching the Marjalese natives eat and make bead bracelets. We met several "Kings" (they are kings of different islands but they have to live together temporarily). They fed us coconuts that the women would cut from a nearby tree and we listened as the native children sang Marjalese songs and old church songs taught by the missionaries. They also sang "Lay That Pistol Down, Babe." But what

I'll always remember is them singing with their accents "Oh how lahvely ees de eeveneeng when the bells are saftly reengeeng" – the high childish voices under the palm trees – it was a magical moment. The women all wore Mother Hubbards so I still haven't had my picture taken with a bare-chested native.

Monday night we had a terrific rain storm so the show was postponed – went to a party at the Officer's Club and met a swell group of guys – 313th Marine Squadron (pilots mainly). They insisted on giving a beer party in my honor. One of the fellows said that I would never know how much the men appreciate "regular guys like you coming overseas." The women they like to see but it frankly frustrates them even more, and they've almost forgotten how to talk to women so they just sit there uncomfortably. But they told me it was so wonderful to talk to a smiling kid who had no griping to do, and who could talk about other things besides "the war, when are we going home, the bad food, and the lousy superior officers." For the first time, I felt honestly worthwhile.

Tuesday, we played for the Marines and Wednesday we went back to Kwajalein. The weather prevented us from flying to Tarawa that we had wanted very much to do. Thursday, we did the show in the pouring rain on the neighboring island of Berlin. We all got drenched since, of course, we're always in the open air with no roof over the stage. That night we had real steak and ice cream made of powdered milk. Friday, we played for the Seabees. Saturday was off so I tried to go swimming but the water was murky and unclean and I felt slimy when I came out. Saturday night both the Marines and the Army Transport gave us a party. Parties, parties, parties – did I ever like them? Well, I've certainly had my fill now.

Well, now you're up to date – so much happens it's impossible to write it all down. I'm certainly grateful for the plane ride giving me the chance to write you a long letter. We're nearing Iwo Jima so I'll close for now.

Aloha nui loa,
Your loving son

12

Tommy in "Junior Miss"

The smell was almost unbearable, but I didn't want the soldier to think I was squeamish, so I crawled after him, scraping my fatigues on the tunnel floor. I swung my flashlight from side to side and saw holes dug in the walls that looked like kennels for small dogs.

"What are those?" I asked in the darkness.

"They were the bedrooms," the guide replied. "Two Japs huddled in each one."

I couldn't conceive of them getting into such a small place. The tunnel itself was only four feet high by three feet wide. As I thought of living there for weeks, I began to feel claustrophobic. Suddenly my light hit the skeletons lying in an opening to another tunnel. Beyond them, I could see bones rotting, remains of food, ammunition, radio equipment, medical supplies, all piled in a heap from which an odor of

decaying flesh emanated. I pulled myself forward away from the nightmare and stopped just short of a skull with just enough skin and hair to
look frighteningly alive. I was afraid I'd be sick.

"Let's go back," I yelled.

"Don't you want to take any souvenirs?" I heard the soldier say. I
had seen everyone else competing for the goriest remnants of the war
but I was disgusted by the hobby.

"It's OK," I answered. "I've got enough."

Once we were out of the tunnel and on our way back to the Jeep, the
soldier told me that the island was completely covered with caves like
the one we'd been in. They were just tiny holes in the ground where the
enemy could fight and still not be seen.

"The Marines hardly ever saw a Jap alive in the whole battle," he
went on, "but there were so many of them, it took them 24 days to
advance less than a mile."

I took deep breaths as if the air of the cave were still in my nostrils,
but the dust of Iwo Jima made me cough. I had been told that the coral
ash in the air was bad for the lungs and doctors didn't want anyone
staying there for more than six months. We'd only be there for ten days
so there was nothing to worry about. I'd heard that many of the men
had been there for over eight months, but it was just another of the
inequities that I discovered every day.

We drove toward the volcano. We saw signs of destruction everywhere, Japanese ships were half sunk in the ocean, and among the rock
piles were pieces of planes and tanks. The road up Mount Suribachi
twisted and turned, I felt like I was in a sightseeing bus as the soldier
kept up a patter of statistics that would have made a tour guide envious.
It culminated with him saying, "The Japs attempted to scale a road up
this peak for 40 years and the Seabees did it in 27 days."

He gunned the Jeep with every bit of power it had. We reached the
spot where the five Marines had raised the flag and created a symbol for
all time. I got out and saw Iwo Jima spread out before me. I thought it
looked like a kitten curled peacefully in front of the fire. On the ocean

side, I could see the crater smoldering and smoking like an everlasting memorial.

I stood in the outdoor shower trying to scrub the dust from my body. The sun had heated the saltwater until it was almost too hot. The slight sting it made as it hit my skin calmed for a moment the itching that was caused by the constant perspiration. As soon as I had dried myself, I was bathed in sweat again. I went to my room to escape the heat. As I sat on the cot, I could see the thick coat of coral powder that covered the sheets I'd made up clean only several hours before. When I had first arrived, I had shaken out the bedding several times a day. As soon as I realized it did no good, I gave it up.

I wondered if the meeting I had instigated the night before would have any results. I knew the actors were shocked when I threatened to quit, but they had immediately started to blame each other. It was only the two older women and two of the boys who were giving the company a bad name, but it still reflected on all of us. *The parties*, I thought, *if only we didn't have to go to a party every night – maybe they'd stop getting so drunk and going to bed with whoever asked them.*

Since I was the only one who worked closely with the men, I had begun to hear the resentment that they felt to the USO groups and the women who were always with the officers. Some of the soldiers worked in the Officer's Club and watched the actresses get so drunk that they could barely walk through the door to get to their rooms. It was only a matter of course that an officer would help them get home, but clearly it would take a long, long time. I didn't want to prevent any of them from doing what they wanted to do. But I had to make it clear to them that they were becoming a laughingstock and hurting the reputation of the unit. I also had to have help.

Moving the show to a new theater every night meant that I worked most of the day. I didn't mind that, but after playing my role and running the show, I still had to take down the set while the others were removing their makeup (I didn't wear any) and sometimes there were not enough men assigned to me and I needed the actors to pitch in.

They had been behaving like prima donnas refusing to get their hands dirty. At least if the meeting had shaken them up enough to lend a hand when I needed help, it was worth the effort.

After the show that night, Bill and Eric at least made an attempt to help me with the set and everyone decided to skip the Officer's Club to have an early night. I took it for what it was – a way of saying they were sorry without apologizing. I knew the next day it would all be back to the usual. When I was in my bed, I thought again about going home, but I knew there was no way I could go unless I was sent back in disgrace. I had no intention of letting that happen.

Going home.... I began to think about what it would be like. *In less than two months when I'm 20, I'll be just about a third of the way through my life on earth*, I thought. *That is If I live long enough to be that old. It's time I began to settle on exactly what I want to be. I've always wanted to be an actor or at least do something connected to the theater. Until now, I've been floundering, helpless, almost afraid to grasp any opportunity that might come my way. I feel the tour has changed me. I'm ready now to do everything I can to get where I want to.*

There was a flash of heat lightning through the screen and I thought of Cass. We had been exchanging letters with plans for an apartment Cass would find with the money I'd been saving. But I began to add up what I would have to spend when I returned: to have the tooth put in that I wanted so badly, to take a movement class, an acting class, to join a gym so I would look better onstage, and get some new clothes to make the rounds. I would get unemployment insurance of $18 a week, but I'd have to live just as meagerly as before. What if all the money went into a place and Cass and I didn't get along? I'd never even considered that before. I'd always thought that love was more important than career, I laughed aloud. I remembered the music teacher in *On The Town* saying, "If sex and art mixed, I would have been at the top of the heap." Maybe I'm just getting rock happy like the men who spend too much time in the islands.

Two soldiers were pacing back and forth outside the building. There was no danger from Japanese snipers any longer. One had been found starving in a cave a month before, but if any were still alive, they would be too weak to pull the trigger. The women across the road, however, had to be guarded so they watched the men as well. I saw the silhouette of a steel helmet and a gun on a shoulder as I closed my eyes.

13

"Pennies in a stream, warbling of the meadowlark, moonlight in Vermont." The woman's voice over the loudspeaker was pure and rich. I lay in the sun listening and luxuriating in the sound that seemed to caress my body. I hardly moved except to get up once in a while to plunge into the enormous pool that had been blasted out of the rock. I felt so content. After the discomfit of the weeks in Saipan, Tinian had been like a vacation. Special Services had given me my own Jeep with a driver. They'd also added a truck that carried my props so I could do all my work in two hours and be at the beach at noon.

On Saipan, the company had been treated badly. Since the unit had been authorized by the Army and Saipan was controlled by the Navy, we had been shunted to a section of a Quonset hut where 50 USO units were billeted. The roof leaked badly and when it rained, we got soaked. Some of the USO people in the other units had already been sent home in disgrace. One older man in a concert group had been discovered sitting in a little shed while a line of men waited outside to be serviced. Servicing the service, I had thought when I'd heard about it. The entire unit was sent back to the States. Each incident gave a bad name to all the USO companies and it was reflected in the Navy's treatment, even of us. Despite *Junior Miss* being a huge success and playing to 8,000-10,000 men a night, we were not given any favors. But Tinian was a paradise. There was actually a mattress on the bed and a flush toilet in the latrine. The shower even had lukewarm water occasionally.

My thoughts were interrupted by a long, nail-file-shaped lizard with an embroidered back who was testing my leg, as if he were trying to make up his mind whether it would be less effort to go over it than around it. I sat up and flicked it on its way. I turned to look at Gordon who was watching the hills of Saipan – only three hours away by boat – change from green to purple in the haze across the water. *How handsome he is*, I thought. Then I realized he was not admiring the view; he was holding his face up to the sun to get even more tanned. How incongruous his vanity was. He was a flight officer on a B29 who had flown 28 missions over Tokyo, and he seemed to care only about getting a great tan and a new bathing suit. But it didn't really bother me.

We had both decided to spend the days I was on the island together, just enjoying each other and forgetting about everything else. Captain Carl had told me in Honolulu that if I got to Tinian, I should look up his friend Gordon. Gordon had a lover at home in Minneapolis who was waiting for his return and I had Cass, so neither of us were looking for romance. I'd been so lonely. Just to be close to someone again made me feel more alive. We were affectionate companions and love was not even considered, nor was fidelity – too many months had gone by and I was sure this respite wouldn't hurt my love for Cass. I had managed for months not to succumb to my strong sexual urges by keeping busy working. But now, I had free time and Gordon was the perfect release. Neither of us wanted anything but the warmth of a few days with someone we would probably never see again. I hoped Cass was doing somewhat the same thing.

The whole experience in the Pacific was an enigma. Tinian housed the greatest number of B29s in the world on the largest existing airfield. I had met night pilots, ferry pilots, transport pilots, but the ones I most admired were the B29 pilots. I thought they had the most extraordinary courage. Quite a few of them, I had been told, were homosexual and their lovers were also part of their crews. It had helped them knowing they were together on the raids over Japan. But now these men, who had fought ferociously, were sopping up sun, exchanging heavy silver identification bracelets, and zipping around the island exploring the gay beaches. There seemed to be a gay beach on even the smallest island.

The men who frequented them managed to sew bits of parachute silk into bikinis that they dyed bright colors. It was a way to pass the time until they went home.

"Let's go for a ride," Gordon said, "I'm bored."

We threw on some clothes and climbed into Gordon's Jeep. Yellow Beach was crowded with many of the men from Gordon's Ninth Bomber Squadron and he waved to them as we drove away. At the wheel, he looked like a leading man in the movies with his black hair combed straight back, his blue eyes piercing his tanned skin, and even a cleft chin like Cary Grant. We had hit it off immediately.

He had taken me on my night off to North Tinian Field to watch the B29s land. I had seen them in the newsreels, but I had no idea of their gigantic size. As one would appear out of the darkness, like a prehistoric bird, and zoom in to land nearby, I felt shivers of exhilaration. I listened fascinated as Gordon told me about bombing missions. It made me think of old sailors telling tales of the sea. Gordon was 22 – most of the B29 crews were in their twenties. I wondered if it hadn't been his youth that had given him the reckless courage to become such a hero.

There wasn't much to see on the island. It was flat with a few rolling hills and very green. It reminded me of Pennsylvania or New Jersey since only in small areas was there tropical vegetation. It was tiny compared to Saipan – only ten miles long by five miles wide – and there were no caves where the Japanese could still be hiding. That was always the fear on Saipan. I had been told that there was a Japanese general who had organized all of the men who were holed up in Saipan and would not let them give themselves up, even though peace had been declared. Some of them would stand in chow lines with the GIs to get food, and even go to the movies without being discovered. I wondered if they saw *Junior Miss* and if so, what they thought of it. A group of them were captured as they stood in a line they thought was for food and discovered was for being paid. It must have been startling for the paymaster to look out his window into a Japanese face.

I had spent all my free time with Gordon – swimming, lying on the beach, drinking beer after the show, talking backstage in between cues, riding around the island late at night. We had found a little beach tucked under a towering cliff, and we would take a supper there at midnight and watch the surf, sparkling with lights from the stars, beat against immense rocks at our feet. One night there had been a torrential rainstorm and we had fled, laughing, to find shelter in a sugar cane field. The whole experience with Gordon was a great release for me. For a short time, at least, I could stop worrying about Cass and the future, and just enjoy the fun of being on a tropical isle with someone I was fond of. I'd worked so hard and been so responsible that it was a relief just to be taken care of for a change.

I hadn't stopped thinking about Cass. I still felt the same way about him, but the sporadic mail delivery had created a schism between us. Cass had written wanting to break it all off because he hadn't heard from me in weeks. I was sure that the letters would eventually be delivered and all would be forgiven. I couldn't allow myself to brood about it any longer. I had begun to feel that there was something preordained about my life. Here I was, thousands of miles from civilization,   where at any moment my life could be over. And yet I believed that I was protected and that it would be all right. I thought often of Hamlet's words: "There is a special providence in the fall of a sparrow. If it be now, tis not to come; if it be not to come, it will be now; if it be not now, yet it will come. The readiness is all."

Gordon said, "What are you thinking about? You look so serious. I'm hungry."

"Let's go get something to eat," I replied.

14

Guam

Guam was so close that we'd barely got on the plane in Tinian before it was time to get off. The island was huge and tropically beautiful. We were taken to an area called Agana, to Quonset huts at the top of cliffs overlooking a pristine bay. All the men bunked together in a huge room, but it was clean, screened, and even had a bathroom of its own. At this point none of us cared. We only had to do our shows and we'd be on our way home. The next few days went well with men assigned to help me so I didn't feel any pressure. The packed audiences roared with laughter and gave us ovations. All looked well for a happy ending.

I was taken by my driver, after a set-up one day, to a native village to meet some of the Comoros who had inhabited the island for thousands of years. They had been badly treated by the Japanese who had controlled the island until just a year before. An old woman who seemed to be in charge introduced a few of the people and we shook hands. She indicated which woman was married to which man and then came to a very handsome young man in his twenties. She pointed at him. "He's not married," she said, "he likes his own kind." She said it with no malice, it was just a part of life.

On my first day off, I sat on the terrace at the Officer's Club looking down at the bay as dusk turned into night. I watched the fishermen, with their torches, making patterns as they moved their boats about looking for fish, It was all too enchanting to last.

The next day, I took off my clothes, made them into a bundle and hoisted them onto my shoulder. I walked into the water and made my way gingerly around an outcropping of coral to a strip of sand at the bottom of the cliff. I spread my things out and lay naked in the comforting sun, completely hidden from the rest of the beach. I had found the place quite by accident and now came to it every day to get away from the others. The month on Guam had gone slowly, but I was all right if I could just be alone once in a while. I was so tired of the actors with their constant complaints and bitching at each other. It never stopped.

The show had finally given its last performance but none of us realized it at the time. We were scheduled to go to one more island. But Brandon, who played the father, had trouble with his teeth and couldn't keep his plate in his mouth, so we closed down. After waiting so long to celebrate our final show, the company wasn't even aware when it took place. And now we sat and waited to go home. The problem was that all the GIs were leaving as well so it was difficult to find space. Many of the ships couldn't accommodate women, and since a great number of maintenance men on the planes had returned to the States, we had been advised to fly only if we had to.

I suspected that the real reason we still weren't leaving was that Peggy, who had played the lead, had fallen in love with a top officer at Island Command. He wasn't about to be separated from her so we were all being forced to stay. Merrill, the effeminate boy, had gotten so impatient that he had stowed away on a plane bound for Oahu. When he got to Honolulu, he was intercepted by the military authorities and was returned to Guam for serious discipline. The actors had forgotten that we had officer rank and could be court-martialed.

I had never felt more helpless. I no longer had any work to do and the tropics had finally sapped all of my energy. I awoke in the morning feeling exhausted and the lethargy pursued me throughout the day. Guam was beautiful, but all I wanted was to go home. I couldn't even concentrate on a book. So, I lay on the beach, sopping up sun and re-reading Cass's letters. They had become more loving since he had finally received mine. I picked up his latest one.

Dear One:

To start with. I can never begin to tell you how much I love you. So let me try in my stupid little way to show you – even a life time will not be enough but at least I think you'll begin to see I'm serious.

Last night I played gin rummy with several friends of mine and had a wonderful time – home to bed around 11:30. I've been thinking quite seriously about us and I wonder if you are going to be content to stay in a lot. God knows I am. My work now requires a good deal of my strength and certainly the new job I undertake Monday carries a much higher requirement in mental and physical work. Assistant production manager of Homemaker Magazine *will sap up a great deal from me. However, I'm not afraid of work and am quite overjoyed with the anticipation of such an authoritative responsible position. I bring this all up now as I know you've been working hard yet still been chasing about, boozing. I'm afraid for a while I shan't be able to go such a pace. Also, you should get a long rest when you return then start working quite diligently and should have little time but I was just wondering how you felt about same!*

I called Marie this morning and told her I had heard from you, also to see when we could get together – and so I'm going down tomorrow night – how perfectly wonderful when Marie, Miranda, you and I can go out together.

Well, it's somewhat colder here today – though I'm not registering a complaint – nevertheless it will be good to have you to cuddle up to this winter.

Have I told you I love you? Yes – completely and wholeheartedly – never doubt that – always I think of you and in terms of how soon you'll be home – now that the end is in sight – somehow it seems utterly impossible.

Then too as I told Marie and Miranda the other night, I become frightened. The thought of your return. Why? Well for several reasons, primarily because I do so want us to last, Secondly, will you still find me attractive. Thirdly, will I prove all you think I am, all you desire – and last, will I be able always to cope with you, to keep you interested in me, keep you in hand, not lose my temper at some of your more prevalent ideas and actions and in a moment of rashness, do something drastic to impair our love? God give me strength. Also, will I be able to subdue this mad jealous flair of mine and settle down peacefully and contented with you – my own?

Well, I wanted you to know I'm thinking in such a vein and quite seriously too. I'm sure that all will work out and we'll be completely happy, but I'm so conscious of the fact that there is more to a happy romance than sex or mutual attraction. So, I'm willing. How about you?

Yours, Cass

The platform was teeming with people by the time I had managed to drag all of my luggage down the corridor and out the door. I couldn't see a red cap anywhere so I looped the duffle bag over my head and took the other two pieces, one in each hand, and struggled toward the sign that said "Taxis." I saw several of the cast surrounded by relatives and friends and I was glad I had told Cass not to meet me. It would have been too embarrassing. I had said goodbye to everyone in the cast who'd been on the train with me from the coast. Some of the actors had to travel later because of limited accommodations. It was all amicable, but I don't think we wanted to see each other again. The one thing the tour certainly didn't do was make any of us good friends.

I had to wait in line for the cab so I tightened the belt on my trench coat to keep any cold air from going through. In the few days I'd spent in San Francisco, my body had not had enough time to adjust to the winter weather. I just couldn't seem to get warm. When I had given the name of the hotel to the driver, I settled back in the seat and tried to relax. I felt very strange being back in New York, almost as if I'd never been there before. The streets were as crowded as ever, and we were held up in a traffic jam near Macy's for almost ten minutes. The Wellington was on a busy side street in the jewelry district. I didn't remember ever having seen it. A torn awning extended to the street, but there was no doorman to take my bags. After the driver helped me into the pocket-sized lobby, I walked over to a partition behind which a woman sat talking on a phone. She put her hand over the mouthpiece and looked at me.

"Yes?" she asked.

"Mr. Stevens made a reservation," I said.

She pushed a pad at me. "Fill this out," she said putting the receiver back to her ear.

I looked at the paper. It had a space for my name and address, but I realized I didn't live anywhere. What would I put down? I suddenly felt so lost, a feeling that had followed me since I got off the ship. It was as if I'd wandered into a world where I didn't belong and no one was paying any attention to me. I wrote down my parents' address and was given a key.

The room was cheap and sparsely furnished. There were twin beds covered by colorless spreads, a dark green club chair with cigarette burns on one arm, and a bay window looking down at the street with drapes that were too narrow to shut out the light. Inadvertently, I shuddered. This was the last place on earth I would have chosen to meet someone after a seven-month separation. There was no point to unpacking since I had to leave for Boston in the morning, but I got out some clean underwear and a shirt. The shower was rusty and the water slightly brown, but it was hot. I stood in it a long time and tried to stop worrying about seeing Cass again.

I lay on the bed waiting for 6:00. I understood that Cass had been too busy with his new job to look for an apartment, but surely there was something better than this. With all the months of planning, in our letters, of where we were going to live, to have to come home to this. I tried to push it out of my head. I didn't want to greet Cass with recriminations. That was not the way to start. I guessed that since Cass was living in a beautiful apartment with his old friend Tom, he just hadn't felt the pressure to do anything. I would find somewhere for us to live as soon as I could.

I heard a key turn in the lock and the door opened. I sat up as Cass walked in, closing the door. He just stood and looked at me for a moment and I was afraid he was thinking that I was not what he expected me to be. But he walked over and pulled me up from the bed and held me.

"I'm so glad you're finally home," he said and I buried my head in his neck. He pushed me away. "I'm filthy," he said, "I've got to take a shower."

I felt as if I were in a stupor as I sat watching Cass tear off his clothes and go into the bathroom and close the door. The noise of the water drummed through the thin walls and I just sat waiting as if I had no will of my own. Cass reappeared with a towel around his waist and walked over to me. He helped me undress and we both got into one of the twin beds. I didn't know where I was or who I was with, but we began to make love. I felt almost as if I were drunk, as if I were enveloped in a gauzy cloud that separated me from Cass.

When we lay still, Cass said, "Oh, that was wonderful. Now, get your clothes on and we'll grab a bite to eat. I'm just exhausted and I've got to get to sleep early."

I sat on the edge of the bed tying my shoes. I stopped to rub the space at the bottom of my rib cage. I felt an ache that seemed to suffuse my whole body. *It'll go away*, I thought.

***

We were in the car for no more than five minutes when the discussion started. My mother was the first. "Well dear," she said, "I know you're older now so I'm sure you'll go to school."

I was totally unprepared. I had thought I was returning as a successful actor who had worked for seven months in a very difficult situation. Instead, they all went at me with the old arguments as if I were a failure. Even my brother's new wife joined in with reasons why I should leave New York and return to Boston, and I'd never even met her before. By the time I had recovered enough to do battle, my father had pulled up in front of the apartment and we all got out. I had felt strained with them from the moment I had walked out of the plane and saw them waving at me from the shed. When my mother had kissed me with tears in her eyes, I had felt nothing. Relations with them had changed so gradually in the three years since I had left home that I was startled at my lack of emotion. Yet everything seemed so different. Since my return to the States, all of my reactions were surprising me.

When I walked through the door into the front hall, I thought of a movie I had seen where a soldier had returned from the war to his home and touched all the pieces of furniture as if he were remembering the past. I looked at everything from the drapes that were too short, to the pieces of cheap broadloom that had been fitted together to try to look like wall-to-wall carpeting, to the marble-topped table, to the Japanese prints. The only sensation I had was a vague memory of once living in this place where I'd had no wonderful experiences. Now that time had passed, there was no meaning here for me. On the dining room table was a cake with a message in the icing: "Welcome home – USO." I was embarrassed.

The next morning my mother let me sleep till noon which she announced was "late enough for anyone to be in bed." As soon as I was seated at the breakfast table, they started at me again. Since it was Sunday, my father wasn't working so he was really able to tear into me about my age, my failure to get anywhere in the theater after three years, my lack of education and a degree. My brother and his wife were there as well and the four of them seemed to enjoy ripping me apart. I finally had enough.

"How can you possibly treat me like this?" I asked. "I've been gone seven months overseas working harder than any of you, without any of the pleasures that make you put up with hard work in the States. I come home to this kind of welcome." I had sworn, since the time my father hit me because I was too nervous about an announcing job to eat all of my dinner, that I would never let any of them upset me again. I walked out of the room rather than let them see that they had managed to get to me after all. I went into the bedroom where I had spent my childhood and adolescence. *This is not my home*, I thought, *and they are not my family*.

In the evening, some of my relatives came by to welcome me home. They asked me a few questions about my trip. As soon as I started to answer them, I saw their faces go blank. When I mentioned Honolulu, one of the men said that his sister, whom he hadn't spoken to in 20 years, lived there. He proceeded to give me her impressions of "The Jewel of the Pacific," as he called it, for 15 minutes. I tried to get a word in but no one listened. I thought *I've traveled 27,000 miles and I've listened to GI's gripes and likes and dislikes, and I want to talk about what I've seen and learned. At least my family should be interested.* I tried again and told the group about the natives in the Marshall Islands and the fact that they had all been segregated in a place where no GI's were allowed to go.

"That reminds me," my father said, "Did you hear about the Texan who was greeted at the Gates of Heaven with 'Well, you can come in but you won't like it as well'?"

I went over to speak to a cousin I had always liked who had gone into his father's business. He flaunted his success in my face and said he'd heard that someone had seen me ushering at a theater in New York, and a lot of people said I was starving in a hovel in Greenwich Village. I tried to make it all as if he was joking, but I knew he wasn't – none of them were. Why was there so much resentment? Was it simply because I hadn't done what everyone else had done?

When they had all gone and I was alone for the first time in my room since my brother had married, I wrote to Cass. *How funny*, I thought, *I wasn't able to talk to Cass when I saw him, but now that I'm away from him, I know just what to say.* I told him of my feelings and said that there was no home for me unless we were together. I promised to find an apartment as soon as I got back. I realized that Cass didn't have the time but I did. When we had talked over dinner, Cass had told me that he had gotten very close to Marie and Miranda while I was away. He was working with them on getting a theater for the summer. If it materializes, he will quit his job and be the business manager.

I had immediately said, "Oh, no." When I saw Cass's expression, I knew that I had said the wrong thing. I had been so grateful that Cass wasn't in the theater. I believed that we had a better chance to have a lasting relationship if Cass were the stable, strong, mature one with a steady job, and I was the "artist." But now it was all changed and I tried to make amends by telling Cass how happy I would be if he were in the theater too. At least we could be sure of spending the summer together after our long separation.

I wrote to Cass about my homecoming and said that Cass and Marie and Miranda were the only ones I could talk to now. I heard a noise in the hall and listened with my pen in the air, but no one came in. Then I went on writing:

This has been my first moment alone to write, and even now, I'm sure my mother will appear and snatch up the letter and insist on reading it. Well, let her – I'm so tired of all this. I love you more than any of these "acceptable" people around here love each other. I don't underestimate their true feelings but my love, I'm sure, is as heartfelt as theirs (and perhaps a little more). Kiss the girls for me and tell them when I come to New York on Saturday, there'll be no sentimental "I've just returned from the Pacific." I'm back now, on my feet, no confusion, eager to get us settled and ready to go to work.

I hid the letter in a book and turned out the light.

15

As long as Cass and I were writing to each other, we could make the most perfect plans. Once we tried to implement them, we faced the fact that there was no money. Cass hadn't worked in his new job long enough to save anything and most of my money from the tour went to my parents, the theater, and the little I had left which would have to be stretched out until I could get a job. Every penny had to be counted and I was back in a $9 a week furnished room near the one I had lived in with Louis. It wasn't at all as nice as that one. Mr. Dorn had taken pride in his house. The woman who owned this one couldn't care less and just kept dodging complaints.

In the beginning, we tried to fix it up. Cass found an old wooden table among some garbage on the street and sawed the legs in half and covered the top with a piece of black felt studded with upholstery nails. I thought it was a handsome coffee table, but a cigarette burned a small hole in it and the coffee cups stained a blotch when we set them down, so it had to be thrown out.

For a short time, we enjoyed playing house, but Cass began to resent never having enough money to go out to dinner or even a drink at a bar. His friends seemed to take little interest in him now that I was around. We spent our time with Marie and Miranda planning the theater. Louis and his friend joined us occasionally, but Cass felt uncomfortable with them. Jackie had met with Cass several times while I was overseas, but they just didn't get along. Jackie thought that Cass was spoiled and not really bright, and Cass found her intimidating, so I stopped seeing

Jackie. Our life together was becoming very strained when something happened that I hoped might change it.

I was making the rounds again on a typical New York cold winter day when I overheard two actors talking. They had just been at the International Theater on Columbus Circle to audition for a replacement in *The GI Hamlet*.

"I don't know how good our chances are," one said, "they're seeing anyone off the street, even if you don't have an agent."

I was out of the office like a shot and hurried to the theater. There was a short line outside the stage door and I just stood there as it moved slowly. Finally, a young guy came out, took my name and phone number and said, "You have to do part of a Shakespeare soliloquy or there's no point in waiting."

"That's OK," I replied.

I started to think. I'd memorized quite a few soliloquies. Which one would be the best? Better not do anything from *Hamlet* since they hear that every night. John of Gaunt, too Englishy and patriotic. It came to me: *Richard II*. He starts out defeated and then builds to strength...if they let me get that far. I began to go over the words in my head and I seemed to remember it pretty well. I didn't think they'd let me do all of it, anyway.

I was ushered onto the stage. I seemed to be at the top of a wooden structure that had built-in stairs, platforms, and niches that had protruding places where one could sit. I noticed one place very near the footlights and walked over to it. I announced my name and sat down. I couldn't see anyone in the dark theater but I began. "I have been studying how I may compare this prison where I live unto the world. And for because the world is populous and here is not a creature but myself, I cannot do it."

I stopped as if I were Richard II and had given up. I was afraid they might just thank me and send me on my way, but there wasn't a sound, almost as if there was no one in the theater. I pulled myself together, as I thought Richard would, and went on. There were many slight pauses in my recitation, where they could have stopped me, but they didn't. I finished the whole soliloquy and there was absolute silence.

Finally, a voice said, "Thank you. That was very good." There was a mumble and then the voice said, "By the way, you have seen the play, haven't you?"

"No," I answered, "I haven't been able to. I've just returned from seven months in the Pacific."

There was another mumble and the voice said, "I think you should know you sat in the place where Mr. Evans does 'To be or not to be'." I felt I'd been reprimanded for invading a sacred spot and I didn't know how to reply. "Thank you," the voice said. "That's all we need."

I got up and tried not to trip going up the stairs and out through the wings. I guess I'd made a terrible faux pas, but how was I to know? I felt terrible...but I got the job! A phone call from the stage manager congratulated me and he said how impressed they'd been with my audition. He also said they had thought I had a lot of courage picking Mr. Evans' spot to do the soliloquy. It seems everyone else had avoided it like the plague as if they were afraid that they'd be compared to the great actor. The stage manager added that they had then been amused that I didn't know where I was sitting.

I was very excited though it turned out all I was to do was understudy a few small roles and be part of the crowd in scenes that took place at the palace. I would get Equity minimum for the few weeks the show stayed in New York and a few more dollars when it was on a short, several-month tour. Cass agreed that I had to do it. We needed the money and it was a good credit. We'd be separated again, but Cass was sure he and the girls were going to finally get a theater for the summer and my tour would just finish in time.

It all worked out as we'd planned. I did have to go on in New York for an actor I understudied, when he had to be away and miss one matinee. It was a short scene in which I was taking instructions from Polonius. I was nervous, but I remembered my lines. The role was usually comic, but I didn't get one laugh. No one seemed to mind since the actor who played the role was old, grotesque and almost a sight gag whereas I was young and fairly good-looking. It just became a rather straight-forward scene. But the stage manager said they were all pleased and luckily, I never had to do it again. It was the first time I had acted on Broadway outside of walking on in *Janie* and appearing in the crowd scenes in *Hamlet*.

I did appear as the Ghost of Hamlet's father, that is as the double of the Ghost. Mr. Evans had wanted to give the audience a moment of magic, so I was costumed the same as the actor who played the Ghost, with the same beard that concealed my face. I would appear in the early part of the play stage left and beckon Hamlet to follow me and within seconds at stage right was the actor who played the role speaking to Hamlet. It was sleight of hand and never failed to get a response. I then appeared as the Ghost again in the closet scene when Hamlet is berating his mother for her marriage to his uncle. Suddenly Hamlet sees me. His mother doesn't know what Hamlet is looking at. Lili Darvas, who had been a Max Reinhardt star in Europe before the Nazis, was the Queen. She had a heavy Hungarian accent as well as one eye that was out of line with the other. At each performance, I couldn't wait for her to say, "Omelette, vere on do you look" as she would stare at me with her crazy eyes. Years later, we acted together and became great friends.

There was one incident that happened that I found out about years later. I bumped into Maurice Evans on the Warner's lot in Hollywood. We had become friendly enough for me to call him Morris instead of Maurice as he was known by the public. As he told me about his living now in Brighton, England where he looked down on a beach "with all these gorgeous men cavorting," he added, "I always think of you in that scene where you doubled as the Ghost. You must have rushed to get into your place where I was to see you and your robe got caught on something so it separated, though the audience couldn't tell. When I looked at you, all I could see was the Ghost with a gleaming white jockstrap. It's one of the few times I almost broke up onstage." I didn't remember it at all.

While I was on tour, Cass wrote that he and Marie and Miranda had finally found a theater near Wilmington, Delaware. It was in a bucolic town buried in trees called Arden and, even better, it was called The Robin Hood Theatre. They had almost all the money, and they were busy signing leases and choosing the plays they would do, again in repertory. Of course, I was to be one of the actors and they were looking especially for a play for me to star in. I couldn't have been happier until I got word from Cass that he had quit his job. What would he do at the end of the summer? There'd be two of us looking for work again. *Oh well*, I thought, *at least we'll have three months together.*

16

With Miriam and Louis in "Dame Nature"

It was so hot and humid that Miranda stopped the rehearsal at 4:00. "Let's all go home and rest," she said, "or we'll be no good tonight."

I slipped out of the theater before the others and walked toward the Pig and Whistle. The trees formed an arbor over my head and I was glad to be outdoors alone. I loved the town of Arden. It was close to my dream of one day living in a tiny English village. There were no grand houses, mostly cottages and many of them concealed by the luxuriant foliage. It had been impossible to concentrate at the rehearsal and I'd forgotten my lines several times – unusual for me.

When I got to the ramshackle house where the actors ate, I saw Hazel, the cook and owner, sweeping the porch. She beckoned me to come over, but I shook my head and walked along. The last thing I wanted to do was listen to her bitching about the theater and how much money she was losing. It was so quiet that I could hear every bird in the forest, but there was a heaviness to the air that was depressing. When

I got to our little house, I pulled down the Murphy bed and stretched out. I kicked off my sneakers and lay quietly trying to clear my head of everything, but it was no use.

I had to face the fact that the summer had not worked out. I should have trusted my instincts and begged Cass not to come, but by the time I knew about it, Cass had given up his job. While I was on tour with *Hamlet,* we had gone back to writing letters to each other and everything seemed all right. I believed I could make our relationship work if we could just be together without worrying about money all the time. But now we had a charming little house and our food paid for by the theater and Cass didn't seem any happier. He kept telling me that it wasn't that he didn't love me, he just felt that Marie and Miranda weren't recognizing his work. I could sense his restlessness and the more he felt ignored, the more he took it out on me.

I was having great success in the roles I was playing and getting a lot of attention. Benn Levy's *The Devil Passes* was my so-called starring role. I was the Devil who becomes a guest in a country home and stirs up everybody. I was able to use my mellifluous voice, that I'd put away since radio announcing, and a touch of the Devil from my high school Prize Speaking. I loved playing it as well as my role in *Dame Nature* by the actress Patricia Collinge. It was the story of two teenagers in Paris who innocently discover that they're going to have a baby. I was their 15-year-old best friend who was a cross between a teddy bear and a St. Bernard.

Both of the plays were very successful. But more and more, as I was onstage in the evening, Cass began to drive into nearby Wilmington. He would come back long after I was in bed smelling of liquor, but I was afraid to say anything.

I got out of the bed and rolled up a newspaper. I smashed it against the wall, killing a wasp that had gotten in. I heard a noise outside and Cass opened the door. I could tell immediately that he was upset. "What's wrong?" I asked. He threw a briefcase down on a chair.

"Can't you even make up the bed?" he said. "This place is a mess."

"I was just resting for a few minutes," I replied and I started to straighten the sheets. "Do you want to talk about it?" I asked cautiously.

"Yes, I want to talk about it," Cass snapped. "Why not? Marie's brother is coming, or did you know that?" I lifted the bed until it fell in place against the wall.

"No, of course not," I said, "but what difference does it make?"

"Only that he's coming for my job," Cass said as if he were talking to an idiot. I closed the doors that concealed the bed and tried to be as calm as possible.

"Cass," I said, "you know that's not true."

"Well, what's the difference?" He was ripping off his shirt. "He's coming to work and there's nothing for him to do but my stuff. What am I going to do? Sit around while he does everything?"

"There must be enough work for two people or the girls wouldn't bring him," I said in an ameliorating tone.

"They're bringing him because he's Marie's brother," Cass retorted. "Don't be stupid." He began to pace up and down in the small room and I leaned against the doors to the bed to keep out of his way. "If her brother had the proper interest," Cass had begun to ramble, "he would have been here some time ago, but the girls don't see it that way. Well, Cass Stevens has taken the last god damn licking he's going to. It's not that I wouldn't be glad to be rid of all the details, but I'll be damned if I'm going to do all the hard work and let them run the show and bring dear little brother along just to be dead wood."

"Cass," I said, "I'm sure if you talk it over with Marie and Miranda they'll understand and it can be worked out." He stopped pacing and looked at me.

"The only smart thing Jackie ever said was that your problem was that you had infinite trust in people."

"But you love the girls," I said, "and they love you."

"I've quit. I'm going back to Texas."

I let out a breath. "Don't you think we should have discussed it first?"

Cass saw the look on my face and walked over and took my shoulders in his hands. "I can't stay here any longer," he said and his voice had lost its edge. "I thought if I was around, I could protect you, but you don't need my help – you're doing just fine."

"But I do need your help," I protested.

There was a moment when neither of us spoke. Then Cass said, "I've got to get back to a job where people respect me and where I can make some money. I hate living like this."

"But what about us?" I asked.

"I just don't think it's in the cards," Cass replied.

"But we have to work at it."

"Look," Cass said as he guided me over to the sofa, "I waited seven months while you were overseas, then we were together for two, then we were separated for two more months while you were on tour, and now you're going to be away for a year with *Hamlet* –"

I interrupted him, "They just asked me if I'd be interested. It's not settled."

"No," Cass said quietly, "but it will be."

"Then I'll refuse to go," I said.

"You're an actor," he replied. "You can't turn down an important role in a play. I wouldn't want you to. And you can't expect me to sit around while you get your career going. I don't want to be depressed all the time. I can get an advertising job in Houston and find a great place and live it up once in a while."

"Without me," I said.

"You want to give up the theater?" Cass said. "Then be my guest and come along."

I didn't say anything. I had the feeling that no matter what I said, it would end in the same way.

17

Fortinbras

"Be delicate and tender," the director George Schaefer said.

I was standing on a stage in a small auditorium where we were re-hearsing for the *Hamlet* tour. Those were the words that Hamlet spoke to describe my character in the play. Schaefer was well-known and had done the play with Maurice Evans for the GIs during the war, but I thought it was a ridiculous direction to give to an actor. I hadn't the slightest idea how anyone could act "delicate" or "tender," but I nodded my head in agreement.

Cass had been right. I was offered the important role of Fortinbras by Maurice Evans himself. He was the greatest Shakespearean actor of the time and had formed a company to bring his production of *Hamlet* all over the country, to places where they had never seen live theater. Of course, I grabbed at the opportunity. We would tour the country for a year doing mostly one-nighters so we would be constantly on the move. That was fine with me. I'd had my fill of love and the dream of settling down with hollyhocks at the garden gate. After two out of two failures, I wasn't sure I could ever make a relationship work. But for now, I wanted to forget all about it and just be by myself.

The stage manager, Bud Williams, of the short tour I had done in the spring, had turned out to be a great friend. He praised my talent and touted me to Maurice Evans. Mr. Evans thought I was perfect for "Fortinbras," so maybe the "delicate and tender" the director wanted was already there in me and just needed to be brought out. I had two scenes in the play, but one of them was really important: the ending and it was all mine. It was a eulogy for Hamlet, and as soldiers lifted the dead Prince up onto his bier, I raised my sword and commanded a tribute of gunfire. The final words were "Take up the bodies. Such a sight as this becomes the field but here shows much amiss. Go, bid the soldiers shoot."

I was to say these words for a year, night after night and I never tired of it. Billy Nichols who played Guildenstern (or was it Rosencrantz, I never could tell which was which) became my best friend on the tour and always made fun of my pronunciation of "bodies" that he claimed I called "bawdies." The truth was that I had to speak loudly and make the words very clear since I was competing with organ music that was playing at the same time. Also, I was way upstage at the beginning of the scene and moved down to the footlights at the end. My father, who as usual was not my greatest admirer, said when he saw the play that I sounded like Colonel Stoopnagle (a popular radio comedian of the 1930's) who did a sketch of being alone at the North Pole and having to yell in the hope of having someone hear him. There were many jokes from my buddies on the tour about my speech that was a mixture of Boston and Shakespeare, but I never minded. It was mid-Atlantic speech before its time.

There was a moment on the tour when my scene at the end of the play became history, at least for the company. As Fortinbras, I had to give the final speech, after Hamlet had died, all the way downstage at the footlights. There were not that many theaters that had footlights at that time to guide me so a spotlight was always installed to shine in my eyes when I reached the proper spot. The only problem was that I wouldn't always feel the light so I walked cautiously. I lived in fear of walking right off the stage and falling into the audience if I missed the light.

Sometimes I would walk a bit too far and often not far enough for the spotlight to hit me. But there had been no problems so far. Since we played a different theater every night, the lighting had to be taken down and put up again every day. One night, the stage manager had neglected to tell me they hadn't been able to put up the spotlight. So that night, as I said my lines, I walked and walked and walked and still felt no light in my eyes. This time there were footlights but they blinded me and I couldn't see anything. Finally, I thought I'd better stop so I raised my sword, said, "Go, bid the soldiers shoot" and the curtain came down right on my head. It knocked me out on the apron of the stage where I looked stunned at the audience as they applauded my solo curtain call. I reached behind me, picked up the curtain and crawled under it. The entire cast was lined up and waiting for me. To make matters worse, I suddenly realized my caracal fur cap, that I always wore at an angle, had been knocked off (it had likely saved me from a concussion) and was lying on the audience side of the curtain. Because I wore the cap at an angle, I only made up half of my forehead and in my stupor, I thought I couldn't let the audience see me half made up, so I grabbed the bottom of the curtain again, reached underneath, found the cap, put it on and returned to my spot with the rest of the cast.

They were all hysterical but hid it when the curtain went up, and after it went down, they all screamed with laughter. Maurice Evans laughed the loudest and couldn't have been nicer. He didn't blame me for a minute. However, it was the beginning of my making laughable mistakes that gave me the nickname "Schnook" or sometimes "Schnookle," but it was used affectionately so I never minded. The actors were all pleasant and very happy to be touring. Quite the opposite of the actors in *Junior Miss*. Mr. Evans created an atmosphere where we all felt secure and admired.

My caracal cap was not the only fur on my costume. The jacket had a fur collar and so did the cape. I thought the black fur, which contrasted with my red uniform, was very expensive until I discovered that it was dyed black and probably from a wild cat. But with black boots and a shiny sword, I had a lot going for me. I still played the double of the Ghost in a gray shroud, but when I took it off along with the beard and put on Fortinbras' glamorous uniform, I became a different person – "delicate and tender" indeed.

I shared a dressing room with Emmett Rogers who played Laerties and lived with Maurice Evans. Emmett told me that the two had driven to the West Coast in a convertible, and since Evans was a huge star with his picture everywhere, they were afraid he would be seen with another man and thought to be homosexual (anathema at that time). Emmett had to scrunch down in the back of the car, out of sight, whenever they drove through a town.

He had the most complicated makeup: a white slash the length of his nose to narrow it, more white covering the circles under his eyes, a lighter brown than his dark brown base on the lines in his forehead. I watched Emmett as we made up side by side in front of the mirrors. I copied everything Emmett did until my face looked like a patchwork quilt. My friend Billy Nichols saw me.

"What have you done to your face?" he asked. I explained I had copied Emmett's makeup since he looked so good onstage. "Schnookle, are you crazy?" he said. "You're doing everything to correct problems on your face that you don't have. Forget it. Just use a little pancake and you'll look better." Billy was right. I was learning slowly, but I was learning.

Along with Billy and the stage manager Bud, I made another friend. I had seen her the first day of rehearsal and was staggered by her beauty and sophistication. She was cast as the Player Queen, a small role, but from the beginning, she was word perfect and in total control. She sat by herself when her scenes weren't being rehearsed, totally immersed in doing what I later learned were Double-Crostics. She spoke to no one and her dark hair and squarish head with its perfect features gave her a haughtiness that seemed to say, "Keep away." But Billy, Bud, and I soon discovered that she was just shy. When we managed to get through to her, she turned out to be the sparkling light of the tour and the bawdy life of the party everyone adored. After the tour, Neva Patterson had a long career on Broadway and in Hollywood.

We finally started out and, not surprisingly because of Maurice Evans' fame and the fact that he had pared *Hamlet* down so that it wasn't tedious to the average playgoer, we were a huge success. So much so that the theaters were filled, especially with young people getting to know Shakespeare as well as seeing a play in a theater for the first time. The only problem was that the kids spoke to each other all through the performance, and the actors were suffering from the distraction.

Finally, Maurice Evans had a brilliant idea: he went in front of the curtain to welcome all the students and then said, "I know you all love to go to the movies but we're so happy you're seeing a play with live actors for a change. The difference is when you watch a movie and talk to your friends and sometimes yell at the screen, the actors are all in their swimming pools so they can't hear you. They don't care. But we can hear every word or sound you utter and that makes it difficult for us to concentrate and give you our best performances." There was always a wave of surprise from the crowd and then they were as quiet as church mice for the rest of the play.

The tour was pretty much the same every day. We traveled by train at night and arrived at a new city with free time during the day and a performance in the evening. We also did matinees so on those days there was little time to explore the city. When there were a few hours off, I would work out at the YMCA or go to the museum. There was usually one in every large city. I also liked going to the tops of things – buildings with vistas of the surrounding countryside, mountains, if there were any – I even went to the top of the Pagoda in Reading, Pennsylvania

– anything to fill the few hours in towns we would probably never see again.

When we stayed overnight in a hotel, we would party. Bud, Billy, Neva, and several of the cast (who were in favor with us that week) gathered in one of our rooms and drank and sang and told theater anecdotes. Another of my "Schnookle" times was at a party in my room when we were all quite drunk. There was a knock on the door. I opened it to two police officers and in my panic said, "Are we making too much noisy?" Another line that traveled through the company. I became the indulged one that everyone patted on the back. After all the time of being in charge and making actors toe the line, I didn't mind being coddled like a child that the grownups doted on.

On another night when we were not sleeping on the train but staying in a hotel, our group went to a club one of us had heard of. As I sat at the bar, two over-dressed, over-made-up women came to me and wanted to know if I was in the *Hamlet* show. I was pleased that they recognized that I was an actor and talked to them. They were un-attractive, almost ugly but very admiring of me. One of them asked my name and after a while I left them to join Billy and Bud. I told them about the odd women and they both looked at each other.

"Are you kidding?" Billy said. "You really are a schnook. They were men; they were drag queens."

I couldn't believe it. I'd never seen one before. The next day there were roses for me at the theater and an invitation to meet. I was relieved that we had to rush to the train after the show. I felt like I barely got out of town before I faced some ghastly confrontation.

Billy was the voice of reason for me on the tour. He looked like the March Hare in *Alice In Wonderland*, not sexually attractive but so witty and bright. He didn't strike me as much of an actor, but he was wildly imaginative. It was put to use later in his life when he did the ideas for *The Hit Parade* television show and produced award winning specials. If there was a piano in sight, Billy would play and sing "Gimme a

Pigfoot and a Bottle of Beer" or "Barrel House Bessie" or any Gershwin or Rodgers and Hart you could think of. Sometimes Neva would sing along and she had a sultry night club performer's style enhanced by her amazing beauty.

Neva was also funny. She would sing "down home" songs in a country style from her native Iowa upbringing. All the glamour would disappear as she acted out the characters of the songs. She would always break me up. Which leads me to the night we made love. Though having sex was more accurate. Of course, we'd had a party and been drinking pretty steadily. Somehow it had seemed perfectly natural to take Neva in my arms and kiss her when we got to the door of her hotel room. We managed to unlock the door without untangling ourselves and headed for the bed pulling off our clothes. I had never been with a woman before but I felt completely in charge of the situation as if I were Don Juan. Who knows? Maybe it was Neva's expertise that made me feel that way. What amazed me was that it all seemed so natural and easy. I didn't have to learn to ride the bicycle, the instructions were already built in. It was highly enjoyable. I kept hearing in my head something Neva had often said: "I like to be kissed when I'm being fucked." So, I kissed her many times and then went on my merry way feeling very grown up finally at the age of 20.

That experience wasn't the beginning of anything. We did it several more times in the weeks that followed but without a great deal of enthusiasm on either part. Then Neva and I went back to being the warm friends we had been and acted like nothing had ever happened. I did, one night in San Francisco, start to try it again but Neva put me off sweetly. She was having an affair with another actor who was appearing in a play at a theater near us. It was fine with me. I did find sex with men more exciting so I continued the short-lived experiences that I'd had so far on the tour.

I did learn more about Neva when we were playing in Iowa, close enough to Neva's family to be invited for Thanksgiving dinner. Our gang – Bud and Billy, Neva and I – set out on an early winter day. There was a sprinkling of snow on the surface of the farmland that made everything look picture perfect, but I could see, underneath the charm, the farmhouses that needed paint and the slanting barns that had to be propped up before they slid to the ground. Neva's parents were a few steps away from Grant Wood's painting *American Gothic*. Neither of them was anything like Neva: the mother, sweet faced, small and welcoming; the father, gray-haired, weather-beaten, a body once strong but now beginning to sag. The house was simple, clean, with comfortable furniture covered in flowered slipcovers that still showed the years of stitches that had repaired them. Neva asked her parents questions about the farm and relatives' health, but though she seemed to be trying to be their daughter, she came across like a glamorous social worker.

The dinner was delicious, great dressing for the turkey and all sorts of side dishes of relishes and jams that the mother "puts up" in Mason jars in the winter. Neva's father insisted we try the hard cider that he had made, and it was practically lethal. I had seen a tall water tower next to the house when we arrived and after dinner I asked if they minded if I climbed it. They couldn't believe I wanted to do such a thing, but they said it was all right. Neva told me later that for years they always talked of "the boy who climbed the water tower."

The tour was coming to a close, and like the *Junior Miss* tour, I was ready for it to end. Actors in plays that run for a long time learn to make each performance new, although they're saying the same words they said at the last performance. The good actor will keep it fresh but, after a year, there was nothing more I could do with Fortinbras. I had gotten good reviews and Maurice Evans praised me. We even became friends. I had to go back to New York to look for another play. But now I had saved a little money, and I had made good friends. The best part was that I had a real credit. I had played an important role with a great star. It might get me an agent or at least a reading for a new play.

18

With Neva Patterson

The traffic was moving too slowly and I was so excited that I told the taxi driver to let me out at the corner of Sixth Avenue. There was a nip in the air, but it was still not cold enough to wear a coat. It had been a magnificent day and I kept racking my brain to remember a poem I had learned in grammar school. I could only come up with the title – "October's Bright Blue Weather." I wanted to recite it into the wind to praise the fall day with its China blue sky and embracing sun. I ran down the few steps and opened the door. There were people waiting, but I passed through to the entrance of the bar. The din was so great that I could barely hear the piano and then I spotted Jackie. We had been seeing each other again now that I was back from the tour and Cass was out of the picture. She was always on time. I walked over to the table, kissed her on the cheek, and sat opposite her.

"You're only 15 minutes late," Jackie said and her annoyance stretched the dimples in her cheeks.

"Wait till you hear why," I replied and gave her a knowing smile, "but first, I've got to have a drink." I ordered a dry Rob Roy, five parts of J&B Scotch to one part vermouth with a lemon twist, straight up with a glass of ice on the side. Jackie had another martini on the rocks with both onions and olives that she always ordered.

"Okay," she said, "don't be coy. Let's have it."

I thought she looked particularly beautiful. She had let her dark hair get very long and it was pulled back and tied with a scarf that almost touched her shoulders. Her burgundy suede suit was set off with gold earrings, the usual gold chain around her neck and a diamond pendant. She was the epitome of the successful New York career woman, and I was proud to be seen with her.

"Well," I began, "I told you I had a reading for a replacement in the Katharine Cornell show yesterday –"

"You got it!" she interrupted.

"Wait a minute," I said annoyed, "let me tell you the whole story. I was just dressing to come to meet you when the phone rang in the hall. and it was for me. A voice said, 'This is Guthrie McClintic. Can you come right over now?' I couldn't believe that the most famous director in America was calling me, but I said, 'Of course.' He gave me the address of the house on Beekman Place where he lives with Katharine Cornell. I tried to phone you, but there was no answer, so I figured you wouldn't mind my being late when you knew what it was for."

"Go ahead, go ahead," Jackie said.

"I started to worry in the taxi," I continued. "Why did he want me to go to his home? Then I thought he probably wants me to read again. But why wouldn't he ask me to go to the theater? Although at 7:30 at night the rehearsal would be over."

"Did you get it or didn't you?" Jackie cut me short.

I ignored her. "McClintic let me in himself to this fantastic brownstone and took me through the corridor into the garden. It was really dark, but I could see the lights on the river and hear the noise of the cars on the East River Drive. You know he's a little man, and even though he's married to Miss Cornell, there are all these stories. I thought he was going to make a pass at me and I kept wondering if Miss Cornell was in the house. He stood with his back to the lamp in the doorway so I couldn't make out his expression. He seemed to be looking at me for the longest time and then he handed me a small book. 'I've marked the roles you are to play,' he finally said, 'be at rehearsal at 10:00 in the morning.'"

Jackie reached across the table and grabbed my head. She leaned forward and kissed me. "That's the best news," she said, "congratulations."

"The funny thing is I remembered the actress, who helped me get into *Junior Miss* in Boston, had said that it would probably take me five years to get a part on Broadway and that's how long it is since I left home."

"No," Jackie replied, "you went on for that one performance in *Hamlet* before the spring tour."

"It was just one time and I was the understudy so it doesn't count. Anyway, I have my own role now and it's at the opening of the play and a famous speech."

Jackie put her cigarette out in the ashtray. "This is the perfect time to say what I wanted to say to you." she said. "I think we should get married." Mabel Mercer sat down at a table near us and began to sing. All conversion stopped and I just kept looking at Jackie. I knew she was being absolutely serious. When Mabel had finished, Jackie went on as if there had been no interruption. "It makes perfect sense. We both want companionship and a home, but we can't seem to find them with anyone else. I certainly haven't and Cass didn't work out for you. We love each other as much as we'll ever love anyone and think of the relief that we'll get from our families trying to marry us off."

I hadn't thought of Cass until Jackie mentioned him. I looked toward the bar where Cass had been standing the night we met. There was a group of good-looking young men laughing. For a moment I thought that Cass would materialize, but I knew I didn't want him to. I had seen Cass once in the year since we had separated. He had been in New York for a few days and had called me. We had dinner and went back to my room. It was a fiasco. I felt as if Cass was trying to force me back into the person I'd been. But I was no longer a little boy hungering to be taken care of.

I'd toured the country with a big star and had made friends with people who were active in the Broadway theater. I was beginning to be known. I was no longer coddled by Marie and Miranda nor was I afraid. I felt myself fighting the old feelings of helplessness that Cass had brought out in me. We seemed like strangers who had picked each other up on the street and regretted it as soon as we walked through the door.

"You're thinking about Cass, aren't you?" Jackie asked.

"You always know what I'm thinking."

"He was a kept boy. I tried to warn you but you wouldn't listen."

"I don't think that's true, Jackie."

"Have it any way you want." She lit another cigarette as the waiter emptied the overflowing ashtray, "but first there was the composer and then the older man while you were away. Cass had rich tastes."

"I think he tried. We both did, but I don't think it's possible for me anymore."

"So," Jackie put up her hand as if she were resting her case, "let's get married."

"What do we do if we fall in love with someone?"

"We'll all live together until the love is over – it always is – and then we'll still have each other. I do love you."

"I love you too," I said simply.

"We can live in my apartment and take the gift money we'll get and fix it up. We can entertain theater people which will help you in your career. And remember, I've worked in an agent's office. They won't send you out for a job if they think you're homosexual."

I took a signet ring with my initials, that Louis had given me, off my finger and held it out to Jackie. She quickly slipped a small gold ring with a tiny diamond off one of her fingers.

We exchanged rings as I said, "Jacqueline, will you marry me?"

"You bet your ass!" she replied.

19

Suddenly in my life, all hell broke loose: I had to be in Buffalo for the pre-Broadway tryout of *Antony and Cleopatra* that would open in New York on November 27th. Jacqueline (I never called her Jackie again) had become Irene Selznick's girl Friday on the production of *A Streetcar Named Desire*, so she was in Boston getting ready for their Broadway opening on December 3rd, a week after our opening.

We would be married on Sunday November 30th in between the two openings. There were just weeks to accomplish all of this. Jacqueline's mother was an invalid who spent her life on the telephone buying things. She acted like the commander of a military maneuver as she prepared for the wedding. She ordered the food, flowers, did the guest list, and even bought Jacqueline's outfit as well as the jewelry she would wear.

I had been living with Bret Morrison, a successful radio actor who was the voice of *The Shadow*. He was famous for his reading of "Who knows what evil lurks in the hearts of men...the Shadow knows," imitated by kids all over the world. We had met through friends at a party and I went home with him in his MG convertible to a stunning duplex overlooking Central Park. He had seemed very handsome in the midst of the group. He was dressed beautifully with impeccable manners. He seemed to be a popular man about town. As we sipped champagne alone in his magnificent living room, I realized that not only was he wearing a full toupee, but he was sad, very lonely, and not terribly attractive.

He asked me to move in with him, no strings attached, just to have company. There was a separate room on a lower floor where I could stay and save rent money. Since the *Hamlet* tour, I had been back in my usual furnished room in the Village and I thought, *Why not?* There was no love involved and no physical demands. He wanted to redo the room that was to be mine and wondered what period I would have liked to have lived in. I told him I had always fantasized about being in New England in the 18th century. Within days there were early American antiques in the room and it had been painted and spruced up.

I felt like the son of a rich father and, after the years of misery in cheap furnished rooms, it was like a fairytale. I had moments of worrying that I was being kept, but I was still looking for work every day and getting unemployment insurance since the end of the *Hamlet* tour. Bret encouraged me to have my friends over so I thought up a Sunday Hunt breakfast. Bicycles were rented for everyone and we rode them in Central Park and returned to the apartment for a lavish brunch with eggs, bacon, Southern homemade biscuits with jams and honey and champagne.

Bret enjoyed it and his home was suddenly filled with people and laughter after what he told me had been a gray, empty period. I paid him back, somewhat, by going with him as he made appearances as The Shadow at county fairs in New Jersey. I put on my radio announcer's hat again and introduced him. He would sweep onto the stage in a black slouch hat and a cape using his amazing voice over a handheld microphone and the crowds loved it. I did tell him immediately when Jacqueline and I decided to get married and that, of course, I was moving out. He was sad but happy for me. He had a set of luggage made with my name embossed on each piece for our honeymoon trip that we never took.

Rehearsals of *Antony and Cleopatra* had gone beautifully, The sets were magnificent – huge columns, copied from the originals in Luxor, went from the stage level to the top of the proscenium. No expense had been spared on the historically accurate costumes. Miss Cornell was especially striking in a black and white ensemble that Valentina had designed for her as a battle uniform.

There seemed to be only one problem: Cleopatra had two hand-maidens – one played by the early movie and stage star Lenore Ulric, and the other by a young woman who seemed to be driving Miss Cornell mad. She kept touching the star and rubbing her arms and back in the scene where Cleopatra dies. We were all sure that she would be fired and finally a young girl McClintic had discovered arrived to replace her. Her name was Maureen Stapleton and the story was that she had telephoned McClintic when he was about to direct an Irish play *The Playboy of the Western World*. With a stroke of luck, he answered the phone himself and Maureen told him how right she was to play the girl in the play since she was Irish. McClintic said he was sorry but the part was cast and started to tell her who he had hired. "I don't give a fuck who's playing it," Maureen said, "if I'm not doing it."

McClintic was tantalized by her boldness and asked to see her. She became the understudy. Now she had arrived in Buffalo to play the handmaiden Iras. The first night she was there she called me. I had never met her, but she acted as if we knew each other.

"This is Maureen. I'm staying in your hotel. Come right over to room 316. I need to talk to you." She hung up before I could reply. I was afraid she might be in some kind of trouble so I went down in the elevator and found her room. She opened the door, a chubby girl dressed in pajamas and with patches of white all over her face that covered pimples. "Sit down," she said. She stretched out on the bed and I sat on the edge of it. "Look, we've only got a couple of weeks before we go into New York so I don't have much time. I figured you'd know who the homos in the show were. I don't have anything against them. I just don't want to waste any time with them or I'll never get laid."

I told her, as best as I could, the ones I knew and she got up and wrote the names down. I figured the men would be just as glad not to be hit on. Maureen was not a beauty, but in the future, when I saw her, she was seldom without some guy in tow.

Maureen came up to me in Detroit, after she had been playing Iras for a week. "Listen," she said, "why can't I get that laugh in the scene with Eli?"

I knew she was referring to a moment in the play when the soothsayer, Eli Wallach, was telling fortunes for Cleopatra's two handmaidens. He examines both their hands and then says, "Your fortunes are alike."

Maureen, as Iras, says, "Am I not an inch of fortune better than she?'

"If you were," the other handmaiden replies, "where would you choose it?"

"Not in my husband's nose," Maureen replies. Typical Shakespearean double entendre.

"Maureen," I said, "You know what it means. Just say it as if it's the capper to a dirty joke. It's so obvious."

"Yeah," she said. But try as she did, she could never get the laugh, not once in 126 performances and she was one of the bawdiest women in show business. Many years afterwards I ran into Maureen. She had become one of the great actresses of her time. The first thing she said to me was, "Why couldn't I get that laugh in *Antony and Cleopatra*?"

At last, we were back in New York and ready for the dress rehearsal the night before the opening. All the men, except for the leads, were in a large dressing room with a row of makeup tables that were connected on either side of the room. We had done the play quite a few times on the pre-Broadway tryout so we all felt comfortable and secure. The rehearsal began and I had the opening speech. As one of Antony's men, I complained to another soldier about Antony's behavior with Cleopatra. It was a strong, angry scene and, as we watched, the two stars came on – two middle-aged people in love. Shortly after that, in the next scene, we heard yelling from the orchestra where the staff was seated.

Everything stopped as we realized it was the director, Mr. McClintic literally screaming, "You're all terrible. What do you think you're doing? This isn't acting. If you're going to give this kind of performance, I'll cancel the opening as well as the play. Now get yourselves together and act, for god's sake."

I was so grateful that someone on the staff had told me that McClintic always did this after the dress rehearsal started on any of his plays. He thought it got all the actors keyed up and that it made the performance much more exciting. It seemed to get results and the opening night began beautifully. Unfortunately, as Miss Cornell and Godfrey Tearle (who played Antony and looked exactly like President Franklin Roosevelt) made love, the enormous columns started to ascend into the fly loft. I heard a gasp from out front. A stagehand must have mistaken a cue. Someone backstage caught the error for the columns were jerked down again where they hit the stage and continued to shake during the whole first scene. It, of course, killed the illusion of Egypt as well as the belief in the play. But Miss Cornell and Tearle worked hard to recover and the rest of the show went splendidly. The reviews were great. It was a success and ran longer than any other production of the play.

Jacqueline was still out of town so her best friend from grammar school, Eleanor Vaughn, had agreed to stand in for her at the opening. She went with me afterwards to Sardi's. Eleanor was an Italian beauty with dark hair and eyes, an aquiline nose and perfect teeth. She was swathed in fur against the winter night and I was proud to have her on my arm as we walked into the famous theater restaurant. I had finally made it to Broadway and I felt no longer on the outside looking in. I was on the inside looking out.

20

With Jacqueline

"Wake up, we're getting married in four hours." Jacqueline shook me until I was able to focus on her.

When I did, I realized what she'd said and felt guilty. Here we were sleeping together before the ceremony. Of course, we'd been in separate beds, and we hadn't physically been together, but now that we were going to be man and wife it all seemed so different. Even though I knew it was a marriage of convenience, I felt as if I were really going to be with Jacqueline for life. So, it just wasn't right to be in her apartment yet. Wasn't there a superstition about seeing the bride before the wedding? I wished I'd taken a hotel room.

"There's some coffee if you'll just get up," she said.

I could see that she was ready under her robe. "I didn't even hear the shower," I said.

As the maid let us into Jacqueline's parents' apartment, we were inundated by the heavy scent of lilies. Flowers were everywhere, on any flat surface that would hold a vase. Combined with the heat, which was always turned up for Jacqueline's invalid mother, it made us feel as if we were walking into a hot house. Jacqueline's mother lay in her hospital bed that had been wheeled into the doorway of her bedroom so she could watch the ceremony in the living room.

When she saw us, she didn't even say hello. She just asked Jacqueline to get her father to give her a shot because, she whined, "the pain is so bad." She was totally hooked on whatever it was her husband gave her. Since he was a doctor, the supply was endless. I tried to talk to her but she was, as usual, far away until the drug took effect. Jacqueline's father, a short aggressive man who was always laughing and snorting as he told jokes, arrived with his doctor's bag. He pushed a needle into his wife's fat arm and within minutes, she was smiling happily.

The doorbell rang and people began to arrive. We had kept the number to 20 so there wouldn't be too much excitement for Jacqueline's mother: my parents; my brother and his wife; Jacqueline's aunt and uncle and their son; Eleanor, who had been with me at the opening of *Antony and Cleopatra*, was Jacqueline's matron of honor; Billy Nichols, my best friend from the *Hamlet* tour; Bret Morrison; several other actors as well as Neva Patterson who had given us a toaster for a wedding present. I guess they run out of Tupperware.

I no longer saw Marie and Miranda since Jacqueline couldn't stand Miranda looking longingly at her, and Louis was away on tour. The agents Jacqueline had worked for before her job with Irene Selznick – Liebling and Wood – were also coming. I was hopeful they would help me get another play. I'd been shocked at my opening night to do my speech at the beginning of the play in almost total darkness. I figured that the lighting cues had gone wrong. It was only after I finished my famous speech and Katharine Cornell started onto the stage that the lights began to come up. It was then I realized why they said a star lit up the stage. The audience must have thought it was Miss Cornell's radiance that was doing it, but in the meantime, nobody was seeing me acting my heart out. I'd have to galvanize my career so the lights would come up on me.

Jacqueline had pinned white orchids on her brown dress that she said was a perfect color for a November afternoon and she had tucked a lace handkerchief into the belt. My mother had forced a carnation into the buttonhole of my jacket. I had worn a brown suit to match Jacqueline's dress, but I'm afraid we both looked grim and somewhat depressed. The man who was to marry us finally arrived from Boston. He was a friend of my parents, and they had insisted he be brought down when Jacqueline's parents couldn't come up with anyone. When we greeted him, he immediately asked us to go somewhere where no one would hear us. We took him into another bedroom and I thought, *Oh my god, he's discovered that I'm homosexual and Jacqueline is a lesbian and he's going to announce to everyone there that as a result, he can't marry us. Maybe I should tell him that we really do love each other and it's much more than it seems to be.*

Before I could open my mouth, he explained that he'd discovered that he didn't have authority to marry us in New York, but if we wanted him to, he would go through the ceremony and a friend of his, who had a license in New York would sign the marriage certificate the next day. "The only problem," he said, "is that you won't be really married on your wedding night."

I was so relieved I blurted out, "Oh that doesn't matter."

He looked at me strangely for a moment and then said, "Well, let's get on with it."

"I do," I said as I looked directly into Jacqueline's green eyes. They were resolute and uncompromising. She was almost dour and I thought of the evening before when she had picked me up at the theater.

As the taxi drove up to the stage door with Jacqueline in the back, I saw the doorman hold the door for Miss Cornell. There had just been a small ceremony as the cast presented me with a silver box that was engraved "Tony and Cleo 11/ 30/47" and I'd assumed Miss Cornell had chipped in. I opened the taxi and told Jacqueline I would like her to meet the star.

She got out and the great actress said in her deep contralto voice, "You must be very excited."

"Yes," said Jacqueline, "we got wonderful reviews in Boston but you know the New York critics. We've got our fingers crossed. Well, I'm afraid we have to run. We're late for a party. Nice to meet you." She propelled me into the cab and we drove away leaving a startled woman looking after us.

After a moment I said, "I think she meant excited about the wedding, not about the opening of *Streetcar*."

"Don't be silly, she replied and she saw no humor in it when I tried to explain it to her.

"I now pronounce you man and wife." I kissed Jacqueline and everyone crowded around hugging and kissing and wishing us well. The waitresses appeared with trays of food and champagne corks popped incessantly. My mother cried and Jacqueline's mother had another injection. The two fathers told each other jokes and the actors got very drunk. When it was time for Jacqueline and me to leave, Bret said he would take us uptown in his car. We kissed everyone goodbye, and a maid threw Minute Rice at us.

When we got to the street, I remembered that Bret's car was a two-seater MG. The only way the three of us could get in was to put the top down and have Jacqueline sit on my lap. The trip to the Pierre Hotel, where we were to spend our honeymoon night, was freezing cold and my legs ached from Jacqueline's weight. The desk clerk smiled at the two of us looking bedraggled and clutching a small suitcase and a bottle of champagne. Jacqueline's orchids were flattened against her shoulder and we both seemed a little drunk.

Once we were in the room and the bellboy had left smirking as if he were in a movie about newlyweds, Jacqueline unpacked our few toiletries and handed me my pajamas. "Why don't you go first," she said.

I brushed my teeth as I looked into the mirror. I had seen the king-sized bed and it made me feel very odd. I wondered if I should do anything. Was it possible that Jacqueline expected me to? After all, I had gone to bed with Neva on the *Hamlet* tour and enjoyed it. It had seemed so easy after all the years of worrying about it. I couldn't get over how well organized a woman was – everything in a convenient place. I had accomplished it neatly and I was happy that I knew that I could do it. I had thought that eventually Jacqueline and I would try and have a child even though I knew of her aversion to men physically. It was the one thing we hadn't yet discussed.

I lay on the left side of the bed, waiting. Finally, Jacqueline came out of the bathroom and walked through the surfeit of French furniture to the large window. She pulled the draperies to block out the view of a wall in another part of the hotel. I watched her as she removed the cork from the half-emptied bottle of champagne and poured it into two water glasses. She went around the foot of the bed and handed me a glass.

"Cheers," she said.

"Cheers," I replied and we both clicked our glasses and drank. Jacqueline sat down on the bed beside me and there was a cracking noise as the bed sank to the floor beneath us. "Think what the maid will say in the morning,' I said and we both collapsed in laughter. It took away all of the seriousness of the occasion and we both slept like babies.

| 146 |

21

In just a couple of days, Jacqueline was going to have her opening night of *Streetcar* and she was so busy, I hardly saw her. In the meantime, I had developed a huge stye on my right eye that looked terrible. I figured all the excitement must have torn my nervous system to bits. Of course, I continued to act. I don't think the audience noticed, and afterwards, I wore a patch and looked like the ad for "The Man in the Hathaway Shirt." Strangely enough, the stye created my first close encounter with Miss Cornell.

She had always been friendly but distant, and she seemed to wear a sign that read, "Don't disturb me. I'm busy thinking about my role." She did have a coterie of actors in the play who had been in her previous productions, and they often surrounded her as if to ward off the unwanted. They called her Miss Kitty. We called her Miss Cornell. Since she and I were in the opening scene, we always saw each other onstage before the curtain went up. Miss Cornell would walk around the stage and, I imagined, she was trying to create her Egyptian kingdom out of the columns and stairs the scenic designed had created. She always nodded to me and sometimes said "Good evening." But the stye changed all that. She must have noticed it because for the first time she came up to me.

"You have a stye!" she exclaimed.

"Yes, I'm sorry," I said, as if I'd done something to upset her.

"Is it very painful?"

"Just uncomfortable."

"You poor thing. But it will go away," she was suddenly acting like my mother. "Imagine," she went on, "when I was in *The Green Hat*" (I knew the play was one of her greatest successes) I had a stye on both of my eyes and I still had to do the performances."

"How did you manage?" I asked.

"I just pulled the hat down lower on my face." I thought for a moment she was joking but I realized she was dead serious. Humor was not her forte. We were interrupted by the stage manager's signal that we were almost ready to begin. We went to our places but not before she said, with a sad expression on her face, "Oh, I hope you'll feel better." She had seemed more animated talking about the stye than I had ever seen her before. I was to experience her penchant for sickness again.

A Streetcar Named Desire opened to fantastic reviews and became a smash hit. Of course, I was acting so I couldn't go to the opening night, but Jacqueline insisted I take her to the party that producer Irene Selznick was giving in her apartment after the show. The stye in my eye was throbbing so I had to wear the patch, and I felt and looked ridiculous. It wasn't a large party, but that made it even worse – just the cast, a few backers and close friends. I felt like a bump on a log. I could only see out of the one eye and I knew no one. Jacqueline was busy with her boss Irene who looked worn out. It seemed more like a wake than a triumph.

Marlon Brando was sulking and quiet, though he'd made what would turn out to be one of the most auspicious performances in theater history. As usual, he looked right through me and didn't even say hello. I remembered my threat of keeping him off Broadway, but I put it out of my head. I had seen his shining talent in school, but he was still a bore. It was a party from Hell, and I was grateful when Jacqueline, exhausted herself, said, "Let's go home."

The next few weeks turned out to be the best of our marriage. We were young, attractive newlyweds, both connected with hit shows, and on the way to being sought out as the young theater couple of the year. Invitations poured in, and Jacqueline sifted through them, tossing away the ones that "didn't make sense," as she said. She had told me early on that her ambition was to make it big in New York. We seemed to be half way there.

With the wedding gift money, we redid her fourth-floor walkup apartment. It was on 45th Street, a half block from Fifth Avenue – a good address, but with only one small bedroom just big enough to store things. There were two studio couches that were lined up on a wall in the living room. They were covered with lush yellow and gray striped slip covers. We slept in the two beds with our feet almost touching and our heads far away from each other. Bright yellow draperies had been made to match the slipcovers. We had spent the most money on what was to be our prize – a Noguchi coffee table. There was a small marble fireplace, but it had a broken top that we removed and replaced with some plants that I pushed into the openings where the marble had been.

By the end of December, we were ready to begin Jacqueline's plan to entertain and conquer the world of the theater. She had accepted several parties for New Year's Eve and would pick me up after the show. As she saw me off to the theater, she said, "I made up something I think is very witty: 'It sure was heaven in '47, but we're going straight in '48.'" She kept repeating it as I walked down the stairs. Jacqueline had a tendency to say things that amused her, over and over.

Jacqueline was waiting when I went down for the curtain call so I dressed as quickly as I could. She was always at me for taking so long when I shaved or showered and she hated standing around in the hall by the stage door. I had made a list of things to change in the new year and "not keeping Jacqueline waiting" was right up there with "give up smoking and promiscuity" and "eliminate sex as a conversational topic." I had taken my makeup off after my final scene so I got out more quickly than usual.

We maneuvered our way from the Martin Beck Theatre through the crowds in Times Square to 54th Street where the audience was just coming out of the Lyceum Theatre. Billy Nichols lived just a few doors up from the Lyceum. Since it was too late to get anywhere else by midnight, Jacqueline had agreed to go to his party first. She didn't care much for him and she said he was "just an actor – no one who can be of any use to us." She knew that Billy was my best friend on the *Hamlet* tour and I told her how bright and funny he was, but she had made up her mind.

Billy had a floor though in an undistinguished building that was part of a commercial block. You wouldn't believe anyone lived there, but after you climbed flights of stairs, you entered an oasis of culture and beauty. Billy had repaired the old wooden floors and waxed them to a sheen. All the furniture was covered with white slipcovers, long before it was fashionable. There were fine paintings on the wall that an art collector friend had lent him. There were artifacts Billy had bought for pennies in flea markets in Europe and wherever you looked – books.

Many of the actors from our tour were there and they greeted me warmly. Some laughingly used my nickname from the tour – Schnookle. Neva, looking glamorous in a long black dress that made her eyes and hair seem even darker and more startling than ever, rushed over and kissed me. I noticed that Jacqueline, who knew we had been to bed together, gave her a frozen look. I wondered if she was really jealous or just pretending to be.

Everyone went out on the balcony from which you could see a slice of Time Square. It was dense with people and there was an expectant din that grew louder as we waited. Suddenly it became a roar and I kissed Jacqueline. She whispered in my ear, "We're going to go straight in '48, and you'll be mine in '49." I hugged her. She had altered her slogan and I was to hear her repeat it many times before the evening was through.

We managed to get a cab on Sixth Avenue and went through the park to avoid the traffic that was still heavy, even though it was after 1:00 in the morning. Our next party was in a huge apartment building called the Wickham Arms. The lobby had thick plaster walls embedded with half timbers and hammered iron sconces that held 15-watt bulbs, obviously to save money. The building must have seen better days. The elevator man took us to the seventh floor and we could hear the noise as soon as we got out.

There was a rack in the hall with coats so we hung ours up with the others. I didn't know any of the people I saw as I pushed my way to the kitchen to try and get us a drink. I left Jacqueline talking to a judge who was a friend of her father's, but by the time I got back, she was gone. I went from room to room looking for her but there was such a mob, I couldn't find her. There wasn't one familiar face I could ask, so I finally put her drink down and walked around, sipping mine. I pretended to look at the art on the walls. No one paid any attention to me. I wished I were home in bed.

Suddenly Jacqueline appeared in the doorway pulling a girl after her by the hand. She pushed her way through the crowd and reached my side. "This is Mary," she said, "she was in that play with Walter Huston last year and she won the most promising actress award and she's going into something with Gielgud." Jacqueline always gave everyone's credits when she introduced them. I said I was glad to meet her and smiled. She was blonde with a big nose and a receding chin. When she smiled back at me, I noticed that she had a full set of white, capped teeth. "She's coming home with us," Jacqueline said.

When we finally climbed the stairs to our fourth-floor walkup, we were exhausted. Mary had told stories about her play in the cab with a slight Southern accent and had made us both laugh with gossip about the star. Jacqueline and I had been sleeping in the twin studio couches that doubled as sofas in the living room. We had only used the tiny bedroom as a place for a cot that was always covered with suitcases. I suggested that I make up the bed in there but Jacqueline and Mary didn't say anything. I went ahead and got out sheets and a pillowcase while Jacqueline made us all a drink. When I had tucked the blankets in, I said that I'd finish in the bathroom unless one of them wanted to go first. Neither of them spoke so I went in and shut the door. I felt like such a fifth wheel – as if they wanted me to leave, but I couldn't go out at 3:00 in the morning.

When I walked back into the living room, Jacqueline and Mary were sitting next to each other on one of the two beds with their arms around each other's waists. "I think I'll just go into the store room and go to sleep," I said. "I'm awfully tired."

Jacqueline got up and kissed me on the cheek and then Mary came over and kissed me too. I closed the door and got into bed. *There's nothing wrong*, I thought. *It's just that I feel so awkward.* I began to hear moaning through the wall. It was Mary's voice. I tried not to listen, but the sound became more insistent. I held the pillow over both of my ears and finally was able to fall asleep.

Mary moved in the next day.

22

Jacqueline said we were now a family: she was the mother, I was the father, and Mary was the baby. "We are a unit," she insisted, "and no one can do anything to break us up."

We had indeed become a unit, but I wasn't sure I was the father. It was Jacqueline who went off to her producer's office early in the morning. Mary and I were left to clean up since we didn't go to work in our plays until evening, except on matinee days. Mary was in a short run of *Crime and Punishment* with the great actor John Gielgud. Jacqueline and I went to see it at a special performance for actors and were disappointed. Gielgud was much too old to play a student and Mary had the small role of Lizaveta, a pathetic creature who is murdered. It was a limited engagement and only ran a month.

As soon as Jacqueline was out of the house, Mary and I relaxed. It was as if the mother had gone shopping and the children had been left to play. We had endless cups of coffee, talked about life and the theater, and admired each other's bodies. Mary, although quite homely, had a magnificent figure. She and I often walked about nude, when Jacqueline was away, and told each other how great we looked. Sometimes we spent the whole day doing nothing and had to rush to clean up in time for Jacqueline's return. Invariably something was left undone and Jacqueline was sure to find it. Then she would suspect that we hadn't been making the rounds looking for a new play. She would berate us with the fact that Mary's play was about to close and mine only had a few more months to go.

"You've just been fooling around while I do all the work," she would say while she inspected the kitchen and the bathroom. She was particularly adamant when she found I hadn't put the top back on the toothpaste, which I always forgot. She found it impossible to understand why I didn't work the tube from the bottom up, rolling it neatly. And yet, despite all the criticism, I still wrote her, when *Antony and Cleopatra* closed in New York and went on a short tour.

How awful it is to leave you – nag though you may be. Would anyone believe I care more for you than anyone else in the whole world? But of course they would, for it's true...I sit quietly in the train reading and thinking of you and our dear 'baby' – what a wonderful family but I am not happy away from it. I miss you.

Jacqueline, however, changed as her relationship with Mary strengthened. All of the plans to be the fun couple that would draw important people to us and help further our careers went out the window now that we were a threesome. Jacqueline no longer made any attempt to be feminine, and she was less conscious of how she dressed or did her hair. I had always been after her to use makeup so her eyes could be even more startling. I had brought her some mascara from the theater to accentuate her thick lashes. She took it from me and disappeared into the bathroom while Mary and I waited for the transformation. Jacqueline reappeared with a full mustache that she had painted under her nose. I never mentioned her looks again.

The winter was harsh, but I went to the theater every night while Jacqueline and Mary stayed home. I found it awkward to have men stay overnight in my tiny room, but I managed several relationships, one with an architect who looked like a greyhound and another with a blue-eyed, blond model who looked like a model. At least it helped blot out the moaning through the wall that had become part of the ambience.

The atmosphere at the theater was a complete change from my home life. Instead of women, I was with over a dozen men in the dressing room who made small talk or played jokes on each other. There was one boring guy who boasted about receiving mail from both men and women who wanted to go to bed with him. He was very tall and not a good actor. We voted him the least likely to succeed. His name was Charlton Heston but fortunately, shades of Marlon Brando, I didn't threaten to keep him out of the movies.

One day there was a huge snowstorm. It didn't keep us from performing, but when we took off our makeup and went out to the street, we discovered that, although the snow had stopped, the roads were impassable. Miss Cornell's car couldn't possibly take her home so someone suggested that anyone who lived uptown should walk with her to Beekman Place, where she lived. There were about ten of us and it was a memorable event. We surrounded the star, who was cloaked in fur, and guided her through the sparkling snow-filled empty streets. It was like a royal procession with Miss Cornell as the Queen. We all laughed and sang. Her usual mien of darkness and almost depression was totally gone and she looked radiantly beautiful. I never saw her look like that again.

We did play Boston on the tour and my parents again barraged me with their usual disapproval of my career. From "You aren't saving any money for your future" to "How can you support children when you can barely keep up yourself?" I had made the mistake of staying with them in Brookline, outside of Boston, so I was a sitting duck for all the venom they'd been storing up. "You said you'd be a star and you've been in New York for five years and you're nowhere near it," was my father's coup de grace. And he was right. I was relieved when we went to our next town.

I got to know a little more about Katharine Cornell as we waited on the stage before it was time to begin the performance. When she spoke to me one night, I mentioned something that had happened in the news that day.

"I don't want to hear about it," she said. "I can't read the papers. I get so upset that I can't act." She also revealed that she didn't read for the same reason.

When Ted, the actor who shared the opening scene with me, got sick and went to the hospital, I went with him. Miss Cornell sent for me before the matinee. She was lying on the chaise that always traveled with her, surrounded by her dachshunds. She grilled me for any detail I could remember of the actor's tumor that had been discovered. I flashed back to my stye after opening night and her sudden concern. I finally told her he would be operated on in the morning. She asked if I would see him again before the operation. I replied that I would go to the hospital between shows. She reached down to a table that was laden with a Kleenex box, candy, and pictures of friends that must have given her a sense of home. She took hold of a small wooden figure of a dachshund and held it out to me.

"Give this to him," she said, "and say I'm thinking of him."

The next evening there was a message with the stage doorman that Miss Cornell wanted to see me. I went to her dressing room, as big as a living room, and found her on the chaise, resting before the show as I imagined she did every day.

"I had Gert (her former lover and now her right hand) call the hospital and they said Ted will be all right. Did you give him the dachshund?"

"Yes, I did," I said and I took a breath. Somehow, I knew what the next minutes would be. "I gave it to him, and he closed his hand around it and held it all through the operation."

Great tears rolled out of her eyes. She was suddenly more real than I had ever seen her on stage.

23

The four flights of stairs to Jacqueline's apartment (I still didn't feel it was mine) had never seemed so steep. I walked in and threw myself into the one comfortable chair to catch my breath. I faced the unmade beds and the breakfast dishes that were still on the table. I would clean it all up in a minute. There had been such a rush to get Jacqueline and Mary to the ship that everything was a mess. I spotted some tissue paper we had used for packing under one of the beds. I got up and reached under and pulled it out. I crumpled it in my hand as if I were putting an end to something. Perhaps, in a way, I was. Maybe it was a new beginning. *I'll sleep in here now*, I thought, *the mattress is more comfortable. I might as well get started.*

I tore off the sheets from both beds. I thought of the ship, out in the narrows by now. I could still taste the champagne they had served in paper cups in the crowded cabin. It had been too early in the day to drink and it had only added to my depression. I felt suddenly so alone, but I supposed that was a perfectly normal reaction. After all, the three of us had been together for nine months, except for the time I had been on tour with Katharine Cornell and the two shows I had done in stock in the summer. Despite the new role Jacqueline had assumed of ordering Mary and me around all the time, I still would miss her. I had grown to depend on her. I had certainly felt more secure financially since we were sharing all the bills together. Now I would have to pay everything, although Jacqueline would still pay half the rent. It was hard not to feel abandoned. Mary had told me repeatedly how much Jacqueline loved me. And yet she had just left me.

The first time Jacqueline had broached the subject of living in Europe, I had thought it was a fantasy made for conversation, but not to be taken seriously. And yet she had never let up about wanting to live abroad. "I want so to live in Rome for a year with Mary," she said over and over. "It's the only time in our lives that we'll be able to do it. I want to learn Italian and write a book." Mary wasn't working at the time, and one day, Jacqueline just quit her job with the producer and started to make arrangements to go. She had saved enough money for them to live for a year. Despite her parents' disapproval, she went ahead with her plans.

I never said a word about it. I didn't feel that I had the right. Although I knew people would think Jacqueline was leaving me after just one year of marriage, I acted as if it were perfectly natural. If they asked me, I said I was so happy she was making a real stab at her dream of being a writer. How could I stand in her way? She had written a book before we were married and I had read it and found it very impressive. It was never published, but I remember it began with the line, "In New York City, no matter what you are doing, somebody else is doing it at the same time." I thought that was a pretty sharp observation. The story was about her affair with a married woman. It was probably ahead of its time.

As I put the yellow-and-gray-striped covers on the studio couches and arranged the matching pillows against the wall, I wondered if I had somehow contributed to Jacqueline's wish to get away. Was it me she wanted to get away from? I flashed on something that had happened that summer. The stage manager of *Antony and Cleopatra* had told me he was looking for a summer theater to rent and I recommended The Robin Hood in Delaware where I'd had such a good season. He rented it and asked me to do several plays there: *The Male Animal* and *The Vinegar Tree*.

Both my roles were typical juvenile parts in comedies of that time. I particularly liked James Thurber's *The Male Animal*. I always got a huge laugh from the audience when I said to a guy who said he was

40, "Oh, that time when all is over and love has turned to kindliness." I was just 22 and 40 seemed like the end the road. When I finished the plays and returned to New York, Jacqueline told me she wanted to share a cottage on Fire Island for the month of August. She insisted I had enough money from my recent job and together we could "make it work," one of her favorite expressions.

The cottage was near New York in Cherry Grove, a burgeoning homosexual enclave that still had its modicum of families with children, as well as the chic set headed by Dick Avedon and his wife Doe. Our roommates were Irving Schneider, Irene Selznick's assistant on *Streetcar*, his present partner, his former partner Clinton Wilder (also a producer) and Clinton's new partner. There were four rooms: Jacqueline and Mary in one, the two couples each with a room and me alone.

It was an odd group and almost like a French farce. All the doors were closed most of the time and one or another would pop open when someone had to go to the communal bathroom. There was some contact at breakfast, but each couple hid behind his or her closed door with his or her partner. I felt like a fifth wheel again. Jacqueline and Mary were more by themselves than they had even been in the apartment.

One day Jacqueline ran into Marlon Brando who had nowhere to sleep so he ended up on the couch in our living room. Again, he didn't speak to me and looked dirtier than ever. He had to get back to New York to perform so we had little time for the pleasure of his company. I found the awkwardness of the situation demeaning and I kept to myself. Sometimes I would go to dinner with Jacqueline and Mary, but their bond seemed to be even stronger and I felt they spoke mainly to each other.

One night they asked me to go with them to the large building that housed the bar and had music on the weekends for dancing. It was almost like being in a barn and I found it depressing. All of the roommates were there drinking and talking to each other or to friends. I stood around by myself until I couldn't stand it any longer. I walked over to Jacqueline, who was holding her after-dinner martini.

"I'm going back to the cottage," I said.

"No, you're not," she replied somewhat belligerently, "you'll wait until we're ready to go."

"I want to go now," I said and started to walk to the door. There was a tremendous crash of glass breaking into many pieces on the floor around me. All the noise in the room stopped. I realized Jacqueline had thrown her martini at me, but she had fortunately missed.

As I stood, almost in shock, the roommate Clinton rushed up to me and said, "I demand to know what is going on!"

"It's none of your business," I replied and walked out the door.

But I couldn't have answered him anyway. I didn't know what was going on. I suppose Jacqueline wanted to be alone with Mary and had just begun to resent our marriage, though she wouldn't deal with her mistake. So, she found a way out – Europe. Well, maybe I could find my way out, but I had to get another play.

The cold weather had returned, but by now I had a heavy coat with a fake fur collar, so making the rounds wasn't quite as horrible as it had been. After a few hours of "Nothing today," I always stopped in to see Bill Liebling and his wife Miss Wood (her first name was Audrey but no one ever called her that). They were famous agents as well as admired personalities in the theater world. Bill was a wiry little man in his late fifties, somewhat common, rather like an old jockey. Miss Wood was the same age but quite elegant and still a reminder of what she must have looked like as a pretty young woman. She had the attitude of a schoolmarm and called everyone by their last name.

They had been to our wedding because Jacqueline had worked for them and they were very fond of her, yet Miss Wood only called Jacqueline by her last name, Babbin. I think she did this to keep her distance from people since she had so much to do. Tennessee Williams was her client, and she was responsible for shaping his career. That was enough to keep anyone busy. I could never get in to see them until Jacqueline kept telling them how talented I was. And now, since we were married, they didn't quite treat me like one of the family but I was spared the "Nothing today" and shown right in to see them.

On this day Mr. Liebling (I couldn't quite get up the courage to call him Bill) greeted me with, "Just the man I wanted to see." He'd never said that before. "I was going to call you. I got this manuscript and I thought it might be something for you." I couldn't believe what he was saying as if I were the Lunts being wooed for a new play. He walked over to his desk and picked up a huge stack of paper bound in a makeshift blue cover.

"It's French," he said. "this famous French playwright," he looked at the cover having obviously forgotten his name, "Giraudoux. It's a big hit in Paris. Anyway, DeLiagre is going produce it here and he says he's going to direct it as well, so I stole a rough translation from the French. It was so boring I couldn't finish it, but there is a boy in it you could be right for. They're having it adapted so maybe it'll be better. In the meantime, try and read it and I'll get you an audition." I couldn't thank him enough but he waved me aside, "Only thank me when you get the part."

I read the stilted translation that was enough to put anyone to sleep, but there was no question I was right for the role. Mr. Liebling came through with a reading for me. He reported that they had liked me so much that I was called back to read five more times. The leading lady was in England so I always had to act with the stage manager who spoke the lines in a monotone. My most important scene was to be with the star when she would try to get me interested in life again after I had attempted suicide. She was to play an old woman and as she talked about the difficulties of her day. I was to realize that my life was easy by contrast and get so moved that I would make up my mind to go on living.

It was almost impossible to work up any emotion, as I listened to the dreary, flat words of the bored stage manager with a cigarette in his mouth. My desperation at wanting so to be an actor was so great that it carried over into the role and I got terribly moved, almost to tears.

DeLiagre, having put up the money and made himself the director, called out from the darkness the usual, "Thank you. We'll be in touch."

I walked back to the apartment, still almost overwhelmed with emotion. Why did they keep having me back when all they ever said was, "Thank you"? It was torture, almost as if they were sadists glorying in what they must have known was putting me through hell. I stopped at the corner of Sixth Avenue and 50th Street to tie the belt of my coat. I'd just thrown it on when they dismissed me so rudely. I noticed a man selling bittersweet and I thought, *I'll buy some to take home.* I loved the bright, yellow-orange tiny fruits – they always cheered me up and they might even keep me from waiting for the phone to ring.

"How much?" I asked the man, whose unshaven face was chapped and red from the cold.

"Thirty-five cents," he replied and held out a bundle to me.

I walked away. That was enough for a whole dinner at the Automat. Tears started to form in my eyes. I couldn't help feeling sorry for myself. I'd been in New York for five years, and I couldn't even afford a lousy bunch of bittersweet.

24

The Belasco Theater was creepy – dark and somewhat neglected. It had a history of ghosts, including a woman who was repeatedly seen in a tattered blue gown. At one time the building even included the lavish duplex of David Belasco. He built high up near the roof so he could look through a peephole down at the stage to see how his actors were doing. As I sat waiting with the others, I wondered whether his ghost was watching us today.

The work light had been lowered, but it still wasn't light enough to cover the stage so the actors all sat in semi-darkness. We had been waiting since the lunch break and she still hadn't appeared. We had already lost a full day of rehearsal because she'd been too tired from the ship's voyage to turn up on the first day, so we had just read through the play with the stage manager taking her part. It had seemed pretty dreary but we hoped the star would pull it all together.

I sat next to Leora Dana, the ingenue who was to play my love interest. We were the only young people in a large cast of character actors, some like John Carradine and Vladimir Sokoloff were well-known from their many movie appearances. Leora had a refined, lovely face without a sign of makeup and rather kinky brown hair that looked like it had never seen the inside of a beauty parlor. She had a flat, thin body, almost like a boy and her schoolgirl skirt and sweater did nothing to help it. But when she spoke, her throaty, husky voice was moving and somewhat mysterious. She was fidgeting, picking at her nails, squirming in her chair.

"What's the matter?" I asked. "Relax. She's bound to get here eventually."

"I'm so terrified she won't like me," Leora said. "You know she can have us fired within the first five days."

That had never occurred to me. I'd been so excited when I got the phone call that I was hired after all the auditions, that I was sure everyone wanted me for the role. But of course the star had never seen me. What if she thought I was wrong for it? I pretended to feel secure. "Why wouldn't she like you?" I said confidently. "Mr. DeLiagre hired us and he's the director so he must think we're good."

"But," Leora said, "she looked so mean in the movie of *Great Expectations*. I know she was great and everything, but I'll just feel better after she sees me."

I pretended to look over my script. Leora had a big speech in the play, almost like a soliloquy, but she was all alone on the stage. I was the one in danger. I played opposite the star in two of her biggest scenes and if she didn't approve me, I'd be out in a second. Not that she was a big star with all that power.

Martita Hunt had made a great success as the crazy Miss Havisham in the movie of *Great Expectations,* but she wasn't a star in the United States and not even in England. Maybe she didn't have the power to fire me. Then I thought, *She's kept us all waiting for almost two days, even the director, while she rests and no one has been able to get her to come to rehearsal. I guess she really does have star power.* There was a stirring among the actors as if they were leaves rustling in the calm air before a storm. A door was heard to open and a deep British voice said, "I'm Martita Hunt."

It had been said quietly, but it reverberated against the bare walls. The director jumped to his feet and dashed to the stage door. He returned with a tall, thin woman beautifully dressed in an obviously tailored black suit with a black hat topped with black feathers and a black veil covering her face. She pulled the veil up to allow the director to kiss her and I could see the huge nose that I remembered from *Miss*

Havisham. It dominated her face and gave her an equine look. But what surprised me was that she was not the old lady she had played in *Great Expectations* at all. Nor was she the aging Countess in our play, *The Madwoman of Chaillot* – she looked around 50 and in great shape. The actors all stood by their chairs and the director walked her around as if she were the queen visiting a military hospital.

As she stood in front of each one, she asked them the name of the role they were to play, and when they told her she would say "Ah yes" and move on. When she came to me, she said, "You're my little Pierre." That was the name of my character in the play. I was so relieved that she recognized what role I would be playing without asking me. She obviously thought I was right for the part.

After the introductions, she took off her hat, fluffed her dyed red hair, and sat very straight in the one chair that had arms as we read the first act. I had never felt so nervous in my life. It was as if she were the executioner and we were all being prepared for the guillotine. I managed somehow to get through the scene in which she coaxed me back to life. When we finished the act, everyone got up to stretch and have a cigarette before we went on to the second part. I walked away from everyone as far as I could and stood at the edge of the stage under the ropes that controlled the flies. I lit a cigarette and drew in a puff and exhaled as if I were getting rid of all my anxiety. I suddenly smelled an expensive perfume. I turned and saw the star approaching me. She looked at me disdainfully.

"I'm at the Stanhope Hotel," she said. "Be there right after rehearsal." She didn't wait for me to say anything.

***

Back and forth, back and forth she paced in the living room of her suite, a cigarette in one hand and a glass of Scotch in the other. She was wearing a long blue dressing gown and her hair was tied up in a matching kerchief. Her face was very shiny. I guessed she had removed her makeup with cold cream.

"I won't do it," she said fiercely. "I'll go right back to England on the very next boat." I sat watching her not knowing what I should say or do. I was afraid if I said anything she would turn all her anger on me. "How dare they give me a company of actors like this?" she glared at me. "Every one of them took my tone. I can't possibly play this part without the proper support. I'm not a star." She paused and I thought for a minute I was supposed to say, "But you are, Miss Hunt." I still thought I'd better keep my mouth shut. She paced some more. "If they'd wanted a star, why didn't they get Peggy Ashcroft? I'm a character actress. I've got to have good actors to give me my cues. Where did they get these people?" She glared at me again and this time waited for me to answer.

"They had a lot of auditions, Miss Hunt," I said.

"Auditions," she snapped back. "That director wouldn't know a good actor if he fell over one. Every one of them has to go." She must have noticed the pain in my face. "Not you," she said, "you're terrible, but at least they didn't give me some little queer boy, so I think I can teach you how to do it."

I felt sick. She had turned away from me and part of me wanted to shout, "I am a little queer boy." But of course, I couldn't. She would get rid of me and the word would get around and my acting days would be over. I'd worked so hard to get this part, my first real chance in New York. How could I give it up? I agonized – why couldn't I stand up to her and tell her she's wrong, but she started up again and the moment had passed.

"We've got to get you to an osteopath first," she said. "There's something wrong with your back."

"I don't think so," I replied but she paid no attention to me.

"You're going to have to learn that all acting comes from the base of the spine – the coccyx – which propels us forward as our torso lifts out of its sockets, the hips. Stand up," she commanded. I rose to my feet and she walked over and put her hands on my back, massaging it and working her palms below my ribcage.

"There's definitely something wrong," she said. "but we'll find it. Just remember, we are placed on two feet, with our head in the air, to remind us that we are only a hair lower than the angels." She was still rubbing my back but the motions had gotten slower and more sensuous. She went on talking but in a quieter tone, "Our body must raise out of its case and strain toward heaven. Have you got a girlfriend?"

"I'm married," I said.

"That's sweet," Miss Hunt said as she removed her hands from my back. "Now you'd better go and let me get some rest."

I grabbed my coat and started for the door. "Good night, Muss Hunt," I said.

"Call me Martita," she replied as she poured herself another drink, "and not a word of what we've said."

I stood in front of the hotel that faced the Metropolitan Museum across the street. I took deep breaths of the night air trying to clear away all that had happened. I wasn't sure what Martita, my new name for her, had said. *Was she going to quit and return to London? Then the play would be canceled. But if she was leaving, why would she talk to me about having my back fixed?*

I looked up at her window where a shadow was moving back and forth. I kept hearing her voice over and over in my head – "You're terrible. You're terrible!" I hailed a cab and went back to 54th Street and the empty apartment.

25

With Martita Hunt in "Madwoman"

I sat on a stool in the shadows, behind the flats that created the set of the Chez Francis. I tried not to listen to the play, but I couldn't help hearing the words that told me how much time I had before my entrance. I kept saying to myself *I must prepare. I must concentrate.* I tried to replay my trip to the 59th Street Bridge the day before.

My part in the play was a young man who was going to commit suicide by jumping off a bridge in Paris. I thought I'd get the right feeling if I could just experience the moment. I walked to the middle of the bridge and looked down at the dark, swirling East River, trying to imagine what it would be like to want to kill myself. Now I closed my eyes, held my face in my hands and hoped to recapture that feeling, but all I could think of was that it was opening night on Broadway and everyone who was anyone in the theater was sitting out there waiting to appraise my performance. I was paralyzed with fear.

I suddenly heard a buzzing sound and I opened my eyes to see Martita standing in the wings waiting for the cue to make her entrance. She was wearing the outlandish costume of the Madwoman's that had been brought over from Paris. Her makeup made her look in her eighties and it was played up by a crazy red wig and objects like a fan, a bell, and ropes of fake pearls that hung around her neck. The buzzing was coming from her half-open mouth as she stood with her eyes closed. I remembered her talking of achieving serenity through certain sounds and this was undoubtedly one of them. She hadn't noticed me in the darkness but she seemed on another planet, far away from everything.

She must be as nervous as I am, I thought. I turned away from her and in a moment heard the applause that greeted her entrance. And then her voice calling out: "Year-ma!" (that was the way she pronounced the name of Irma, the waitress) "Are my bones ready?"

I only had a few moments before I had to go on and then it would all be over. Four weeks of rehearsal and one week of previews. Money had been saved by not trying out in Boston or Philadelphia. I had waited every day to be fired. Leora also continued to complain that she was the one who would be fired until one day she said, "Do you think I should get a press agent?" I was dumbstruck, but in time she actually did get one and became a great success. Martita didn't manage to get rid of anyone, but she did give everyone directions, summoning them to her dressing room, one at a time, and telling them how to read their lines. She spent most of her time picking at me since I was alone with her in two of her biggest scenes.

When she didn't have me nearby to lecture me, she wrote me notes: "My sweet boy – imagine you are lying on the back of a black-white seagull that is taking you away away away – you need make no effort to be heard – Do nothing." I didn't see how I could do nothing since I was stretched out flat on a bench and she was sitting next to me, far back, so I had to turn upstage to speak to her. If I didn't speak loudly the audience wouldn't hear me. Still the notes came every day: "Remember – don't fight your boring Martie. Just lie back in the arms of Jesus. Count sheep. Don't act. They can see you. Forget them. Safe in the arms of Jesus and his loving servant and yours – M."

It had gotten to the point where I dreaded coming to the theater for the previews for fear the stage doorman would say, "Miss Hunt wants to see you in her dressing room." I'm sure the director knew what was going on and that everyone was miserable, but he was weak and I guess, at this point, just hoped to get away with a mild flop for which he wouldn't be blamed.

Meanwhile, I couldn't avoid going in to see Martita and I'd stand there while she made up and complained about every one of the actors before starting in on me. She knew I had plenty of time. I didn't have to get made up since she'd put the kibosh on that. I'd used some light pancake for the dress rehearsal and when she saw me, she said, "You look just like one of Bebe Berard's little boys. Take that mess off!" I knew Berard was the French designer of our sets and I'd heard he was a famous homosexual, so off went the pancake. Martita only stopped her negative reviews of almost everything when she took a swig of her cough syrup that I finally realized was straight Scotch.

Several nights before, in the scene where she tries to persuade me to go on living, tears came streaking down her face from all the liquor. The speech was supposed to be about joy, not sorrow. Instead of finding it strange, the preview audience thought she was wonderful. After all, she was a madwoman so she could do anything – crazy or not. I heard the audience laughing at her now. She must be feeding her imaginary birds. It was time for me to go on.

The actor who played the policeman appeared and hoisted me onto his shoulders. I closed my eyes. If only I could forget all those people out there judging me and just be the character. I felt myself being laid out on the bench and I tried to go into an unconscious state. In the play, I had been knocked out by the policeman before I could dive into the river. I was almost calm when my mother's cough ruined the mood. She always coughed to let me know she was in the audience when she came to see me in a play. I had begged her not to do it, and she swore it wasn't her. I knew better.

I tried to forget her and everyone and think of nothing when I heard the cue to open my eyes. I saw Martita, now the grotesque Madwoman of Chaillot. I raised myself up on one arm and looked at her as if she were an apparition in the afterlife, since my character thought she had died. Martita had managed to sit even farther upstage on the bench than usual, so I had to keep turning my head to see her until I got a sharp crick in my neck. I had to hold my head in that awkward position for what seemed like forever.

I listened as she began her speech that would become famous – she even recorded it later with me for Harvard University. As Martita said "To be alive is to be fortunate" in her deep theatrical voice, I forced myself to forget the audience and opening night, and my mother, and just really listen to the words as she spoke them beautifully: "Of course in the morning when you first awake, it does not always seem so very gay. When you take your hair out of the drawer, and your teeth out of the glass, you are apt to feel a little out of place in this world." As she continued, I felt increasingly moved. When she finished the long description of her day and finally said. "How does life seem to you now?"

I could feel my eyes shining, holding back tears as I answered her emotionally, "It seems marvelous!" I felt truly in character and didn't find out until later that most of the audience had only seen the back of my head.

The rest of the act was a nightmare. Martita was so flustered that she kept dropping her props and forcing me to pick them up. I'd be in the middle of an important line when she'd hit me on the back and point at a fan that had just fallen. I would have to stop everything and retrieve it. In addition to the fan, she dropped a bell, an umbrella, a scarf, a comb, and a glove. When she took my arm and we walked offstage to resounding applause, I knew it was not for me.

After the final curtain, I went back to my dressing room. I didn't have on any makeup so I only had to change my clothes. My mother came rushing in with my aunt who was visiting from San Francisco. She threw her arms around me and gushed – mainly about the audience.

"I've never seen so many stars," she said.

My aunt pushed her way in. "Wait till I tell you what happened," she said. "In the intermission, we saw the great musical star Mary Martin, so your mother went up to her and said, 'Mary Martin – can I shake your hand?' Well, of course, Mary Martin put out her hand and your mother shook it. As she backed away, I went up to Mary Martin and I said, 'That was the boy who's playing Pierre's mother.'"

"Oooh," I groaned. "What do you mean?"

My aunt said, "I'll bet she was very glad to meet your mother."

Eleanor walked in and my mother recognized her as Jacqueline's matron of honor at the wedding. They embraced and then Eleanor put her arms around me. I felt the fur of her collar against my neck and I inhaled her perfume.

"You were wonderful." she said.

For a moment I forgot the opening and the embarrassing Mary Martin story, and even Martita. "Thank you for coming," I said.

"I wouldn't have missed it for the world," Eleanor replied.

26

Something was burning. I had to find out what it was. It was probably just leaves in the yard. I thought I'd better go into the other room and see. Just as I was about to turn the doorknob, I opened my eyes. Eleanor was smoking a cigarette and looking at me.

"You slept well. You were exhausted," she said. I pushed myself up against the headboard and propped the pillows behind me.

"What time is it?" I asked.

"Almost 8:00," she answered.

"I've got to get home," I said starting to pull back the covers.

She held my arm. "Why? You have all day."

"Jacqueline wrote that she'd call me from Rome to get the reviews about 10:00 our time," I explained. "I've got to be there." She looked disappointed. "I don't want to go," I said and I took her in my arms.

It had been so natural to make love to her. When I'd taken her home after the opening night party at Sardi's, we both had been so exhilarated. The newspapers had been read aloud to the cast and we realized the play was a hit. Despite my misgivings, I'd gotten excellent reviews. I had finally made it to Broadway in an important role, and I'd have the money to pay the rent, as well as to be able to take acting classes.

After we'd dropped my mother and my aunt at their hotel, Eleanor had said, "It's silly for you to go all the way downtown and then back to 53rd Street at this hour." I insisted. Jacqueline had made me promise to see a lot of Eleanor while she was away. "She's my best friend since grammar school," she had said. "She knows everything about us and she can be a perfect sounding board for you when you need it."

I had started to have dinner with Eleanor during rehearsals. She had been helpful in getting me through the problems with Martita. She taught psychology at Hofstra College on Long Island. She was able to make me see what a neurotic woman the star was and get me to stop blaming myself for everything. When the taxi stopped in the middle of Nineth Street, Eleanor said, "Well now that you've come this far, do you want to have a nightcap?"

Her apartment was one huge two-storied room with beams in the ceiling and oak paneling half way up the walls. There was a kitchen arrangement behind a screen. Eleanor went behind it and reappeared with a split of champagne that I opened. She took a stack of books from a chair so I could sit down. She perched on an ottoman at my feet. We talked over the evening and laughed at my having to pick up all of Martita's props.

"Let's forget about *Madwoman*" for a change," I said. "I want to talk about something else."

"What?" Eleanor asked.

"Oh, anything," I replied. "What did you do today?"

"I had my hair done,' she said. "You didn't even notice."

"I told you how beautiful you looked," I replied, "everyone said so."

"I hate being coy," Eleanor said, "forget that I even mentioned my hair."

"Is that the only thing that you did?" I asked.

"No, I had lunch with my father's partner and it was awful."

"Why?" I asked.

"He's so sick, poor thing. Hunted, suspicious, fearful, deluded, and as a consequence, so unhappy. It's so frightening when you think of it in terms of 'There, but for chance and individual difference, go I'"

"Can anything be done?" I asked.

"Well," she said, "I'm trying to convince him to get help, but he resists it. He only wants to see me because I'm a psychologist and he thinks it's going to help him just to sound off. He needs to be in a hospital for a while. Do you realize that one out of ten in the general population spends some time in his life in a mental hospital?"

I looked appropriately shocked. "Are you saying that I need help?" I said with a smile.

"I'm not going to answer that now," she said also with a smile.

I thought how smart Eleanor was, in a different way from Jacqueline. Jacqueline was filled with statistics and memorized quotations, but Eleanor seemed truly wise about the serious things in life.

"I'd like to sit on your lap," Eleanor said.

"What a nice idea," I replied and pulled her over onto my thighs.

I held her shoulders. She seemed so soft next to my chest and the back of her hair was against my mouth. She started to slip down so I grabbed her to keep her from falling. As she turned her head, I kissed her. It was a long kiss and her tongue melded with mine until there was no doubt of our passion. She pulled away from me.

"I have to go into the bathroom," she said. "I won't be a minute. Why don't you get undressed?"

***

The bus inched forward in the heavy traffic, stopping and starting like an old ragpicker sorting his way through the city's refuse. There had been a slight snow during the night and a sifting of powder still remained in places where people hadn't walked. I kept looking at my watch. The doctor had said if I was early, I'd have to remain outside since there was no place to wait, but it looked like I might be late. At 64th Street, I jumped out and ran the rest of the way. I'd make much better time. I was out of breath when I got to 73rd Street, and I stood for a moment pulling the piece of paper out of my pocket and looking at the address. I had memorized it, but I wanted to be sure. I didn't want to make any mistakes this first time. I found the house. It was of gray stone with four windows on each floor. It was 10:55 so I walked to the corner of Park Avenue to kill time.

I couldn't stop thinking about the night before and the euphoria I had felt from the whole experience. I knew it was an evening I would never forget. Eleanor had looked so beautiful with her olive skin and dark hair framed by the silver fox coat draped over her shoulders. I was proud to be with her, and I introduced her to many people, when we got to the theater, who came up to congratulate me on *Madwoman* being such a success. Most of them praised Martita and said how much I must love working with her. I simply smiled and agreed with them. Martita was almost as difficult as she'd been before the opening. The difference was that she was now being interviewed and photographed by all the magazines so she was often too tired, when she arrived at the theater, to have the energy to bawl us all out. And then her lover had arrived from England. She had raved and raved about him. When she summoned me to meet him, she said proudly, "This is Arthur!" I saw a fat, balding man with quite a few missing teeth prancing around the dressing room with Martita's feather boa twined around his neck. She giggled girlishly. I hoped he would stay for a long time and keep her busy. But unfortunately, he didn't.

Everyone in the theater was there that night. *South Pacific* was the hit of the season and it was the first actor's benefit on a Sunday when we were all free to see it. I was so excited to feel I was at last a part of the theater community. From the time the overture began, the actors applauded at every possible opportunity. When we ran into Maureen Stapleton, who had been with me in *Antony and Cleopatra*, she said, "They're even applauding the applause." We laughed. I sat holding Eleanor's hand as Ezio Pinza sang "Some Enchanted Evening" and the moment seemed to symbolize for me all of the yearning I had felt in my life to love and be loved.

Later, when Eleanor and I were in bed, we each seemed to express that yearning, and the physical pleasure peeled away the layers of our reserve. I still didn't feel the intensity that I did with a man, but I thought in time it would happen. And the very next day I would start to work on it with the psychologist Eleanor had recommended. When I pulled out of Eleanor and lay back in bed, she began to cry. I put my arms around her.

"What's the matter?" I said as soothingly as I could.

She answered through her tears, "That would have been the most beautiful baby."

I walked down the few stairs to the doorbells and found Doctor Byron's name. My ring was answered immediately and I went up the wide staircase where she was waiting for me. "Hello," I said.

"Come in," she replied as she held the door open for me.

I walked into a large room facing the street, with Oriental rugs on heavily waxed floors and comfortable sofas grouped near a grand piano. Paintings were placed on the walls, far enough apart, so it was clear they were not just for decoration but were serious works of art to be studied. I heard her close the door and I turned to face her.

"What do I call you?" I asked.

"What would you like to call me?" she responded.

"I mean, do I call you Doctor, or Doctor Byron, or by your first name?"

"Which would you rather call me?"

"Well, it's really what you want," I said, "I haven't done this before."

"Why don't we sit down," she said as she placed herself in a chair in the curve of the piano.

"Where would you like me to sit?" I asked. "Or do I lie down?"

"What would you like to do?" she said without any expression.

"It's up to you," I replied.

She looked at me from behind rimless glasses. I couldn't tell what she was thinking. "Why don't you sit there on the sofa to begin with," she said and I settled myself trying to get comfortable.

There were several moments of silence while I just looked at her. She had pale, wispy brown hair parted in the middle and pulled back and pinned to her head. Her powder-white face was innocuous. She looked like any other average housewife except that she had a huge bust that was obviously her pride and joy. It was accentuated by a tight lavender sweater that she was wearing. Since she said nothing, I broke the silence.

"What do you want me to talk about?" I asked.

"What would you like to talk about?" she replied. I was getting exasperated.

"I don't know. I thought you were supposed to tell me."

She sat quietly and watched me as I lit a cigarette. I was determined not to break the silence and finally she said, "Why don't we talk about why you're here? What is it that you want?"

I immediately answered, "I thought Eleanor would have told you when she asked if you'd see me."

"Eleanor has nothing to do with us," the doctor said.

"Oh I know, but she must have told you that we're having a relationship."

"What she told me has nothing to do with what goes on here," her voice was as measured and cool as it had been since I arrived. She continued, "The only thing that matters is what you tell me. Now, what is it that you want from me?"

"I guess I want to be cured," I said sheepishly.

"Of what?" She asked. I felt as if I were a bug being pinned and put into a collection.

"Eleanor must have told you that I've been homosexual," I said looking out the window at the bare branches of the trees. "I'd like to not be anymore."

"Are you sure?" She asked.

"That's why I came here," I confessed.

"You're married," the doctor stated rather than asked.

"Yes," I replied.

"How do you feel about your wife?"

"Oh, I love her very much, but not in the way I love Eleanor." Doctor Byron sat very straight in her chair holding a pad and pencil but not using them. I wondered why she didn't write anything. I thought I must not be doing the process correctly. I reached in my pocket and took out several pieces of paper. "I brought you a dream," I said enthusiastically. The doctor said nothing so I went on. "I thought you would want me to tell you my dreams." She still didn't say anything so I asked her, "Don't you?"

"Since you arrived," Doctor Byron said, "you've been trying to please me. You wanted to address me in the way I would like, you wanted to sit where I would want you to sit, you wanted to talk about what I wanted you to talk about. Now you've even brought me a present of a dream to help me do my work."

"Then let's forget the dream," I felt hurt. "I'm just trying to find out how you do all this."

"Why don't you read me the dream?" she said.

I hesitated for a moment and then read the pages I had brought with me.

Jacqueline, that's my wife, and I were walking through a park – green with summer – in the late afternoon. We heard voices screaming and saw adolescents running along a road. Some man told us that the kids were pursuing movie stars for autographs. He said Clark Gable and Tyrone Power were there. We saw Gable go by in a slouch hat and he was wearing a mustache. We bumped into an actor I had toured with in Hamlet *who had escaped from the crowd – torn and happily tired from the attention of the mob. The three of us walked along the road and I secretly worried or hoped that we would be stopped for our autographs. Although small groups passed us constantly, no one noticed the actor or me. We watched a large group of children hovering around a celebrity on a hill overlooking a valley.*

It was getting darker and the trees were almost black. Suddenly Jacqueline and I were alone. We stood on a hill and watched a young boy in a circular, flat-bottomed boat float down a labyrinthine river that wound over little hills. Appearing and disappearing from our sight. It was like an amusement at Coney Island. I wanted very much to do it, and I begged Jacqueline to do it with me. She refused utterly, and although I didn't press the point, I was disappointed. We walked through the heavy growth, over hills and along twisting paths, and arrived at a low, rambling house. It was brightly lit as if a party were going on. It appeared to be an inn or a dance hall. There was some kind of celebration or reception for the movie stars. Photographers were there and people were drinking cocktails. I found I was alone, wandering through the many rooms of the party.

On an enclosed porch, lit dimly by an overhead lightbulb, I met Eleanor. She was shadowy, vague and spoke very softly. Her dress was to her ankles. It was white with a pastel print of pale flowers. Her hair was lifeless and her skin was transparent. I told her about the little boat floating down the river and begged her to try it with me. My description of it was animated and excited. I tried to show her what fun it would be, though I think it mattered little to me that Eleanor would be the one to be with me. I just didn't want to do it alone. Jacqueline wandered up to us. She was in her party mood, unsmiling but exhilarated. She had been talking to many people, enjoying herself, but she was composed and detached. She left us and Eleanor agreed to take the boat trip. I was calmly determined rather than overjoyed at having found a companion. We went off together in search of the little river. It was evening and the moon was shining.

I folded the pieces of paper. "That's all," I said. I was happy to see that Doctor Byron had been taking notes. I had obviously been doing the right thing.

"Did you and your wife have sexual relations?" the doctor asked. I felt embarrassed and I wanted to explain the whole situation, but I didn't know where to start. "Did you?" She repeated.

"No," I said. "Not yet."

"I'm afraid our time is up," she said. "I'll see you on Thursday."

27

Jacqueline and Mary were standing at the railing looking for me and, for a moment, I had a wild urge to just turn around and disappear into the crowd. But they had spotted me and had begun to wave enthusiastically. Mary blew kisses that I half-heartedly returned. There was a traffic jam at the gangplank so it was some time before the women could get off. When they reached me, they kissed and hugged me. I tried to say something but Jacqueline cut me off.

"We've got plenty of time to talk later," she said. "I've got to get the car and there's not enough room in it for the luggage, so you'll have to take a cab." She directed Mary and me over to where the suitcases and trunks were being sorted. People were pushing and shoving each other as if they were in a food line during the war. There was such a din in the vast shed that we couldn't hear each other without shouting, but Jacqueline managed to identify their baggage. I put it all in one place. When Jacqueline was satisfied that she had everything, I got a porter with a handcart to take me to a taxi. Jacqueline hurried Mary toward where the cars were being unloaded and yelled over her shoulder, "We'll see you at the apartment."

There were so many bags that some of them had to be placed in the back of the cab with me and I had a moment of feeling trapped. As soon as the car started, I opened the window wide to try to get some air, but the rain poured in and I had to close it. I sat, trying to be calm. I thought I would suffocate in the heat. I wanted to give myself courage so I thought of Doctor Byron and the months I'd been climbing the stairs to her perfect living room. Funny, in all that time, it never occurred to me to question the marriage until I had the dream. Eleanor and I seemed perfectly happy, and there were never any discussions of my marriage to Jacqueline interfering with our relationship.

Jacqueline had written long letters from Rome with plans for our life together when she and Mary returned. She had not had much luck with her novel, and the two of them had been so cold during the winter that they stayed indoors most of the time, ignoring their plans to visit all the museums and churches. I wrote back mainly about going to the gym to try and build myself up, my search for the right acting teacher, and my attempt to give up smoking and drinking. I couldn't very well tell her what was really going on – that I was having an affair with her best friend and going to a shrink to try and become normal. I still thought I'd continue to live with Jacqueline and Mary, but I couldn't imagine Eleanor wanting to join our little family.

Jacqueline answered my letter from Paris, where they were spending a month before returning to the States. She wrote mainly with instructions as well as criticisms: "Be sure you take care of the insurance," she directed me, "we should have four policies: fire insurance that covers everything in the house, loss insurance that covers theft or any mysterious loss, insurance for furniture, (don't get too much because they can't easily carry it down four flights of stairs), and insurance for silverware, my camera, furs etc. Get in touch with the insurance man immediately. Don't put it off!"

Then she addressed herself to what I'd written that I'd been doing:

You made me furious with your self-inflicted punishments of not smoking or drinking. You are an adult human being with a will of your own and a good head. Why in hell try to prove that you exist to yourself by these little games that are really quite childish. If you aren't smoking because it affects your voice and, as an actor, you feel it is important for you – then don't smoke. But then don't talk about it either as if you are the great martyr of all time. It is extremely immature and actually quite pointless. That sort of game only proves that you need title dramas in your everyday life to make yourself exciting to you. They certainly don't impress other people because these things are really pointless. I see no reason why you have to cut yourself off from things for the simple reason of playing a game with yourself. You are not proving anything to anyone – not even yourself – and you certainly don't need that type of self-discipline. There are many other ways of doing that. Try seeing how many days you can put the cap on the toothpaste, not lose things, hang your clothes up. Basically, I think it would be more constructive. I'm sorry to be so repetitious and insistent on this but, to me, this whole thing is just nonsense. Have missed you terribly. Seriously can't wait to see you. Am really excited about coming home and, if we can only make sense about the closet space, the three of us will have no trouble.

I began to sing softly to myself, "If you leave Paris, you'll take away the sun." I still smiled whenever I thought of it. I had been having a session with Doctor Byron but I just had nothing to say.

I had sat there looking at her when she said, "Have you been having any dreams lately?"

"Nothing I can remember," I replied, "except a song, but it doesn't mean anything."

"What's the song?" she asked.

"Oh, it's just a Mabel Mercer song she used to sing at Tony's," I said.

"Why don't you tell me the words if you know them," she encouraged me.

"It's just a dumb romantic song," I said deprecatingly. "It goes: 'If you leave Paris, you'll take away the sun, the shining lights, the dazzling nights, the fun. You'll take the moonlight from the Seine, the sparkle from champagne.' That's all I remember."

"What do you think it means?" Doctor Byron asked.

I lit a cigarette. "I don't think anything," I said. "It's just a love song. I must be in love with someone in Paris."

"Who do you know in Paris?" she asked with the lack of inflection in her voice that I had grown accustomed to. I began to laugh.

"Jacqueline, of course," I said. "She's in Paris for a month. I guess I'm saying I love her and want her to come home."

"Are you?" she asked. "Doesn't the song say that if she leaves, Paris will be destroyed?"

"Yes," I said trying to follow her, "then I don't want her to leave Paris? Oh my god – I don't want her to come home." The revelation made me sit absolutely still for a minute, and then I said again, "I don't want her to come home."

The taxi stopped in front of the apartment house on 54th Street. The driver and I carried all the luggage into the front hall. Everything was soaked from the rain. After I had paid, I had to lug it all up the four flights of stairs to the landing. When I had opened the three locks, I pushed through the door and stacked everything in the tiny bedroom. I went into the living room and sat in the club chair, waiting. I thought of calling Eleanor, but I was afraid they would walk in while I was talking.

I looked around the room. Jacqueline and I had worked so hard to fix it up. The bright yellow curtains that pulled across the whole window wall and the yellow and gray striped covers on the two studio couches, the Eames chair with the painted red seat near the Noguchi coffee table, and above one of the couches the Georgia O'Keefe print of a Canadian Barn. I was so proud of the full effect. It was the first real home I'd had in the seven years I'd been in New York. The doorbell rang and I ran down the stairs to help Jacqueline and Mary with the few things that were left.

"I had to put the car in that garage on 55th Street," Jacqueline said as they walked in. "It's too expensive, but we'll find a cheaper place tomorrow. Wait'll you see it – it's an absolute doll and we saved so much money buying it in France."

I got the door closed and Mary rattled on about how well I looked and how excited they were to finally see my play – they'd heard so much about it. I kept trying to get a word in but both of them were too busy going to the bathroom and unpacking.

Finally, I couldn't stand it any longer. "I'm leaving you," I blurted out.

Jacqueline stopped what she was doing and looked at me. "You're what?" she asked as if she didn't have any idea what I was talking about.

"I'm not going to live with you anymore," I said.

"Are you crazy?" she replied. "When did this happen?"

"I want to live alone," I said firmly. Jacqueline stopped in the middle of what she was doing.

"Why didn't you write me if there was a problem?"

"I wanted to wait to tell you face to face," I said. "I thought that was the fair thing to do."

"Did Eleanor put you up to this?" Jacqueline demanded.

"Of course not," I said, "it was my idea." Jacqueline walked over and unzipped a compartment on a suitcase.

"We'll talk about it at dinner," she said, "we have to get caught up."

I could feel it all slipping away and I was determined to get it back. I took off the diamond ring Jacqueline had given me in Tony's when we decided to get married. "I want you to take this back," I said. "I don't want to be married to you any longer." I forced the ring into her hand, and she glared at me before she threw it as hard as she could at me. I ducked and it hit the wall and bounced back across the room.

"Get out of here," she screamed.

I walked over to the door and opened it. As I started out, I heard Mary pleading, "Jacqueline, don't – please."

I shut the door on the two of them, walked down the stairs and around the corner to the furnished room I had rented several days before. I unpacked the things I had brought there that morning. I suddenly remembered that Jacqueline hadn't given back my ring. It didn't matter.

28

My new furnished room was the worst place I'd lived in since I'd been in New York. It was in a pleasant enough apartment building and was owned by an elegant elderly woman who had just lost her husband and didn't want to be alone. She was very cold and sedate and so was the furniture, especially the heavy draperies crowned with their fancy pelmets. Not a particle of dust anywhere nor was there any sign of human life. It was like a mausoleum that had been closed up for years.

I had to tiptoe to my room since the woman was in bed by the time I arrived after the theater. She was everything that had made me want to escape from my nouveau riche relatives. The atmosphere was so depressing and claustrophobic that I almost regretted having left Jacqueline. But that feeling didn't last long. The next day I had a phone call from her. I had left my number in case I got a call for a job. Her voice was steely. No "hello" or "how are you doing?"

"Did you happen to see the diamond ring you gave back to me?"

"No," I reminded her, "you threw it across the room."

"Well, I've searched everywhere," she said, "and I just can't find it. I thought you might have seen where it went."

"No," I repeated, "I didn't."

She hung up and I didn't see her or hear from her any longer. To my knowledge, she never did find the ring. Certainly a sign of an ending, if there ever was one. But then it turned out that it wasn't the end of the whole unpleasant episode. Shortly afterwards, I was served with annulment papers. Evidently her parents thought she might want to marry again, but the chances of that were pretty slim. I read through the documents to discover that they were asking for the annulment on the grounds that I had refused to have children. What a facade. I signed the papers and sent them back.

Despite it all, I had really cared for Jacqueline. I even believed, in time, we might have been able to have a child together. But she had changed so much since we were married. She no longer made any pretense of being feminine. She had cut off the beautiful hair that she had brushed religiously 100 times every night before she went to bed. She never wore a dress anymore, only jeans, and space shoes, never heels. She was still, somehow, the Jacqueline I had known in the beginning. I don't think I dreamed her up.

I had found some letters of hers a few weeks earlier. She had written to me when I was on tour just before we were married. They were full of love and a real sweetness – an almost childlike quality. I wonder if she hadn't met Mary so soon after we were marred, whether things would have been different. But she did met Mary and now, instead of Jacqueline and Mary, there was Eleanor and Doctor Byron.

I had to get away from the widow and the feeling in the apartment that life was over. I had posted on the bulletin board, which hung in the stage doorman's cubicle, that I was looking for some place to live. The actor, Ralph Roberts, who played the policeman who carried me onstage every night, said that a one-room apartment had just come up in the house he lived in. I knew he was in the Village and I hated to go back there. I was so much happier living uptown, but I asked him if I could go with him after a matinee and have a look at it.

"Why sure," he said with his slight Southern accent. We called Ralph "the gentle giant". He was about 6'3" and solid muscle. His massive head looked like the Indian on the buffalo nickel. He'd told me he had Native American ancestors. He had a soft voice you had to strain to hear and the shyness of a milquetoast. Since we both waited offstage for his cue to carry me on, we had got to talking in the wings and had gradually become friends. He, little by little, revealed his problems that had driven him for help. I never did figure out if he went to a psychiatrist or a psychologist or just some faith healer, but he did trust me enough to talk about his leaps in whatever it was he was going through.

His first "breakthrough" came when he was advised, because he was afraid to touch people physically, to take up massage. He studied and became a superb masseur to the point, later on, of massaging celebrities including Marilyn Monroe. The next event he recounted was that he was told he was ready to stop living alone and could get a dog. He did and, in the years I knew him, he never lived with anyone except Bridget, a Kerry Blue Terrier.

Ralph took me to a converted brownstone where Fourth Street ends at 12th Street, right off Abingdon Square. It was weird that it was near the furnished room that I had lived in with Louis. The apartment for rent was in the front of the basement floor, just under the sidewalk, so you could see the shoes and ankles of the people, who walked by, through the bars on the two windows The one room had a stove and a small refrigerator. I thought I could disguise them with a screen. The dishes would have to be washed in a small sink in the bathroom. There wasn't much room there, barely enough for a shower and a john, but I was thin and I could manage. Jacqueline's place was no Versailles, but it was luxurious compared to what Ralph showed me.

He lived in the back of the basement, next door to where I would be. I thought this would be a plus. I would have a friend if I needed some help. The rent was $35 a week. I might be able to save a little on my minimal salary in *Madwoman* now that I wouldn't have extras like paying part of Jacqueline's expensive insurance. I had nothing to insure. So I put down a deposit, the first and last month's rent, and moved in as soon as I got a bed delivered.

As I continued to act in *Madwoman*, I kept hoping I would be offered a role in a new play but it never happened. I continued to make the rounds and agents were much more pleasant to me, telling me how much they had admired my performance, but somehow there wasn't a role in a new play that was better than what I had. So I stayed listening to Martita, telling me how wonderful life was, eight times a week for over a year in New York and then a short tour and then back to New York for several weeks at the City Center. I even played the Subway Circuit: Long Island, Brooklyn and the Bronx with Eleanora Mendelssohn in Martita's role.

Unfortunately, Eleanora, a lovely actress who had fled the Nazis, didn't have the hauteur that was Martita's strong point. She made her Madwoman sentimental and pathetic, and as much as I enjoyed being free of Martita, I missed her amazing performance. By the end of the New York run, Martita had pretty much let up on me. She never mentioned sending me to an osteopath again, nor did I ever figure out the key to her acting from the base of the spine that she had threatened to teach me.

Audiences loved Martita Hunt no matter what she did. When Leora Dana left the company to do a play opposite Henry Fonda, Roberta Haynes, a very pretty girl from Hollywood, took her place. There is a moment at the end of the play when the Madwoman tells me and the girl I had fallen in love with to kiss each other. It was always a tentative, sweet kiss of beginning love. Roberta, though playing a waitress, had long fingernails painted red. One nights as I kissed her, she ran her fingers down my back passionately and Martita, aghast at the girl's misplaced sensuality, slapped Roberta's face so hard that it resounded throughout the theater. The curtain fell and the audience applauded as vociferously as ever.

I only saw Martita once after the play finally closed in New York and she had returned to England. She was flying to the coast to be in the film of *Anastasia* and had a stop-over in New York. She cabled me to ask if I would have lunch with her at Sardi's. I put on my best suit and found her already sitting at the most visible table. She was beautifully dressed (she had all her clothes made by "a little dressmaker in Paris") and sat as erect as a queen trying to impress her subjects. We kissed on both cheeks and had an hour of laughter and good will. Not a sign of the ogre who had upstaged me so much that I had to twist my neck, night after night, resulting in pain that I have to this day. I watched her chattering away, being charming and acting the captivating leading lady. But I thought as I marveled at the prow that was her nose, if she hadn't looked that way, maybe everything would have been different. She had said so many times, jokingly, that she wanted so to be beautiful and loved. But I knew it wasn't a joke. She looked like a prison warden all dressed up in expensive clothes that didn't change who she was at all. We did the usual two cheek kiss goodbye and said we'd keep in touch. But, of course, we didn't.

I heard of her death in 1969 from a literary agent who was a close friend of hers. She said that Martita had burned up in her apartment from probably forgetting to put out a cigarette and falling asleep. Her friend and I both agreed that she must have had, as usual, too much to drink. The papers, however, said she died from bronchial asthma. In the almost two years that I saw her every day, I never saw or heard of an asthma problem. I like to think Martita, just like her most memorable character Miss Havisham in *Great Expectations*, did go out in a blaze of glory.

29

With Eleanor

The wind was whipping across the lake sending the dried leaves scurrying across the icy path. Eleanor was nestled in her furs and I was snug in a coat lined with lambswool. We had both been advised to prepare for the famously cold Chicago weather. We walked so closely together that we must have looked like one figure from a distance. We were oblivious to the cold that was particularly bitter for the end of March. Every once in a while, one of us would start to laugh and the other would join in.

"I'll never forget it as long as I live," Eleanor said and we both began to laugh again.

Since I was appearing in *Madwoman*, I had been asked to do a television play at the local station. Television was in its infancy and I had never done it, so I was eager to get the experience, even though I wouldn't receive any money. Since Eleanor was visiting me, she came to the studio to watch it.

I had rehearsed for a few hours on Friday before I had to be at the theater for *Madwoman*. We had Sunday off so we could rehearse the television all day and then go on the air live in the early evening. It was a two character drama about two prisoners trying to escape from Devil's Island. They had been struggling to break through the wall of their cell for years, and finally, at the end of the show, they manage to get through. Only one of them can escape, so the older one sends the younger one to his freedom. John Carradine, who was playing the Ragpicker in *Madwoman,* was my costar and we went on the air live with two cameras following us.

As we began to act, I noticed Carradine behaving very strangely. He was changing all the positions we had rehearsed for the cameras. I suddenly realized he was blocking me from Camera Two, the camera that was supposed to be on me, so that all the shots had to be on Camera One, the camera focused on Carradine. It was just like acting with Martita who was still upstaging me after a year of playing. I couldn't do anything about her because I was trapped stretched out on a bench with nowhere to move. But I decided that I could fight Carradine.

I knew that a little red light went on when the camera was activated in the control room, and that was the picture that went over the air. I watched out of the corner of my eye and whenever the red light went on one of the cameras, I eased over to that camera and got in front of it. That way I could be sure I got into the shot. I also kept as close to Carradine as I could so that the active camera would be forced to get us both into the shot. Carradine realized what I was doing so he tried to get away from me, but I just followed him. The tension between us enhanced the saccharine script and there was a great deal of excitement right up to the end when we were to break through the wall and I could escape.

The dress rehearsal had gone very well and I had slashed through the plaster wall with a rock that, according to the script, we had managed to hide from the guards. It all worked perfectly and a stagehand then sealed up the hole for the actual performance. When the moment came for my final break through, I slammed my rock against the wall and nothing happened. I hit it harder and still nothing. I couldn't cut into the wall. I realized that the stagehand, who had sealed it, must have used a stronger plaster than he should have. I kept hammering and hammering but nothing happened. The whole ending of the play was my breaking through the wall, saying goodbye to the old prisoner and then wriggling out through the hole we had created. But no hole.

Carradine, who was supposed to be too ill to get out with me, saw what was happening and slid over to help. We both started to beat together at the wall, but we couldn't make a dent in it. Suddenly, as we were both getting desperate, there was a crash. A huge hole appeared and an arm came through from the other side holding a sledge hammer. It was a stagehand saving the day, but unfortunately being seen by the camera and the entire TV audience. Carradine and I somehow finished the play and the minute the director yelled cut and the show went off the air, we got hysterical. The thought of people watching the show, seeing us digging the hole to get out of Devil's Island and then a hand coming through with a hammer from the opposite side to help us – we couldn't stop laughing. It became part of television lore.

**

We pushed through the revolving door, out of breath, and still laughing and feeling that we were celebrating. The week had gone well. Eleanor had visited me in several cities of the tour but never for so many days. She had her classes to teach and, though we'd had a relationship for almost two years, we never had been able to spend more than a couple of days together. I liked having her with me and it had been fun to see all the sights of Chicago with her and go to the best restaurants. I had been staying at the YMCA to save money, but I'd gotten a small apartment on the near North Side where the actors had a rate. As we walked into the lobby, I saw an actress I knew who was appearing in a pre-Broadway tryout. She rushed over to us.

"Oh," she said to me ignoring Eleanor, "just the man I want to see. I'm having such trouble with this part and I thought you could help me." I introduced the two women and said I'd be glad to help her. "Could you come up to my room now?" she asked.

"Maybe for a little while," I said, but I felt Eleanor kick my foot. "I think it would be better tomorrow," I added.

"But that may be too late," the actress said.

"I'm sorry," I replied, "it's just not possible."

When we got into the automatic elevator and the door was closed, I could sense Eleanor's anger. I reached over and stroked her head. She swung her purse and hit me in the arm. "Don't you ever do that to me again," she said. "I'm not a dog to be patted."

"I'm sorry," I said. "She asked for help. What did I do that was so wrong?" She didn't answer. We got out at our floor and went into the apartment without speaking.

I sat in the small sitting room smoking a cigarette and listening to drawers being opened and shut noisily in the bedroom. Eleanor was packing and I could tell from the sounds that her anger had not abated. A part of me would be relieved when she went. I cared for her, but a steady diet of being with her every day was more than I could take. I felt claustrophobic, as if I couldn't breathe, and I began to long for her to leave. We enjoyed being together but the physical part of it still was not as thrilling as being with a man, and sometimes it became a chore. I couldn't seem to shed my homosexual skin no matter how hard I tried.

I know Eleanor was disappointed when I stopped going to Doctor Byron. I thought the analysis would help but it didn't. The doctor just listened and listened and after two years, I left. She hardly said anything. I told Eleanor it was the doctor who suggested we stop. She had felt that I really wanted to leave the marriage and once that was accomplished, there was nothing more to be done. Eleanor didn't agree with my stopping the analysis, but she said it wasn't her business. There had been something unspoken between us for some time that we both had tried to ignore, but I knew it would have to be faced eventually.

Eleanor walked into the room. She had put on the white silk pajamas that she always wore, and on top of them, her blue robe. "Are you still angry?" I asked cautiously.

"You really hate it when I get emotional, don't you?" she answered. "You're always so threatened by emotion – you're so afraid to express your own, for fear it won't be real. One day you'll get to know the luxury of indulging in your emotions without any fear that they might not be real. They are real, when they are there, and no one could ask for more." I felt she was lecturing me as if I were a student in one of her classes, but I sensed that she had to get something off her chest, so I kept silent.

"If you question your emotions," she went on, "and wait for proof of their reality, it merely deprives you of the wonderful experience of the moment. Of course, the next moment is never like the last one because it must build on it, or it too is lost." She raised her hand and shook her finger, "This is what keeps love at a minimum in the world, since it seems to me, that in order to experience any emotion, we must be without defenses – that goes for fear, anger and love." She lit a cigarette and I waited a minute to see if she was finished.

When she didn't say anything, I said, "You know that girl didn't mean anything to me."

"Don't you know why I was angry?" she asked. "Because it's my last night with you, and you were going to spend part of it helping some little nothing with her silly part."

"Actually, she's a very good actress," I said. "I don't care if she's Helen Hayes. You still don't get it." Eleanor began to walk about the room.

"It's a matter of priorities." she continued. "I wasn't going to go into any of this. I was just going to send you a letter and explain it all, but maybe it's better this way. I'm going to live in Paris."

I got up and went over to her. "Eleanor," I said, "isn't that a rather dramatic way to react to my talking to a girl?"

She took my hands. "I love you and I thought I would be able to go on making no demands on you and be perfectly happy. After all I knew everything about you when we began, and I didn't set out to change you. Maybe I hoped the analysis would but I don't think I even said that to myself. I never told you but I walked into the Five Oaks Restaurant in the Village one night when you said you couldn't see me because you had an early appointment the next day. You were sitting there eating with that handsome boy who I call the jack o' lantern because he's always smiling. You seemed so happy being with him. I got out before you saw me and burst into tears in the street."

I tried to put my arm around her. "No don't," she said, "it's all right. We never had a commitment. I knew what I was getting into and I cared so much about you that it was worth it."

We began to feel awkward standing in the middle of the room, so Eleanor sat down on the sofa and I perched on a chair opposite her. "You know I've always told you," she said, "that I believe real love is when two people are equals – when neither of them needs anything from the other. They are together only because they love each other. That's not true of us."

"But I do love you," I said.

"I'm afraid I need more than that," Eleanor said softly. She looked away from me for a moment and then said, "I was wrong. I do need something more than love from you. I want to get married and have children."

I felt a rush of panic that was almost physical. I wanted to hold my stomach to stop it, but I couldn't move. A suburban street with houses lined up on both sides flashed through my head. Children riding bicycles on the sidewalk went by, as I saw myself coming home every night for the rest of my life to the same kitchen and the same bedroom. It was an image I'd had before and it made me feel like my life was over. Eleanor watched me as if she could read my thoughts.

"I know it's not in the cards for us," she said without rancor, "but I'm going to live abroad where I can't see you. One of my great maxims is 'you finally get what you want, and I'm going to go in search of it.'"

I got up and walked over to the sofa. I sat down beside her and held her as tightly as I could.

Eleanor did go to Paris. I didn't hear from her for several months and then a short letter came. She had met a man, through some friends of hers she was having dinner with in a restaurant. He turned out to be a count but, she it made clear, he was not an elegant one or a rich one. He looked, according to her, rather working-class and he was somewhat older than she was. They were married almost immediately and I didn't hear from her again for some years. She had become close to the wife of an actor friend of mine when we both were in *Madwoman*, so I would get an occasional report. She never did have a child and in time, she ran a small antique shop.

A few years later, when I was earning extra money working for a photographer, we went to Europe on assignment for *Life Magazine*. Since I had to be in Paris overnight, I got Eleanor's phone number from my friend and called her. A very deep smoker's voice answered the phone and I could barely tell it was Eleanor. She seemed a little distant but agreed to have a drink with me before my train left. We made a date for her to come to the Pont Royal on the Rue du Bac, where I was staying, and she arrived with her husband who looked like a baker or a cook. He was terribly nice. Eleanor had streaks of gray in her beautiful hair and was turned out in a chic suit that looked, to my eye, like a Chanel.

I asked her, with a smile, if I should call her Countess. She replied with no amusement that it wasn't necessary. She lit one Gaulois after another and she now had, added to her smoker's voice, a slight French accent. We made pleasant small talk for a half an hour until her husband got up and said he had to leave for an appointment. Eleanor insisted on staying and taking me to the train. She seemed much more sophisticated than when I'd known her. We both behaved like old but distant friends, until I was about to get into my compartment on the train. I kissed her on the cheek and said goodbye. She immediately burst into tears and threw her arms around me. For a few minutes we just hugged without speaking. I got on the train and she walked along beside it, tears streaming down her face. We just kept looking at each other as the train moved slowly out of the station. When she came to the end of the platform and could go no further, she waved and disappeared from my sight, and from my life.

30

With the final closing of *Madwoman* and the end of the ignominious Subway Circuit performances, it was almost the end of summer – too late to look for work in summer stock. Out of the blue, a new door opened and I walked through it to the place where I would spend the next few years: television. Because of *Antony and Cleopatra* and *Hamlet*, I was asked to be in a TV version of *Othello* starring Torin Thatcher. I played Roderigo who the villain Iago dupes into giving him money in return for his help and guidance. There has always been some suspicion, from literary critics, that the two were more personally involved with each other, and in this version, though the audience didn't see it, we were.

Since Eleanor, I had been exclusively with men and I just treated it as a part of my life, but in no way a serious part. The show went well. I had learned a lot from my experience in Chicago, so that I was able to hit all the camera positions we had rehearsed without thinking about it. So my concentration could be completely on my character. It was like being in a play onstage. The director, Delbert Mann, was very professional as were the actors, so there was no nonsense about hogging the camera. The show was live, as most of television was at that time, and there were no mishaps.

I didn't have any work to look forward to so I decided to fix up my little apartment to take my mind off the worry that all actors face when a show closes: "Will I ever work again?" I saw a way of minimizing the double bed that took up most of the space that the kitchen didn't use. I built a structure that I nailed to one wall. It had a shelf at the top and attached to it was a board the length of the bed. The bed could slip under it as far as possible and the hanging board rested on the bed and supported pillows. It turned the bed into a sofa and left enough space on the other wall to build a corner desk. I covered the top of the desk with linoleum tiles so I could also use it for plants. Once a week a horse-drawn wagon would come by with Boston ivy and some other greenery that was very inexpensive.

I also made a large screen out of poles I bought at the hardware store to block the kitchen. They were held together with large blue tape. At least the place was getting to be presentable enough to entertain a few friends.

I was barely finished when I got a call to audition for another television show, this one was for a role of an Italian. I practiced the accent the entire day before the reading. I had rushed to the library and skimmed the book the TV was to be based on, Nathaniel Hawthorne's *The Marble Faun*. I had gleaned from the book that my character, Donatello, was a child of nature, always lighthearted and sunny, until he was forced to kill a man who had been making the woman he loved miserable. He then lost his innocence. He was transformed from the happy, adorable faun-like creature into a guilty, miserable human being, no longer the "happy native."

With all this knowledge, I was able to reach into myself and use the part of me that was joyful and innocent – very much the way I had been on the *Hamlet* tour when I earned the nickname "Schnookle." The transformation into depression was easier – starving in New York and trying desperately to be an actor had taught me, in spades, what it was like to be depressed and morose.

The reading went well, and I was ecstatic when the call came that I was hired. The week's rehearsals went perfectly. Franklin Schaffner, who became an admired movie director, was so supportive and the cast was filled with the best stage actors. Anna Lee, who was already known for her many films, played opposite me and I fell in love and so did she. It's not that unusual when actors are together working and the rest of the world is blocked out. Anna was in an unhappy marriage and she commuted from Connecticut to rehearsals. I persuaded her to stay in town one night so we could be together. She agreed but at the last moment she canceled. She told me it would only make her marriage more difficult. Of course, she was right.

Looking back, my acting was getting confused with real life. It's a danger. Anna and I did see each other many years later in Hollywood. She invited me to dinner to meet her new husband Robert Nathan whose book *The Portrait of Jennie* was one of my favorites. Anna was just as beautiful as when we had both been young. I wondered if she remembered my crush on her.

The Marble Faun was one of the high points of my life as an actor. The dress rehearsal went without a hitch. After a few notes and some repairs by the makeup woman, it was time for the show. I sat listening to the Richard Strauss music from *A Hero's Life* that introduced the show at the beginning of the live telecast. I can still hear it when I close my eyes and I remember how thrilled I was at that moment.

It was as if my whole body was expanding and filling the studio. I wasn't nervous. I wanted more than anything for the play to start. I felt my life was just beginning and everything was going to be all right. Most of the time, as I had waited to begin acting in a play, I would worry about forgetting my lines and go over and over them. But this time I was Donatello, not myself. I was in Rome, the most beautiful city in the world and I was about to meet the woman I loved. Everything was perfect. I said a prayer of thanks, and then stood up to get ready for my entrance for the most exciting time in my life so far. The rest was a dream. I never questioned what I was doing. It wasn't acting – it was living.

There was a curtain call when the show finished and the camera went from face to face as we all stood in a line. I noticed that Wesley Addy, who played the villainous man I pushed off the Tarpeian Rock to his death, was missing. They had not wanted to tell me that he was taken to the hospital. The mats to break his fall had gotten moved and he hurt his arm, but fortunately it turned out to be a slight wound. Everyone congratulated everyone but unlike a theater opening, there was no Sardi's and no newspaper reviews. None of my friends could afford TV sets so I had no feedback until several days later.

My agent called excitedly to say that Mrs. Samuel Goldwyn had seen *The Marble Faun* and told her husband I was going to be a big movie star. He was on his way to New York and wanted to meet me for his new movie *Hans Christian Anderson* that was to star Danny Kaye. I could barely breathe. He was the most important producer in Hollywood. After I wrote down the time and the name of the hotel, I hung up and started to shake. It was going to come true – all my dreams and the hard work. But what if he didn't like me? How would I behave with him? He was so famous. I worried and thought of nothing else until the days had passed and the meeting was finally to take place.

Going up in the elevator to Mr. Goldwyn's suite was an ordeal. I had shaved and showered and put on my best suit. It was a little heavy for such a warm day and it made me perspire, so I tried to be as calm as possible. Mr. Goldwyn answered the door himself and instead of the big cigar-smoking mogul I had expected, there was a warm, smiling man with startling blue eyes. He couldn't have been more welcoming. He sat me down, talked of how talented he heard I was, and how much his wife had liked me. He described the movie he was doing and I relaxed, as I realized he was acting as if I already had the role. At one point he mentioned that his wife had said that I wore tights in the television show and she thought I must have been a dancer. He went on to say that he needed an actor, of course, and he was sorry, but he couldn't possibly use a dancer. I went berserk.

Suddenly all my dreams of the world I thought I was about to enter were shattered. I felt like a delicate glass that had been admired and then crashed against the wall. I had to put the pieces back together again. I heard myself screaming, "I'm not a dancer, I'm an actor! I only took a few lessons at Katherine Dunham's. They were just to help me move. I'm actually a bit of a klutz. The director wanted me in tights because

I was the faun. I mean not a real faun but faun-like so he wanted me to have the lightness of a faun and thought tights would free me and give the illusion that I was a wild thing. I'm an actor." All the calm and confidence I had walked in with had flown out the window. I behaved like any other desperate actor looking for a job.

Mr. Goldwyn reached over and patted my hand. "That's fine," he said. "I've sent for the kinescope and I'm sure you're just as good as my wife said you were. Thank you so much for coming to see me."

His eyes were so comforting and friendly that they made me realize even more what a horse's ass I had been. I knew I had behaved ridiculously, but anything further I could say would just make it worse. So I said "goodbye."

Several days later, the agent called to say Mr. Goldwyn had liked me very much in the television show, but I would have to play opposite Danny Kaye in the movie. He had felt that my nose, though a very good one, was as big as Danny's. He couldn't have two big noses in the film. He was going to use a contract player – Farley Granger.

When I hung up the phone, I remembered a talk I had once had with my grandmother when I was a teenager. "Am I good-looking enough, Nana?" I asked.

"Your nose is too big," she answered heartlessly.

Still, I'd had many compliments about my nose. Some even saying my profile was in a class with Barrymore's. But I guess it was good enough for the stage but not good enough for the movies. And then I realized, it wasn't my nose. It was my losing complete control of myself and seeming like anything but a talented and sensitive actor. I thought, *I really should get someone to embroider a pillow with "Life is full of missed opportunities" to always remind me of what I did.*

31

With Gaby

I had been studying acting with Sanford Meisner at the Neighbor-hood Playhouse. It was possibly the best drama school in the country and Sandy, as everyone called him, was the preeminent teacher. I had to work to keep alive so there was no way I could take the two-year course. But Meisner gave me a scholarship to his professional classes that met twice a week, so it didn't cost me anything. He said that one day he would be paid back when I was a success and he would visit me in my palatial Hollywood home and swim in my pool. The chance of that happening, at the time, seemed remote.

Years later some friends did bring Sandy to my home in Los Angeles (there was a swimming pool), but by then Sandy had to use an attach-ment to be able to speak – cancer had destroyed his larynx – so he wasn't up to swimming in my pool. Sadly, he didn't even remember who I was or that he had ever taught me.

In the years I studied with Sandy, he was so encouraging and so congratulatory when he saw something he liked. We did improvisations and scene study. I took forever, when he called on me to perform, prolonging the agony by lighting a cigarette and blowing out a lot of smoke before I even began. We all put off starting to perform out of fear that Sandy would excoriate us in front of the class. One boy began his improvisation sitting in a chair facing the class. He took off his shoes, then his stockings and then he would begin to walk around the room on his bare feet. Finally, he worked up enough courage to begin. Sandy let us take our time. He knew we were all terrified of his reaction to what we were going to show him. He was tough and uncompromising and was not without a sadistic streak that frightened us all. But it was worth it – even the nights when I couldn't sleep, after a class, when I knew how inept I'd been.

But then, there were the great times when I got it right and the character came alive. Sandy made fun of our tension and nerves by clenching his jaws together and screaming at us, "RELAX!" which was enough to send us all into spasm. There is sometimes a single image in a remembered life that is the essence of the person and to me, "RELAX" is Sandy's. When I think of him, I see him slouched in his chair watching an actor get ready to perform for him, knowing the agony the actor was going through and relieving the pressure by yelling, clenched jaw and all, "RELAX!"

One of the great things in Sandy's classes was the people. Joan Lorring had just been in the film of *The Corn is Green* with Bette Davis and was nominated for an Oscar for her amazing portrayal of a slut. She was anything but. She had come to New York because she wanted to do plays as well as movies. She joined the class, although her technique was already perfect. Joan was enormously talented and in addition, acting was so easy for her. She had immediately auditioned for radio soap operas and was in great demand. She told me how simple it was: "Just audition with four characters, each having a different emotion 'mad, sad, glad and bad.' It's a snap."

I tried, but I didn't yet have the acting facility that Joan had. She made us all call her Dellie, a nickname based on the real name she was given when she was born in Hong Kong. When I did a scene with her, I was always better than I was with anyone else. She had a way of bringing out the best in you. She had had a big nose in *The Corn Is Green* and decided to have plastic surgery when she finished the picture. She told me that she went to see the film in a New York movie theater and heard two women talking in front of her. One of them said, "That girl should have her nose fixed. I wanted to lean over and say to them, 'I did!'"

Dellie, or Joan, was endearing and became a good friend. She cooked a few of us incredible Chinese food from recipes she had learned in the Orient. I'll always remember an astonishingly generous thing that she did for another of our classmates, Gaby Rodgers. All of us thought Gaby was not only a beauty, but a wonderful actress as well, and Joan was a particular fan. Joan got a role in Lillian Hellman's *The Autumn Garden* on Broadway with Fredric March and Florence Eldridge. Using her influence, Joan got Gaby the job of her understudy. Some weeks into the run, Joan had a slight cold and called in to the stage manager to say she couldn't perform that night and Gaby would have to go on. Joan wanted to give Gaby a chance to be seen – something I've never heard of another actor ever doing. (It is done in *All About Eve* but that was a movie, not real life.)

I later asked Joan how she could stay home when she was hardly sick – what about "The show must go on?" I said.

"The show went on," she replied. "It just didn't go on with me. I had a cold and I knew Gaby would be great. Why not give her the opportunity?"

When Gaby found out she was to play that night, she called me and I got a ticket. She was superb, different from Joan, but just as interesting in her own way. She had a scene where she had to keep bending over Fredric March who was in bed. There was no time to refit Joan's costume for Gaby and reduce the large neckline, so every time Gaby bent down, she started to spill out of her dress. The audience had a special treat of not only observing Gaby's talent but also being tantalized as they waited to see how much more of her would be revealed. Gravity, however, didn't win out and Gaby finished the scene without the audience seeing any more of her than she would have wanted them to.

Gaby became one of my closest friends and a great influence on my life for the next few years. She was having a relationship with Jerry Cooke, a magazine photographer. who did many assignments for *Time* and *Life*. When Jerry looked for an assistant to help him on shoots and take care of his office and billing, Gaby came to me. I was beginning to work on television but the pay was minimal so Gaby knew I always needed money. I took the job and stayed with Jerry for many years, even when I was involved in a play or a television show. I could always arrange my schedule to get Jerry's work done. I usually worked for him in the morning so I was free for matinees and evening performances. At least I knew I would be able to pay the rent even if I were temporarily strapped.

I had gotten to be comfortable enough in my Village basement. I even saved up enough money to get a television set and have friends in to sit on the floor and watch me kill my father on a filmed episode of Ralph Bellamy's series *Man Against Crime*. Having Ralph Roberts next door gave me someone to always help me if I needed to fix something or wanted a ride to the beach. We stayed friends for years though I never knew much about Ralph's life. He was more of an observer than a doer and he always seemed to enjoy me and the activity that I engendered. Ralph had a garden attached to his basement flat that was next to mine. I had the brilliant idea of having a party and inviting casting people, directors and anyone who could help us get work. It would be in Ralph's garden but since our apartments lined up, we could have 50 people and they could wander about.

The day before, we had everything organized: the wine, the hour the sandwiches would be delivered, the ice – it was all going to be perfect.

Then we suddenly realized there was nowhere to sit. We raced about getting folding chairs that people were getting rid of but they looked pretty awful. "Let's paint them," I shouted. So we were up most of the night making everything look great. Only when people had arrived, sat down and then moved about did we see streaks of green paint on everyone's back. They all made a joke of it, but it was a Schnookle moment for me, rearing its head again. I don't think either of us got a job from that party, but we were sure talked about.

I was beginning to have a few really good friends. Billy Nichols was becoming even a better friend than he had been in the *Hamlet* days. He had given up acting to create the ideas for *The Hit Parade* for television. Every week Billy thought up the plots for the sketches behind the singing of the top tunes. He was brilliant and the show became an enormous success.

The top singers Dorothy Collins and Giselle McKensie had to have an actor to sing to, although he didn't sing or speak. Billy got me the job whenever he could, so I made a little money and had a great time acting without words. Dorothy and I worked together quite a few times. She was serious about acting, so the two of us put our all into the shows when we were together. The television critic of *The New York Times*, John Crosby, did a whole column about how I reacted to Dorothy when she sang. He was very complimentary and seemed surprised that an actor could express so much without saying anything.

There were other friends from Sandy's class. Barbara Ames, the daughter of the movie actress Adrienne Ames, was very much into The Method. We sometimes auditioned together. We were endlessly going over in our minds our characters' backgrounds before doing a scene. I think we were exhausted by the time people actually saw us perform and we never got a job from our efforts. Barbara was close to Phillip Loeb, the husband on *The Goldbergs*. He was blacklisted by Red Channels and McCarthyism. After Phil took his own life, Barbara never quite recovered. My other friend, Joan Lorring, went from play to play and then married so it was hard to spend time with her, but she remained a close friend as did my next-door neighbor Ralph. We talked together, had meals together and shared our triumphs when we got a job and our failures when we didn't. And there was always Gaby.

Gaby, who had been born in Germany and had fled with her family from the Nazis, was always quirky and fun. She was in analysis which she continued for years. She called me very late at night. She sounded desperate.

"Can I come over?" she pleaded.

"Of course," I said.

She arrived and told me breathlessly that she had awakened from a terrible dream and felt that she was going mad. She decided she had to put herself in an institution for the mentally disturbed. She dressed, got a taxi, and went to Bellevue Hospital that was famous for its work with mental health patients. She waited and waited to be admitted. She started to get annoyed. Didn't they know who she was? How could they treat her this way? Finally, she got up and left, furious with the hospital staff and bristling now with her newfound energy.

As she told me this, she began to laugh at how ridiculous she'd been and her laugh was very contagious. We both ended up screaming with laughter. So typical of Gaby – a mixture of neurosis and humor that enchanted everyone. It didn't hurt that she was so pretty with her gamin look, tousled short hair, and full figure. Her life was a series of adventures and most of them also with their funny side. She told me once that she had met the famous actress Edna Best. The star was in a rest home for mentally ill patients but was allowed to come out and mingle with people occasionally.

Gaby, feeling sympathetic for a fellow sufferer said, "Miss Best, what do you do in the rest home all day?"

Edna Best answered, "Well, there is a small studio where I paint a little."

Gaby, to make the actress feel better said, "Oh how wonderful. I would love to go there and just be away from everything and paint."

"Oh my dear," Miss Best replied, "Don't consider it. The brushes are not very good."

Gaby came through for me again. At a party she found out about an apartment uptown between 51st and 52nd Streets on Second Avenue. She knew I wanted to live uptown again near my day job at Jerry Cooke's office and the theater district. There was no lease and the present tenant wanted $200 to let someone take it over. It was all illegal but the chances were it would work. I would just say I was subletting and in time I would become a fixture. The rent was $50 a month, $15 more than I was paying, but I thought I could go out on more photo jobs with Jerry and make up the difference.

The Healy family owned the building. They ran the bar at street level and paid little attention to the three apartments above in the old brownstone. Mine was at the top, a fourth-floor walkup. All of them were old cold-water flats that now had heat and hot water. The bathtub and the toilet were in the bedroom blocked off by doors that opened into the room. You had to go into the kitchen to wash your hands. The space was enormous after my one room in the Village.

As I walked through, I could see that everything was in bad shape. The big wall in the bedroom was covered with a message in red paint from the former owner to his lover saying how much he hated him. Gaby, who had gotten the keys so I could walk through alone, told me that the owner had painted the letter when he was quite drunk and the two continued to live with the letter above their beds for several years. Since I had been getting some television work, I was able to scrape together the $200 and the place became mine.

The first thing I did was paint out the message of hate on the bedroom wall. I hoped, in time, it would become a place of love.

32

I ended my first year on television with a Christmas play, *A Child Is Born,* in which I played Joseph. It was mainly about the innkeepers who opened their door one night to find Joseph and Mary looking desperately for a place to sleep. I, as Joseph, pleaded for a room for my pregnant wife, while the people from the inn, Fay Bainter and Anna Maria Italiano (who later changed her name to Anne Bancroft) gradually realized that they were in the presence of something holy. Fay Bainter told me afterwards that she was so moved by me that she couldn't hold back her tears. The reaction to the show was incredible. There was an audience demand to see it again, but because it was live, not on film, we had to perform it two more times for the following two Christmases.

After a bitter winter of living on unemployment checks, I suddenly got called for a variety of parts. The first was the brother of the mad wife in *Jane Eyre.* The show turned into a love fest due to a well-known British character actress named Viola Roche, who was to play the housekeeper. She was in her eighties, very fat, as was her 60-year-old daughter who delivered her to rehearsal each morning. The first day, Miss Roche arrived pulling an old dog on a leash.

The director rushed over to her and said, "Oh I'm sorry, Miss Roche, but we can't have a dog at rehearsal."

She looked up at him with a wide smile, "Don't be silly," she said, "Sal loves *Jane Eyre.*"

The director stood for a moment nonplussed. The dog stayed. Viola Roche entertained us all with stories of her great romance with C. Aubrey Smith, the actor who played many British stiff upper lip roles in films like *Rebecca* and *Prisoner of Zenda*. She told us she had called him "Ever-ready" and had us roaring with laughter at the antics of their long affair.

One day she said to me, "Oh ducky, it's so good not to want fucking anymore."

The next job came from the *Philco Playhouse*, a prestigious showcase for actors. I was a kid in a Southern prison where the inmates contracted pellagra. Then I was a young Irishman in Paul Vincent Carroll's *The Old Foolishness* with Una O'Connor, who I'd seen in so many movies, as my mother. For *The Ed Sullivan Show*, though I looked nothing like him, I was cast as the young Oscar Hammerstein in a tribute to him. He was introduced and said I was much better-looking than he had ever been which got a big laugh.

On the show, I did a sketch Hammerstein had written and performed in college. I was in a restaurant and called the waiter over to complain that there was a spot on my soup plate. He replied, "That's not a spot, that's the soup." Not the most promising beginning for the writer of *Oklahoma*, but the audience loved it. After that, Mr. Hammerstein recited the words to his "The Last Time I Saw Paris." It was only six years since the end of the war and many in the audience had tears in their eyes.

In the fall, I got one of my best parts, the lead in Galsworthy's *Justice* for Kraft Television. I was the lead, a young Englishman who forged a check to get the money to take care of the woman he loved. He was caught and sentenced to solitary confinement, a totally unfair sentence for the small crime he had committed. Galsworthy had written the play to expose the horrible conditions in British prisons and the harsh treatment of the poor, while the rich were let off easily for greater crimes. The director, Stanley Quinn, treated me like a star, encouraging every idea I had. Instead of telling me what to do, he let me find my own way.

The most crucial scene was when the young man, who had been in solitary for some time, went almost mad from his isolation. Stanley had a set built for my cell that was totally shut off from the rest of the studio and the other actors, so I could feel what it was really like to be alone. There were holes in the walls big enough for the camera lenses to look in, but when I was in the cell, I was truly in solitary. I tried to relate it to my own life, a feeling that was similar to something I had experienced. I had to end the scene screaming and beating on the walls, trying to get out.

I came up with a memory of masturbating when I was young: the locked door, the fear, the pressure of trying not to give in to the desire of my body, then the force that propelled me on and the sounds that came out of me uncontrollably. Naturally, I didn't tell any of this to the director. He kept the studio as silent as possible whenever I did the scene in rehearsal.

On the day that we ran the show for the camera people, just as I was going into the cell for the scene where I was to go mad, I heard Stanley whisper to the camera operators, "This is the masturbation scene." I was surprised that Stanley had recognized what I was doing but didn't discuss it with me for fear of destroying my sense of creative secrecy. The show went perfectly and the cast and crew applauded me when we went off the air.

Stanley, who was never effusive, shook my hand and said, "You gave a truly great performance." People stopped me on the street and for a few days, it was almost like I had performed in a theater and people were coming backstage to congratulate me.

There were three more shows before the end of the year: two for Studio One – *Coriolanus*, not one of Shakespeare's best and also not one of the best efforts of the handsome movie star Richard Greene, who seemed stiff and uncomfortable. The other Studio One was *The Idol of San Vittore* starring Maria Riva, Marlene Dietrich's daughter. CBS was trying to build Maria into a major star, but it wasn't working very well. In the play, Maria was an Italian woman in a small hill town where the Americans had taken over.

On the day of the show, I ran into her on my way from the makeup room. Her blonde hair was covered with a long black wig and she looked quite authentic. "Maria," I said looking at the wig, "It's great."

"Oh, I always bake bread for the cast and crew on the day of the show," she said modestly. Only I hadn't mentioned anything about bread.

My final show of the year was the lead opposite Janet De Gore in Booth Tarkington's *The Wren*. Janet was the most adorable 20-year-old, beautiful, petite with a mass of brown curls. Everyone commented on our being the perfect young couple. It was such fun to do a light comedy romance after the seriousness of the other shows. Janet and I played off each other as if we were having the time of our life. It was an audience favorite, bright and cheery – perfect for the holiday season.

33

With Joseph Welch on Omnibus TV

I was becoming known in television, especially by the casting people. I still tried out for an occasional play, but they were few and far between. Theatrical agents considered me a classical actor with my Giraudoux and Shakespeare backgrounds. They even thought my biggest successes on television, *Galsworthy* and *Hawthorne*, were classics as well. At least on television I could do a variety of parts – Italian, British, Southern, French – it got so I thought I could play anything anyone asked me to.

I was awakened one morning with a call asking me to be at a reading for a radio show later that day. The casting person said, "You're a 12-year-old boy who believes in Santa Claus." I hung up, wrote the time and address down and went back to sleep. When I woke, I thought about the message. I was 27, but I guess I could sound much younger on radio, but the Santa Claus thing. What did that mean? How could I indicate that with just my voice? I spent the time getting ready testing different levels with my voice, searching for youth and some childish belief in Santa. Was he coming down the chimney or just whipping the reindeer? The phone rang and it was the same casting director.

"I'm terribly sorry," she said, "there's a young actor with a similar name and I mixed you up with him. Forgive me, but just ignore my earlier call."

Boy, I thought, *I really am getting a swelled head. Did I believe I could play a 12-year-old? I'd better come back down to earth.*

Two more costume dramas came along on television: I was Joseph of Arimathea begging Pontius Pilate to let me bury Jesus, on Studio One, and then I played Chopin opposite Sarah Churchill (Winston's daughter) as George Sand on Hallmark Hall of Fame. The show was called *Prelude*. The plot was Chopin trying to get his lover George Sand, an attractive woman famous for wearing pants, to put on a dress. She kept refusing. But in the last scene, as I was playing a somber piece at a recital, I saw George walk in wearing a beautiful dress. I quickly switched to a triumphant polonaise for the happy ending. Probably iffy as far as history was concerned, but it did get Chopin's music out to an early television audience.

The day of the show, Sarah appeared made up with almost every inch of her face a different shade of grease paint. She was such a good-looking woman that I wondered why she had to make herself over. It reminded me of my early days in *Hamlet* when I copied every actor's makeup, not realizing that they were trying to fix facial problems that I just didn't have. But Sarah looked beautiful anyway when she appeared in her 19th century gown as I played the piano. Of course, it wasn't me making the music. My hands were bouncing around silently as someone else played a piano out of sight. At least Sarah and I looked like the romantic artists from another time and the show was labeled "a charming success."

Man Against Crime, starring Ralph Bellamy, asked me to do another murderer and it was a real education. Since it was not live television and on film, all my classes (I studied at one time not only with Stella Adler and Sandy Meisner, but with Herbert Berghof and Uta Hagen as well) all my improvisations and sense memories turned out to be hardly necessary. The director stood over me as I was doing a close-up and said,

"Look up. Count to five. Now look down. Count to seven. Now look up again."

I did as he told me though it was against everything I had studied. The result was really amazing when I saw the film. I hadn't been thinking about anything, except counting, when they filmed me. But it was a lesson in just how much the camera can do to make an actor look even better. The camera made me look like a terrifying killer. Of course, this only works when you're doing a close-up. The director can't very well count for you when you're acting in a scene. But every little bit helps.

***

Kenneth Banghart, a popular radio announcer, offered me a job at a summer theater he was running as a hobby in Olny, Maryland. He was getting stars to do popular plays and there were some good roles for me. The summer in New York was suffocating. I had no air conditioning, although I had managed to create a makeshift shower in the old bathtub that cooled me off. Nevertheless, I grabbed at the chance to get out of town. The theater was one of the better ones in the country with a very professional stage and pleasant living quarters. I shared a large, sunny apartment with another actor, Geoffrey Barr, who later became a well-known manager in Hollywood with clients like Jean Simmons and Elaine Stritch.

The first play starred Eva Gabor in a French farce and I had a small role of no importance. Miss Gabor was charming and quite beautiful, although I was surprised to see her costume hanging on a rack when I went to collect mine. Clearly visible was the inside of the dress that was stuffed with artificial padding for the breasts as well as the hips. I thought of the saying, "Don't believe everything you see." I remember my shock when I discovered Maurice Evans had a whole undergarment as Hamlet that gave him magnificent legs and a bigger chest.

The second play was more interesting: Willian Inge's *Come Back Little Sheba*. I had a good part as the boyfriend of the young girl that my friend Joan Lorring had played on Broadway. Joan Blondell was the star. She was down to earth, with no pretensions or any of the accoutrements of a movie star. She seemed like a middle-aged woman who was running a small beauty parlor. Perhaps that was what she was affecting in order to play the lead of a beaten-down woman, but if so, it was really working.

She joined several of the actors and me for breakfast and acted like just one of the boys. She told us that the morning after her ex-husband Dick Powell married June Allyson, June telephoned her and said, "Oh Joan, I'm so happy, but tell me, what did you do with Dick, he's so big. I don't know what to do with it." I was startled by Miss Blondell's intimate disclosure, but she went on about June Allyson in words that were hardly complementary and quite specific. Obviously, she had loved Dick Powell very much and was quite bitter about losing him.

The third play affected my life the most. *The Happy Time* had been a huge hit on Broadway. It was a coming-of-age story of a little boy growing up in a French-Canadian family. His uncle, my role, was a young, attractive womanizer who thought of little else than conquering women. It was great fun to play, using a slight French accent and flirting with the mother of the little boy, played by Mary Fickett who was beginning to get attention as a promising talent. Mary was attractive, tall, blonde, and full of energy and fun. She was hardly an ingenue, more a leading lady though she was still in her early twenties.

We all would pal around after the show and sometimes go off to a roadhouse for a sandwich. Geoff had an old convertible and one night Mary and I found ourselves in the rumble seat while Geoff and another actor were up front. It had suddenly turned cold and we were freezing. We huddled together and suddenly it became more: we began to hug each other and that turned into kissing and suddenly we were just about making out. The next day, when we saw each other, instead of pretending it didn't happen or saying anything about it, we rushed into each other's arms. We began an affair that was to last for five years.

34

Mary Fickett

Mary and I were making plans to return to New York together when Ken Banghart summoned me to his office. He told me that the next play, that I knew was Luise Rainer in S.N. Behrman's *Biography*, was having problems. It was arriving totally cast, which was the reason I was free to go home, but the actor playing opposite Miss Rainer was leaving. He was going to appear in Olny, but he wouldn't do the rest of the tour. Would I be interested in replacing him? I was thrilled. Luise Rainer had won two academy awards in a row. I had seen her in both *The Good Earth* and *The Great Ziegfield*, and she was great. Just to be on the same stage with her would be a dream come true. Banghart told me I would have to read a scene for her, but she had been given my picture and thought I looked just right for the part.

She would arrive on Sunday, after *The Happy Time* had closed. If the reading went well, I would rehearse during the week, while the other actor played, and then open in Easthampton, the next theater on the tour. It all seemed so exciting. Mary was disappointed that we would be separated so soon, but she agreed it was too good an opportunity to pass up.

I read the play. My part was an angry young writer who disapproves of a famous woman though he is trying to get to write her biography, but falls in love with her, nevertheless. Everyone is in love with her, and I could see the adorable, delicious Luise Rainer winning all of us over and the audience as well. I had heard the rumors that she had been run out of Hollywood because she had been so difficult, but there was always gossip about movie stars. I did remember that the director, Bobby Lewis, whose classes I had begun to take, had told me a story about Miss Rainer when she was married to the writer Clifford Odets.

Odets had to fly to New York so he asked his friend from the Group Theater, Bobby, to take Luise out to dinner one night so she wouldn't be too lonely. Bobby agreed and after the dinner, Luise didn't want to go straight home. So, Baby drove them up to Mulholland Drive where the view of nighttime Los Angeles was so spectacular. As the two sat in Bobby's convertible with the top down, Luise looked up at the sky. "Look at all the stars," she said. She paused for a moment and added, "And I am a star." It was a good story, but Bobby ate out on his anecdotes so it may not have been true.

I waited for Miss Rainer who was a half hour late and breezed in with no apology. She was tiny but a dynamo. She immediately complained about the apartment they had given her, that there weren't enough vegetables at lunch, and that the theater was in the middle of nowhere.

Then she turned to me as if I had kept her waiting. "Don't you think we should begin? I have other things to do."

I picked up the Samuel French paperback version and read while she responded from memory. It was a little disconcerting to read while she acted what she did every night, but I adjusted to it and we went along for a few pages. She stopped.

"It's all right," she said. "You don't have the character, of course, but we have a week and I will help you to get it."

"Won't the director be here?" I asked.

"I am the director," she said as if challenging me.

The week was hideous. We did rehearse every day, but we all had to stand around while Luise stood on her head before she could start rehearsal. Then she always stopped for a phone call to her agent or her husband while we waited again. We seldom got through a whole scene before she had to stop. Her sweetness and adorable quality had obviously been left at home. She seemed to invent things to do while I had my big scene, bits of business to engage the audience as Martita Hunt had. I watched her rehearse her entrance and it was an example of what was to come. She swept in wearing a hat with a veil so the audience couldn't see her face. She walked to center stage where a mirror hung, turned her back to the audience, and fussed with her veil and hat, not letting her face be seen until she turned around.

When we did the play, on a good night, she was greeted with applause that continued until she turned and faced the audience. On a bad night it didn't work at all and there was just a smattering of hands clapping as she entered and then it stopped before she got to the mirror. One night I was standing in the wings watching when she came on and the applause was meager, just a few hands slapping together. I heard her say to herself, as she faced the mirror, "What's the matter? Don't they ever go to the movies?"

The week of performances in Easthampton was unbearable. Few people came and within a few days, we were all told that the tour had been canceled and we were closing Saturday night. It was a relief. I had avoided the actor who had been playing my part. It was an awkward situation. I should have asked him why he was leaving, but I thought he had been fired. Now I realized he had had the guts to refuse to put up with Luise any longer. I suppose, even if I had known how impossible she was, I still would have done it. However, I didn't learn anything. I already knew too well that stars are not necessarily wonderful people.

35

Life with Mary was a total change but a happy one. We were together constantly. A great coincidence was that Mary was sharing an
apartment with Neva Patterson, the first woman I had gone to bed
with on the *Hamlet* tour. Of course, neither Neva nor I ever mentioned
that to Mary. The two women were total opposites: Neva – bawdy, fun
loving, devil may care; Mary – proper, elegant, well-bred. The difference
between them was spelled out in an incident that Mary laughingly
told me.

They were both in their small studio apartment, next to the Cherry
Lane Theater in Greenwich Village, when the phone rang. Mary picked
it up and a man's voice uttered the worst sexual commands imaginable.
Mary, without thinking, called out, "Neva, it's for you!"

Mary was extremely sexual, but it was hidden from the world. She
looked like she went to church on Sunday, though I don't remember
her ever doing that. She dressed beautifully and her blonde hair was
always coiffed perfectly. She looked like the quintessential hostess for a
morning television show: beautiful but not disturbingly so, bright but
never making you think she knew more than you did, a Democrat but
conservative, a homemaker but ready to look glamorous for a night on
the town. In a word she was "perfect."

Our schedules were quite different. I had to be at the photographer's
office quite early every day, and Mary had appointments and occasional
television shows as I did. We also had to dress up in those days. You
didn't go to an agent or a director in jeans and a torn shirt, so Mary had
to wake up in my apartment, dress, and then go down to the Village,

change, and be uptown at whatever appointed time. She couldn't do this every day so we worked out a timetable: we would only spend certain nights together, mainly on weekends.

We usually cooked together to save money. Since we were spending so much time in my apartment, I decided to fix it up. I got an actor friend, who had talent as a carpenter, to tear out walls that separated the small rooms, in what was really a railroad flat, and create a large L-shaped living room. There were so many doors from the old labyrinth of rooms that I had him create a wall of pecky cypress to conceal them. The apartment turned out to be really attractive with its working fireplaces in both the living room and the bedroom.

Ken Banghard, my producer from the summer theater, opened a play on Broadway that flopped in a couple of days. I had told him about my new apartment so he knew I needed furniture. He offered to sell me a few pieces from the show for practically nothing – a chaise, a club chair, and a table. They were French style and very elegant. When I got them home, I realized that they were stage furniture so the bottoms of the chaise and the club chair were wood, rather than something soft. This was done so the actors would sit up straight and not sink down out of sight. You couldn't sit in them for long without getting a cramp, but they sure made the room look terrific.

I can't say that being with Mary was the passionate dream of my youth. I liked her enormously and we were perfectly content sexually. But the best thing was that I finally felt more a part of society than I had when I was with men. We were a good-looking and amusing couple, welcomed by everyone, and there was no question that I was looked at differently by agents and casting people. I did wrestle with my attraction to men that, despite all my efforts, just wouldn't go away. Mary was so happy and loving that I kept it from her, but my neighborhood, in those days, was a hot bed of homosexual cruising, as was the 63rd Street YMCA, where I worked out in the gym. It was impossible to ignore it completely, and I sometimes churned with sublimated desire.

Meanwhile, television had turned upside-down. Movie stars, who had disparaged the new medium in the early fifties, suddenly discovered it. Roles that I would have gotten were being filled by actors with big names who could lure the growing audience. TV sets were affordable and everyone was buying one. More and more the advertisers wanted stars. My phone barely rang anymore and I began to worry that the money I made at the photographer's would barely keep me going. In a phone call to my parents, I made the great mistake of sounding a little worried about money. I had always been careful not to do that, but I was beginning to feel depressed.

My father got the opportunity he had been waiting for. He had left his years of being a portrait photographer to join a large insurance firm where he thrived, first as a salesman and then as a teacher. He was gung-ho about the insurance business and started a campaign to enlist me. "Just for a sideline," he said. "You'll make good money and you can do it in your free time."

I resisted as long as I could, but as the days went on, I began to think I might as well give it a try. The capper came when Maurice Evans' office called. Maurice was doing *Hamlet* on television and wanted me in the cast. Unfortunately, they had had to cut out my role of Fortinbras because of time, so the only thing available was a small part. I had to accept it because I needed the money but it was such a comedown. I called my father. "All right," I said, "I'll try the insurance business. What do I do?"

After *Hamlet*, and my ignominious role, I started classes given by the insurance company and learned a selling tool that was bound to get people to sign up. It was a speech, brilliantly crafted, anticipating all the objections the potential buyer might have. My acting made me a natural, and I came out the head of the class. My job, unpaid, was to go see people who had answered an ad promising information. Instead, they got me. The only rub was how to get to all these people's apartments that were all over New York City. My father wasn't going to let this get in the way of his plan to get me out of acting. He was making a little money at last so he loaned me enough to get a tiny, used Morris Minor car that would do the job.

I had to buy from the company the names and addresses of people who had written in. If I sold a policy, I would then be paid. I would set out in the early evening, when most people were home, with my forms and my memorized speech. Most of the time, people would let me in. I had surprising success, but I hated it. Most of the people were poor and lived in shabby places. Part of me felt I was taking money they could ill afford, but I tried to rationalize that they were getting some health protection. It was an inner battle that made me feel even more dejected.

To add to all of this, I was seeing Mary less. My mornings were spent working in Jerry's office, my evenings selling insurance and during the day I worked out or went to acting class. Several days a week, I was in a new workshop that the director Bobby Lewis had put together to perform seldom-done classic plays. Mary was a member so we sat together for a few hours, and I felt I was an actor again. We were to do the play *Cock-a-Doodle Dandy* by Sean O'Casey. After many hours of Bobby Lewis explaining the play and acting out parts of it, readings were held for the roles as if they were going to be done on Broadway. I lost the role I wanted to the actor who had played Iago in the television *Othello* when I was Roderigo. He was a name actor so I felt I was losing work again to a star.

Gaby called to tell me she was going to be in a play off-Broadway and said there was a good part for me. A new group called the Artists Theater was doing three one act plays by poets. Gaby got me an audition and I won the role. Our play was *The Bait* by James Merrill. We were only scheduled for a few performances. Gaby and I were so happy to be working together, but neither of us understood the highly intellectual play, and that must have shown in our performances. The opening night is remembered primarily for the sight of both Arthur Miller and Dylan Thomas fleeing the theater. James Merrill became a great poet and even won a Pulitzer Award. Gaby and I went back to the drawing board.

I was getting fed up with trying to fit everything into 24 hours: Mary, the job at the photographer's, acting classes, the gym, selling insurance and the occasional audition for television. I suddenly was offered a way to escape from all of it. *Macbeth*, starring Charlton Heston, was to be done in Bermuda. The great movie actor Burgess Meredith was to direct and I was offered the role of Malcolm. It was a good part as he becomes King at the end of the play. I pushed everything aside and accepted. I had done a few plays in Bermuda a few years before, and I had loved the British atmosphere of the island. It would be a way to clear my head. Better still, Mary thought it was a good idea for me to be acting again, so off I went.

The weather was like it was nowhere else – constant sun but always a cool breeze from the surrounding ocean. I loved riding around the island on a rented motorbike. Everything was perfect – every cottage and garden was cared for lovingly so you felt like you were in a land out of a fairytale. St. Catherine's Fort, where we would rehearse and perform, was in the eastern part of the island only a couple of miles away from the town of St. George where we all would stay. Everyone got together the night before rehearsals were to start.

Chuck Heston, as we had always called him in the *Antony and Cleopatra* days, came over to me and greeted me warmly. He had already become a movie star. How wrong we were when we all voted him the least likely to succeed. We had ignored his magnificent looks that the camera ate up. After a few words, Chuck started to walk away. He turned back for a moment and said, "I'd like you to be in all my Shakespeare productions."

No one had ever told me that this was a Charlton Heston production, but stardom had obviously not diminished Chuck's sense of self-importance. Many of the other actors, who were there, I had worked with, and some, like Nancy Marchand and her husband Paul Sparer, were good friends. Burgess Meredith took charge and made us all comfortable with his humor and unpretentiousness.

Rehearsals went swimmingly except for the blazing sun. All the scenes were on the ramparts of the fort, so going over and over a scene was often exhausting in the heat. We all got tanner and tanner and drank gallons of water. I was only in the beginning and the end of the play so I escaped, when I could, to a shady spot. Meredith might suddenly skip to my scene, and they had to try to find me. He got exasperated one day and yelled, "Where the hell's Malcolm?" (That was the name of my character.) It became a catchphrase and the actors would yell, "Where the hell's Malcolm?" to fool around. I felt cosseted by everyone, even Heston was complimentary, and it was a relief not to worry about money, or at least for the moment, getting a job.

The excitement in Bermuda about *Macbeth* was intense. Nothing like it had ever happened on the island. Tickets were almost impossible to find and the opening night was to be a gala for all the important people on the island. The play was in great shape. Nancy Marchand as Lady Macbeth was brilliant. Heston was strong and his movie stardom had made him even more confident of his acting. The costumes were of Broadway caliber and the fort was the perfect backdrop for the time and place that the play described.

There was a theatrical tradition that *Macbeth* was cursed. So much so that actors were not supposed to say "Macbeth" and only use the name for it as "The Scottish Play." Theater lore is that the actor who played Lady Macbeth died the day of the first performance in London and Shakespeare himself had to play the part that night. Be that as it may, it was certainly cursed on our opening night in Bermuda. The weather turned out to be miserable, rainy and windy – almost hurricane strength. All the actors huddled in the caves cut into the rock under the fort. We had to put on our makeup with the help of flashlights.

There were spotlights on the fort itself, but they gave it a ghostly patina. Every seat was in the open air with no cover to hide under. Brave people arrived in heavy rainwear and everyone carried an umbrella. Music on loud speakers tried to create a festive air for what had been advertised as a festival, but the wind accompanied it and gave it a mournful sound. The men, except for Heston, were all dressing together. We waited to get word of whether we would have a show that night or not. A boy ran in every few minutes and announced that there was no decision yet.

Meanwhile the islanders piled in, drenched but eager to see a movie star no matter what. One of our drivers arrived and told us Heston, already in costume and sitting bareback on a horse, getting ready for his entrance, suddenly screamed, "Get me out of these tights! I'm being burned to death!" Evidently, they had used a kind of cleaning fluid that he was allergic to and it was burning his legs and loins. He was not hurt, but I suppose a few people got a look at what he had always shown off in our dressing room every night during *Antony and Cleopatra*. Well, if you've got it, flaunt it.

Word came that we were going forward, so we all girded our own loins and started out into what had become a serious storm. We could see that every seat was taken under a mass of umbrellas. The play began with a recorded fanfare. Then Heston made his entrance on the horse to wild applause. The famous scene with the witches began. But as soon as the witches started to speak, we knew we were in for it. The wind had gotten much worse, so it drowned out some of the actor's words every time they spoke. You only heard part of a sentence. You couldn't make any sense of what the actors were saying.

The first witch said, "When shall we three meet again, in thunder, lightning or in rain?" But what the audience heard was, "When shall – again in – or in –?" Then they heard the second witch say, "When the hurley – lost or won." This continued throughout the evening. You would have had to be a Shakespearean scholar to follow the plot, but the good people of Bermuda sat there without leaving, just trying to keep warm and as dry as possible.

During the intermission, Burgess Meredith came running into our cave. He had the look of a madman. He screamed above the wind, "Everybody speak up. The more they hear, the more they like it." He ran out, I supposed to spread his brilliant advice to the others. I still laugh when I think of it. It should be embroidered on pillows for actors to put on their sofas.

The curse of *Macbeth* wasn't quite over. Burgess had had a brilliant idea. In the play we know that Lady Macbeth has killed herself, but we don't see it. We just hear about it. Burgess said, "I want to see it as well." He had a dummy made copying Nancy Marchand's Lady Macbeth, costume, wig and makeup. It looked just like her – he had a rig of wires put together that was attached to the dummy. At the proper moment, a spotlight would hit the dummy as it plunged over the cliff, where it would rest unseen until it was used in the next show. But no one had planned for a hurricane. Her death was described by the actor as the spotlight lit up the dummy. It shot over the precipice, and before the light could be turned off, the dummy was blown back up by the wind. Lady Macbeth had returned from the Netherworld. The audience roared.

Burgess had another great idea. He had a wooden façade made of the front of the fort, and at the very end of the play, it was set on fire and was to go out in a blaze of glory. The wind, as if signaled, turned its force to behind the burning set so all the smoke and some flames went right toward the audience. No one was hurt but they must have heard the coughing in Miami.

The night before we left Bermuda, there was a huge party to celebrate us. Despite the storm, *Macbeth* was a huge success and Heston's name spread the news of it not only to New York and Hollywood but to London as well.

As a special treat to all of us, Bill Dana, who was an actor in the cast and later became a famous comedian when he assumed the character of Jose Jimenez, did a short version of *Macbeth* with the wind erasing most of the words. It was hilarious, the perfect conclusion to a happy time.

Who says there is a curse on *Macbeth*?

36

While I was in Bermuda, Mary had phoned me with the good news that she had landed a job as Deborah Kerr's understudy in a new play, *Tea and Sympathy*. The role was for a leading lady and Mary was just 25, but understudies seldom got a chance to go on. Still, it was good auspices with the playwright Robert Anderson and Elia Kazan directing. The play was a hit, and Mary and I faced another separation of time as she had to be at the theater every night except Sunday. We did continue to go to Bobby Lewis' workshop in the afternoon as he painstakingly examined every line of the O'Casey play.

One day I noticed a new actor who had just joined the group. He was extremely handsome and wore what looked like an expensive tan suede jacket that set off his darker brown hair and eyes. He seemed quite sure of himself, although he came to sessions without speaking to anyone. I kept watching him as the weeks went by and became fascinated by his looks and bearing. There was something about him that made me feel inadequate and at the same time attracted to him. I finally managed to talk to him and discovered he was a model and just beginning as an actor. He longed to know some of us but had been afraid to be rejected since we were all so much beyond him. I brought him over to where our little group always sat and introduced him to Mary and the others. He joined us and from that time on, he always sat with us.

I suppose it was bound to happen. Jim was everything I had wanted to be. I wasn't unaware of my attractiveness, but he was a model. Everyone looked at his picture and wanted to be him, wear the clothes he wore, brush their teeth with the same toothpaste. He was the mold and the rest of us were just poor copies. I developed an obsession that wouldn't go away. I was still in my relationship with Mary and Jim knew it, but we became lovers.

Now I not only had to balance my commitments to Mary, my job at the photographer's and selling insurance – I had to be with Jim whenever I could. Of course, it was doomed. Jim refused to commit himself because I was still with Mary, so we struggled about that, as well as my wanting to stay home after hours of peddling insurance. Jim, bored from waiting around, wanted to go out on the town. It was a constant argument. I was also dealing with someone who was nothing like me – our backgrounds couldn't have been more different nor could our egos.

One day Jim said to me, "Don't you notice anything different about me?"

I looked at him carefully. "No, I said, "I don't."

"My imperfection, don't you see that it's gone. I had it removed."

"What are you talking about?" I asked. "What imperfection?"

"I had a little spot on my cheek, didn't you see it?"

"No, I never noticed anything," I replied.

"Well, it's gone," he said.

I was horrified. It's one thing to be thought perfect by others but quite another thing when you think it of yourself. It was as if I were being tortured, but I was doing it to myself. I was miserable, wanting Jim, having him, but never really. He was a will-o'-the wisp. I knew I would never possess him and there would just be disaster in store for both of us. After a final frustrating drunken evening with Jim, I went back to my apartment, took the picture of him I had kept on the table next to my bed, and set fire to it. I watched it burn in the fireplace and said a prayer not to see him anymore. My prayer was answered.

I felt like a weight had been removed from my body. The holidays came and Mary and I were closer than ever. Her father, Homer Fickett, had died a few months after her play opened. He had been the director of *The Theater Guild On The Air*. Every Hollywood star had been eager to do the program. Radio meant that they could have a thorough rehearsal period, but they didn't have to memorize their roles or take the time to learn camera positions. The best plays and novels were done by actors like the Lunts, Helen Hayes, Gertrude Lawrence. They all loved Homer as did Mary who was shaken by his early death and reached out even more to me. We started a routine of having dinner with Mary's mother often. Her mother wasn't crazy about me, but she made an effort to be friendly, and so did I.

The Artists' Theater asked me to be in another poetic play. This one was a full-length play unlike *The Bait*. It was also written by a poet, V.R. Lang (known as Bunny). The author had taken the Orpheus and Eurydice legend and moved it from Greece to an amusement park. Eurydice worked there and Orpheus fell in love with her. The story was mainly about Orpheus who, in the play, became a major figure in the music world, like Leonard Bernstein. He seemed to care more for himself and his career than he did for Eurydice. It was to only run for a week, and I was happy to be acting again. I enjoyed playing it and I never forgot one line in the script that I loved. It didn't make much sense, but it seemed to me truly poetic and funny at the same time. The line was: "Later in their love, she learned to play the glockenspiel." The usual poets and writers and Village people came to see it and found it very talented and promising. Unfortunately, the young author died of cancer a few years later.

***

The director, Iza Itkin, for whom I had done *Angel Street* some years before, asked me to play the lead in Jean Cocteau's *The Infernal Machine*. Again, it would be off-Broadway, but this time it was uptown and a full production. Cocteau had taken the Oedipus legend and turned it into an entertaining, funny but still tragic story. I couldn't resist playing Oedipus, but again I would have to fit it into my working for the photographer and still go on selling insurance. I hadn't been paid for acting on the stage since summer stock in Maryland. I loved working on the role – Oedipus kills his father and marries his mother with no knowledge of who they were. When he discovers what he has done, he blinds himself. I had the idea of using ketchup on my eyelids and under the eyes because it looked so like blood. The opening night the effect was great, but I was miserable. The ketchup was heavily spiced and I was in great pain. Fortunately, it was the very end of the play or I would have had to stop and bathe my eyes before I could go on.

The production got a rave in *The New York Times,* but the gods were against us. There was a newspaper strike and nobody got to see the review or even find out we were doing the play. The producers couldn't afford the empty houses so we closed very quickly. I've always regretted the fate of *The Infernal Machine.* It was a real showcase for me with so many different moods and emotions to play. I began as a bumptious young man and ended as a tragic king – not that many parts outside of Shakespeare have that kind of range.

Mary got a chance to go on in *Tea and Sympathy* when the lead was ill, and though she couldn't come to my plays because she was in one, I was free to see her. She was phenomenal. She became a leading lady with incredible grace, dignity and beauty. She played an older woman who, recognizing the agony a young man is going through in his fight against being homosexual, goes to bed with him to save him. Today, this story would be unacceptable, but in those days, it was believed that just having sex with a woman was enough to cure a man of what was still a criminal offense. Mary knew I had been bisexual, and I wonder how much that had affected her performance. Elia Kazan was in the audience that night when Mary was so brilliant. The next day *The New York Times* published a long article by Kazan raving about Mary's performance. No director had ever done such a thing for an understudy, and it changed her career overnight.

A phone call came from Mary. We hadn't seen each other for a week or so. Our schedules had been at odds and there had been all the excitement of Mary's success. I was glad to hear from her, but not for long. She said she didn't want to see me anymore. When I asked what was wrong, she said she didn't want to discuss it. But I said, "We've been together for too long to just say goodbye in a phone call. Can't we meet so you can tell me what's bothering you?"

"No," Mary said, "I don't want to see you."

"All right," I replied, "then just tell me what's wrong."

There was a long silence and then she said, "I know all about Jim." I was shocked. I had thought I'd been so careful.

"What do you mean?" I said.

"You know perfectly well what I mean," she said. "I'm going to hang up."

"Wait a minute," I said, "that's all over. Why are you bringing it up now?"

"Because I just found out about it, and I don't want to live this way."

I took a breath. "Mary," I said. "you knew about my past life –"

She interrupted me, "This wasn't the past," she said, and I thought she was crying.

"But it is the past. I told you it's over."

"You were seeing him while you were seeing me," she raised her voice. "How do you think that makes me feel? I'm not going to live this way."

"But what if I tell you it won't happen again?"

"I don't believe you anymore."

We stopped talking for a moment. Then an idea struck me. "Do you think your play has anything to do with this?"

"How dare you try to use my play as an excuse for what you did? My friends told me you'd have a thousand excuses."

"They must be good friends to want to break us up –"

"You broke us up. I can't talk to you any longer. Don't try to reach me. Just leave me alone." I heard the phone shut off.

I was shattered. I knew it was all my fault. I didn't blame Mary. I was so used to meeting married men who had sex with men when their wives weren't looking, that I guess I hadn't thought enough about the wives. Most of them never knew, but they were still deprived of the full sexuality that they deserved. I realized that a double life isn't fair to someone, or in truth to anyone involved in it. But I was torn. Somehow it was part of my DNA. What could I do?

Jerry Cooke, the photographer, got an assignment from *Life Magazine* to do photographs for an article on vacationing in Italy. And coincidentally, an assignment from *Time Magazine* to do pictures of Yugoslavia. He needed someone to go with him, help him drive, carry equipment and write captions. He asked me if I wanted to go. I jumped at the opportunity. Mary wouldn't answer my calls, and I decided a trip to Europe would be the perfect way to clear the air between us. Also, summer was approaching with no jobs for me in either summer stock or television.

There were a few hectic weeks of getting everything ready, including a car Chrysler was lending us, since we were to do some work for them in Italy as well. Jerry was flying over and I would accompany the car, take it off the ship and then drive it to Paris, where I would meet Jerry. The only problem was that I knew practically no French and the ship docked at dusk. It was a nightmare driving through dark villages, screaming at any people I saw, "Ou est Paris?" It was the only French I could remember from high school. But finally, I saw the Eiffel Tower and my heart almost burst. Paris, an impossible dream come true.

37

Jerry had made a reservation for me at the Pont Royal on the Left Bank. Somehow, I found it by stopping people on street corners. None of them spoke English, but finally one recognized the name of the hotel. The valet put the car in the garage, and I signed in and went up to my room. The elevator was an old-fashioned glass and gold contraption that creaked dangerously. My room was minuscule, just under the roof, but high enough so I could see the Eiffel Tower through my small gable window. It was a dream come true.

Jerry, who had been born in Russia and spoke five languages, knew Paris well so I was excited to go to dinner at his favorite place. It turned out to be a Jewish kosher delicatessen and the only thing I could read on the menu was "Le Bouillon avec le Kreplach." My fantasy of eating at a great French three-star restaurant was quickly forgotten. I hid my disappointment. Jerry was my boss, not a friend I could share things with.

I did have an ace in the hole. Before I left New York, my friend Billy Nichols came to the boat to wish me bon voyage. He reached into his pocket and took out an envelope. "I want you to have a great time," he said, "and I know you'll be eating wherever your jobs with the photographer land you. Most of the restaurants will probably be pretty terrible. I want you to have one great dinner in Paris, so there is $100 in here," he tapped the envelope. "You can't spend it on anything but a dinner for yourself and it must be in a great restaurant. I want you to feel what it's like to be pampered and rich and not have to worry about how much the dinner costs. You have to tell me all about it when you return." It was the nicest present anyone had ever given me.

The day after I arrived in Paris, I got a recommendation from the hotel and that night, since Jerry was seeing friends, I went to Le Grande Vefour in the gardens of the Palais Royal. I felt like a king sitting all by myself at a table in a room that had been there since the 18th century. The ceilings were decorated with garlands of flowers, the furniture elegant. I felt like I was in a museum until I began to eat what the Captain had helped me choose. Then I was very much in 20th century Paris with the best food I'd ever tasted.

***

We drove over the Simplon Pass through Switzerland into Italy. Jerry had to do a job for Chrysler to photograph at the Ghia factory in Turin. Ghia make the bodies for some of the greatest automobiles in the world at that time, and they were doing some for Chrysler. We had two days scheduled because we would be using flash on the cars and it took time to set up the stands and change bulbs after they went off. Everything was packed neatly in cases in the car and my work was to carry them in, set them up, and exchange the flash bulbs each time Jerry took a picture. Often, I would be screwing in a fresh bulb when a trigger would accidentally set it off, burning my hands. I learned to wear gloves, but it still hurt. We worked tirelessly for the two days and finished everything.

The head of the factory, Giorgio, a charming, very sophisticated Italian with pictures of his wife and many children cluttering his massive desk, had invited us to dinner to celebrate. We were much too tired, but Jerry said we couldn't refuse. We thought we were going to his house, but several of his staff joined us and we were taken to a busy restaurant where heaps of pasta, chicken, fish dishes and rich desserts made me even more exhausted. Giorgio seemed to have taken a shine to me and aimed many jokes at me, teasing me constantly through the endless meal. When we finally finished, Georgio announced that we were going somewhere to have an after-dinner drink.

I whispered to Jerry, "Can't we get out of it. I'm collapsing."

Jerry said, "So am I, but we can't be rude."

We seemed to be driving out of town – there were fewer and fewer lights. We stopped at what looked like somebody's house and followed Giorgio and the others up the front stairs and into an overstuffed living room where a half dozen women were playing cards, some with each other and some by themselves. They were all in their twenties or thirties, dressed alike in kimonos with slits exposing their legs. Several of them had pushed back the kimono to expose their bare breasts. *Oh my god*, I realized, *it's a brothel*. A lovely woman around 40 and looking chic in a pale blue dress with a jacket over her shoulders, pushed through some curtains and greeted us all.

"I heard your car pull up," she said as she and Giorgio kissed on both cheeks. "I have some Strega ready." She disappeared for a moment and reappeared with a bottle and some small glasses. The girls didn't make a move to help her. They just continued with their cards and looked up occasionally with bored expressions.

We all sipped our drinks and then Georgio announced, "This is my party so who wants to pick first?" No one said anything so Georgio demanded, "Come on, Jerry, you're the guest." Jerry looked blank, then he finally raised his hand and pointed at one of the girls. She stood up and he followed her to a staircase at the end of the room. "Alan," Georgio said, "your turn. This is my present to you for your hard work."

I didn't know what to do. The last thing in the world I wanted was one of these women. But I was stuck. Jerry had made clear that we were guests and on an assignment. I couldn't make a fool of Jerry and myself and refuse. I looked at the women who were left. They were all unattractive, but one was almost ugly. I felt sorry for her. *She, at least, would be grateful if I picked her*, I thought, *so maybe it won't be too unbearable*. I chose her and followed her up the staircase.

As soon as she closed the door to a bare room with a sink and a bed, she said something in Italian to me. I didn't have the slightest idea what she was saying. A bell kept ringing as she repeated whatever it was. She started to get angry when I didn't answer her. She had a beak of a nose and she scowled.

"Pagare, pagare," she shouted.

"Oh," I said, "pay, Giorgio will pay." She didn't understand me.

"Il tempo!" she screamed. I knew that word meant "time."

Oh, she wanted to know how much time I would take. How did I know how long it was going to take me? How could I explain it to her when I didn't know any Italian. Finally, she gave up and pulled me over to the sink. She yanked down my pants and underwear and took a large rag, wet it and pushed it around a bar of soap lying on the sink and started to scrub my penis. She did it roughly as if she were beating me up. She then dried it with a much-used towel and pushed me over to the bed. She slipped off the kimono and kneeled down, made a few halfhearted slurps at my penis and then stretched out on the bed.

The bell kept going off and I guessed it was telling the customers how much time they would have to pay for. *I can't make Giorgio pay too much*, I thought. *I might as well get it over with*. I lay on top of her and touched her breast that was at least somewhat attractive.

She slapped my hand away and screamed, "No, no. no." She grabbed hold of me and started trying to arouse me. At last, with a lot of my desperately trying to think of someone else, she shoved me into her and it was over.

Back downstairs we all gathered, worn out warriors after the battle. Giorgio appeared with the lady of the house adjusting her jacket over her shoulders as if she were a queen. One of the girls said something to the girl I had been with, mentioning my name. My girl said something back. I asked Giorgio what they were saying. He answered sheepishly that the girl said she'd heard my name was Alan, like Alan Ladd. My girl had replied, "If only it had been Alan Ladd." That really rankled me so I thought, 'I'll get back at her for that.' I stole a card from the solitaire she had been playing when we arrived. 'That'll fix her,' I thought. "She won't be able to finish her game." I kept that card for many years.

The next morning, Jerry and I were up early and went right over to the factory to pick up the car. Giorgio had been kind enough to offer to go over it and be sure it was ready for us to continue on. When we got there the car was waiting, washed, waxed, the top was down and all our equipment was loaded in the back. Georgio was sent for so he could come and say goodbye. In a few minutes he appeared with what looked like the entire workforce of the factory. Jerry and I were so touched at the turn out of so many people.

As we were about to get into the car, Jerry opened the door on the driver's side and Georgio said to him, "You look exhausted."

"I am," Jerry replied.

"Why don't you let Alan drive and get a little sleep."

"That's a great idea," I said and went over and got in behind the wheel.

Georgio shook Jerry's hand and helped him in beside me. He closed the door and I turned the key. There was a tremendous boom like a bomb going off and billows of smoke poured out from under the bottom of the car. I was terrified. What had I done? Through the smoke I heard screams of laughter and applause, and as the smoke cleared, I saw dozens of faces, all laughing, some so hard there were tears running down their faces. I felt like an idiot and I realized what had happened.

Georgio wanted to have his final joke at my expense. That's why he had gotten me to drive and had kept the car overnight so he could plant a device. People kept coming up to the car and clapping me on the back. I laughed along with all of them.

Giorgio said, "I wish you could have seen your face."

Then he reached in and gave me the warmest hug, and we were off to Rome.

38

The trip to Rome took seven hours. We stopped several times and took turns driving so we wouldn't get too tired. When we got there, the city was dazzling in the bright sun. I couldn't believe my eyes when suddenly there was the Colosseum right next to us as we drove by, and then the Arch of Constantine so near it. They were both in travel books I had grown up with, but now to be really seeing them!

Luckily, Jerry was driving. I was so overwhelmed, I'm sure I would have crashed into someone in the heavy, late afternoon traffic. Our hotel, the *d'Angleterre*, was near the Spanish Steps so I got to see them too and the twin towered church that looked down on them. My room had double doors that opened onto a terrace that seemed to surround the building, so you could wander by other people's rooms and, I guess, look in to see what they were doing. I didn't try, but I had read famous people like Tennessee Williams had stayed there. So I'm sure, in those wild days, there was a lot of traffic from room to room.

Jerry was spending the evening with friends and asked me to join them, but since we were leaving for Capri in the morning, I wanted to wander about and breathe in the history that seemed to be everywhere. I went down and talked to the concierge about the best way I could spend my few hours. The tours were pretty much over for the day so that was out. He told me *Aida* was being performed at the Baths of Caracalla and I might enjoy that. It was outdoors with the ruins of the Baths as a backdrop and, since there would be almost a full moon, it would be an enchanting way to see how the Romans, as well as the tourists, spent their summer evenings. I got excited and said I'd go.

"I don't know if I can find you a ticket," he said. "It's very difficult now in the summer."

"Oh," I answered, "it sounded so great."

"Of course I am going to try," he said, "but it may take a little time. Where are you having dinner?"

"I don't know," I answered.

"Look," he said taking over, "there's a little restaurant called Otello a few blocks over in the Piazza di Spagna. You go there and I'll send you a ticket if I can find one. Otherwise, I'll send you a note."

Otello was a small but perfect Italian restaurant with an arrangement of fruit in a fountain at the entrance, as if it were being washed to be ready for you to eat. Of course, I had pasta and the waiter, who fortunately spoke English, recommended carbonara that was the best pasta I ever tasted. I asked what was in it and it was something about adding eggs. I was almost finished when a boy from the hotel arrived and handed me an envelope. There was no note inside, just a ticket to the opera. I couldn't wait to go so I quickly paid my bill and hired one of the many taxis arriving to show tourists the Spanish Steps.

It was much too early when I reached the Baths of Caracalla – I'd forgotten that Romans ate very late – but I just wandered about looking at the romantic ruins nestled among the famous pines of Rome. It couldn't have been a more beautiful night with the full moon rising and bathing the ancient stones in an ocher light. As the mobs of people arrived, I thought I'd better find my seat. It was a great one. The concierge had managed to get me into the center of the huge amphitheater and I'm sure in the most expensive section. I didn't care. I had a little money saved for a special occasion and this was certainly it.

Every seat was filled and the music was gorgeous. I didn't know much about opera, though as a kid, my father had taken me with him to operas when he photographed them for the WPA. I paid more attention to getting autographs of the cast, at that time, than I did to the music. But somehow the music must have found a storage place in my brain and I often could hum along with tunes I didn't even know I

knew. This was certainly true at *Aida* and I remembered every note of
the sublime love song "Celeste Aida" and the "Triumphal March." The
March certainly was triumphal – including an elephant being in it. It
took place in the second act and it looked like there were almost as many
people onstage as there were in the audience. Horses and chariots and
wild animals in cages and musicians and dancers. They kept parading
onto the stage in a spectacle unlike anything I'd ever seen. The audience
ate it up and kept applauding each new surprise.

I tried to walk around in the intermission but the aisles were jammed,
so I started back to my seat when I was stopped short. There was a
small group of young people gathered around one of the handsomest
men I'd ever seen. He seemed to be my age, in his late twenties, and he
wore tailored clothes – a dark blue linen jacket he had arranged over his
shoulders. This was obviously the way the Roman men were wearing
their jackets in the warm summer night. His pants were pale blue and
his shoes were shined to perfection. All of this subtle elegance clothed
a man of incredible looks. His features were like a Greek sculpture and
his hair was a burnished brown with a few streaks where the sun had
touched it. He was one of the few men I'd ever seen who almost took
your breath away. I could hear the group all speaking Italian, but there
was no question of their origin. They shared a similar elegance and
sophistication that was clearly European.

I couldn't help staring at them as if I were watching a group of actors
on a stage who only pretended to be unaware that they had an audience.
I was sure they knew their aura seduced everyone, but they paid no attention to me or any other onlooker. The lights signaled the beginning
of the next act and I went back to my seat. I was really staggered by the
man I'd seen and I kept thinking about him through the next two acts.
I looked for him at the end of the opera, but he was nowhere to be seen.
I wished I could have seen him again, but I realized I was behaving like
a silly adolescent. I was leaving Rome in the morning and would never
see him again. I was too excited by the evening to go straight back to the
hotel. I remembered the name of a bar that friends in New York had

told me to go to if I got to Rome. "Victor's, it's the place to go," they said. I found a taxi. *Why not?* I thought.

Victor's was in a handsome house near what looked like the busiest place in Rome. The broad avenue was lined on either side by chocka-block parked cars, and on the wide sidewalks were tables crammed together, filled with people on what the driver told me was a *passeggiata*, a promenade in Italy. Elegant shops and a huge hotel created a back-drop. The driver said it was the Via Veneto when I used my few words of Italian to question him. I paid the driver and walked up the stairs past high bushes into a room with tables on one side and a long bar on the other.

The bar was crowded, but I squeezed into an opening and ordered a Negroni, a drink I had discovered in Turin. I looked around at a well-dressed crowd that was predominately Italian and sipped my drink. A group that blocked my view of the end of the bar moved away and, as if a curtain went up, there was the young man I'd seen at the opera. This time he seemed to be alone and, as if he felt me looking at him, he turned and stared straight at me. I was embarrassed for a moment that he'd caught me looking at him, and then he smiled. I relaxed and smiled back and he walked around the crowd and came over to me.

"I saw you at the opera," he said in a slightly accented English, "are you American or British?"

I was stunned that he had noticed me. "American," I said, "from New York."

"Ah, I thought so. Did you like *Aida*? he asked.

"Yes, it was amazing." I felt tongue-tied.

"It's such an old warhorse," he went on, "but we all love to see the elephant and the dancing once in a while. I'm sure it's better at your Metropolitan."

"I don't know. I'm not much of an opera goer," I confessed.

"How long have you been in Rome?"

"Just a couple of hours."

"Have you seen any of the city?"

"Well, not very much," I said. "I did pass by the Coliseum on the drive in and the Arch of Constantine, and the Spanish Steps near the hotel, and, of course, the Baths of Caracalla."

"But that's just scratching the surface," he scoffed. "Come, I show you Rome by night, unless you'd rather drink."

"No, no, I'd love that. I have to leave in the morning so I won't have a chance to see much more."

"Then let's go."

I'd already paid for my drink so I set the half empty glass down on the bar and turned to follow him. As we walked out, the bartender raised his voice above the noise and said, "Addio, Principe."

We walked a few blocks, the moonlight sifting through the leafy trees that lined the street. I felt lightheaded as if I were floating on a wave that was carrying me out to sea. We stopped at a small Fiat with a sun roof. There were just two seats inside and the stick shift barely kept our legs from touching.

"I'm Alessandro, he said as he settled in the driver's seat and put out his hand.

"Alan," I replied as I shook it.

There was no overt pressure in his hand to indicate anything and I felt relieved. Somehow the last thing I wanted was any obvious physical overture. I was too enthralled with my fortune at meeting him and now just being able to be beside him. Rome, the opera, the moonlight and to be with the best looking, elegant man – it was all out of a fantasy.

Alessandro drove and for a few minutes neither of us spoke. "The bartender called you Principe – doesn't that mean something royal?" I asked.

"It means nothing," he said, "my family has been in Italy for centuries so I inherited the title. I don't use it, but people who know of it, like to say it. I no longer bother to tell them not to. It has nothing to do with my life."

We started to talk about what we did – I, about being an actor and working with a photographer on a *Life* assignment, and Alessandro, who was a writer and a poet and lived in a tower in the middle of a vineyard near Florence. He had been visiting friends in Rome and was returning to his home in the morning. So it turned out we both were spending a last night in Rome together.

I told him about playing an Italian in *The Marble Faun* and he exclaimed, "How wonderful! Hawthorne is one of my favorites and I know that book well. Good. The first stop will be the Campidoglio right next to the Tarpian Roch where you pushed the man over to his death."

I got terribly excited as he pulled up at the base of the stairs leading to the piazza which he told me had been designed by Michelangelo. I got out, while he waited, and walked up until I could see the beauty of the square, surrounded by magnificent period buildings, with the bronze statue of Marcus Aurelius on horseback. It was framed against a palace that had a double staircase. It was all lit so it looked like a stage set.

The next hour was a miracle. We parked near the Coliseum and Alessandro took me in a side door so we were able to see the enormous inside that was now full of the ruins of a complex of rooms, some used by the gladiators and some to hold the animals that they were to fight. Then we saw the Forum, the Castle Sant Angelo, the façade of the Pantheon, and the Piazza Navona – all illuminated like stage sets and all incredibly beautiful. Each one seemed to draw Alessandro and me closer together and I basked in his wonderful looks and sensitivity and great love for Rome.

"It's getting late," he said but we have two more stops." He drove to the Trevi Fountain with its statues and columns and water splashing in the spotlights' glare. I was open mouthed and Alessandro put his arm on my shoulder. "Here is a coin," he said handing it to me. "You throw it with your right hand over your left shoulder into the fountain and it will bring you back one day to Rome." I did as he told me and said a silent prayer that I would return. "Now," he said, "the piece de resistance."

When we stopped again, Alessandro said, "You've been to some of the seven hills of Rome – the Capitoline where you saw Michelangelo's Piazza, the Quirinal where you threw your coin in the fountain, but now you are at the top of the Aventine and I'm going to show you the most beautiful keyhole in Rome."

We walked across to a magnificent villa that Alessandro said was the Knights of Malta Institute. In the elaborate iron door was a small shield with a keyhole. "Put your eye close to the keyhole," he said.

When I did, I felt like I had the first time I'd looked through a stereopticon as a child. Through a long vista of bushes that had been trained to create a tunnel, way in the distance, was the basilica of St. Peters at the Vatican. It gave me a chill. I was looking at an image of perfect beauty created by man and overseen by God. It was a truly spiritual experience but in no way connected to a specific religion. It was a sign of what man could do with the gift of genius. But everything Alessandro had shown me that night was created by people who'd been given that gift. I told Alessandro what I was feeling and what the night had meant to me. He was very moved.

"It's 2:00," Alessandro said, "I have to take you to your hotel – you have an early start (I had told him of the pictures we had to take in Capri) and I have to be off to Florence in just a few hours. I would have loved to be with you through the night, but we can't go to my friend's house and you can't take me to your hotel. They're strict at this hour and would not let me go in with you. Perhaps it's just as well. We would have to part in the morning and probably never see each other again. It will be hard enough now to forget you, but at least it can remain part of a dream that could have happened rather than a reality always haunting us that it couldn't be continued."

I sat stunned, realizing how close we had come to something that was impossible to continue and that would only make us miserable. It was better this way. I had kept fingering a ring on my finger as Alessandro talked. I seldom wore jewelry, but I had found an old silver ring in an antique shop, that also had a lot of junk, on Second Avenue.

It was heavy and worn and I fantasized it was from the Crusades. I wore it sometimes when I was all dressed up as I was tonight. I slipped it off my finger.

"Alessandro," I said, "I want you to have this ring. It isn't worth anything and I don't expect you to wear it. But it will remind you of me and how you gave me Rome, and also a perfect relationship for one night that time will never alter."

He took the ring and held it in his hand. We didn't say anything more as we drove to the *d'Angleterre*. I got out of the car and we looked at each other for a moment, thinking, I suppose, of what might have been. I started to go in, but I stopped and turned back. I hadn't heard the car leave. Alessandro was sitting there, just watching me. I didn't know what to do. I automatically touched my fingers to my lips, turned my hand and held it up toward him, almost as if it were a blessing. Then I went into the hotel.

39

Capri

We drove to Naples where Jerry had hired a boat to take us to Capri. The day was bright and sunny but the water was rough, making us both feel a little seasick. It did calm down as we approached the Marina Grande, the harbor on the island. The thrill was when I saw the Faraglioni, the famous rocks bursting out of the sea. They were to Capri what the Eiffel Tower was to Paris or the Coliseum to Rome – a symbol of the place known all over the world. The Captain of the tiny boat steered us right through the opening in the rocks, and I forgot Alessandro and my night in Rome, Mary, television, theater, acting, everything. The sun was beating down on me. I was being splashed with water from the Mediterranean and I was free as a bird.

After we landed, our first stop was La Canzone del Mare owned by the British comedienne Gracie Fields. There was a huge pool open to the public for a fee and it was a meeting place for the chic Italians we were looking to photograph. I had felt I was one of them in our private yacht on the way over, but now it was all business. I had to find some attractive girls to sit by the pool for a shot Jerry was planning. I found two quite beautiful girls. They were perfect for the shot, but their hairy armpits, which were fashionable in Italy at that time, were a turnoff for me. Jerry also needed some attractive men to sit with them but the men, who were there, were business men with large bellies from eating too much pasta. Jerry had me change into a bathing suit and staged me talking to the girls. It began my short modeling career. He then got me to jump in the water at the Blue Grotto and waterski with a gorgeous girl in Positano. All three pictures ended up in the *Life* essay when it appeared.

Our trip through Italy was a whirlwind. I didn't have a minute to sightsee as I was busy lugging heavy equipment in and out of hotels, and pursuing people who had been in Jerry's photos, for their names and where they were from. Our days were busy from early morning, when we had to get up to catch the good light, to dusk for sunset shots. In between there was the driving all over Italy from Naples to Lake Como to Cortina d'Ampezzo. Most of what I saw was the Autostrada. After two weeks of this, we were off to Trieste and Yugoslavia. More of the same, working down the country and photographing everything from Lake Ohrid in Macedonia to Belgrade to Titograd in Montenegro.

Jerry had been suddenly notified that he had to spend a few days in Istanbul photographing a wrestling match. Since someone had to stay with all the equipment, as well as the car, I would be left alone in Titograd. We were in what passed for a hotel in those days, but I said, "How am I going to eat? No one speaks English. How can I order food when you're not here?"

Jerry said, "Don't worry, I heard the maître d' speaks English."

That's a relief, I thought. I would be in a city where I couldn't speak to anyone, but at least I wouldn't starve. That night, after Jerry left, I went happily into the dining room. I found the maître d', who was used to taking orders in Russian from Jerry, and I said with a smile, "You speak English."

"Small," he replied. It was the last English word I heard for the week. I didn't know what to do with myself. I couldn't read the papers or find any books in English. I was hesitant to wander in the city without being able to speak to anyone if I were lost. Besides there wasn't anything to see. Titograd, named of course after the leader of Yugoslavia Josip Broz Tito, had been occupied by the Austrians, the Italians and the Germans and practically destroyed in the Second World War, so everything was new or being built. I felt I was in a strange world where I was the only one who didn't speak the language. I had become an outcast.

After a few days of just wandering around the colorless hotel, I thought there must be something I could do. *I have the car. Why don't I drive up into the mountains and have a picnic lunch?* I somehow communicated to the kitchen staff and got a paper bag with hardboiled eggs, several pieces of heavy peasant bread and a bottle of something with a Cyrillic name. It was a glorious day, so I got into the car and took the one potholed road out of the city. It started to climb up gradually. I had put the top down, and I thought how clever I had been to think of this excursion. An old jalopy came weaving down the hill in my lane and smashed right into me. Hysteria broke out.

There must have been at least a dozen people who jumped out of the old car. It was almost like a circus stunt and they were all screaming. I started screaming too, and they couldn't understand me anymore than I could understand them. I examined the car. There was a gash along the right side that was on the door as well as the body. I must have unconsciously tried to get out of their way when I saw they were going to hit me. They all came over and started to rub their hands on the gash. I couldn't tell if they were examining the extent of the damage or trying to rub it away. I tried to talk in sign language to tell them it was their fault, but I realized there was no way these poor people could do anything to repair the damage. I said "police" thinking that might have some equivalent in the Serbo-Croatian language and sure enough they started to scream "no polis."

I looked over the car and saw that everything else was in good shape so I made motions for them to go. Several of them grabbed my hand and kissed it and they raced to their car and sped off. The damage wasn't great, but what could I tell Jerry when he returned? It was a mess. I drove back to the hotel, put the car in the garage and never wanted to see it again. I went to the lobby. Maybe there was a body shop, but no one understood me, so I was stymied. I went to my room feeling miserable.

Several hours later I went back to the lobby to see if anyone had arrived who might speak English. A tall man in his thirties, with a lot of black hair and a burgeoning mustache, was talking to the woman at the desk. He walked over to me and banged his hands together with appropriate sounds, and I realized he had heard about the accident. I suppose everyone in Titograd had heard by then. The man then took my hand and led me out onto the street where the *passigiatta* was taking place.

I had seen this in Italy. At the end of the day everyone parades up and down the main street, talking, flirting and having a wonderful time. The man, who I now figured had something to do with the hotel, led me along with the crowd, still holding my hand. I felt uncomfortable but he wouldn't let go, and I did notice other men holding hands so I assumed it was all right. I just felt I couldn't be rude and tear my hand away.

Finally, he stopped and took out his wallet. He showed me a red folded card, tapped it and said, proudly "Communist." I guessed he was either trying to impress me or he was showing me that he was part of the government. He then, with a lot of sign language, told me that he could get my car fixed. I asked him how much it would cost, and he led me to the garage where he examined the gash. He felt it with both hands and, with his fingers, signed 35.

"Dollars?" I asked. He shook his head yes. What luck, I thought. I didn't have much money but that much I could certainly afford. I agreed and he grabbed my hand and shook it. "How long?" I asked pointing to my watch. He indicated two or three days. He rubbed his fingers together to indicate that he wanted the money now, so we went to the cashier's desk where a middle-aged woman, with a pencil in her thick hair, cashed my travelers' checks. I gave him the keys to the car, and I felt relieved. Jerry would be back the end of the week and the car would be all fixed.

Several days went by. I saw the man several times and asked in my hand language how the car was doing. He smiled broadly, clapped his hands at me and beamed. I felt sanguine and relaxed. But on the third day, the car had still not returned. I looked all over for the man and finally found him. I somehow communicated to him that I was leaving the next day and had to have the car. He said it was ready and he would go and get it. I waited in front of the hotel for an hour and finally the car drove up. The man parked and I rushed over. The gash was little changed, but a coat of paint covered it somewhat. The color was not quite the same and it looked like what it was – a botched job by an amateur.

At that moment, a young, good-looking woman arrived, went to the back of the car, opened the trunk and took out a keg of almost empty of wine and several shopping bags. She grabbed them all, gave me a haughty look, and walked away. When I turned back to the man, he shrugged his shoulders and gave me a wide smile. He went over to the gash, ran his hands over it, nodded at me approvingly, grabbed my hand, shook it and walked away. Even if I'd known the language, I couldn't have expressed my feelings of disgust at the way he had taken advantage of me. I figured he had had the car painted over in one day and used the rest of the time to take his girlfriend up into the hills to picnic and make love.

The car must have so impressed the girl. An American convertible was a rarity in Yugoslavia. When we drove through villages, the people all stood at attention and saluted, thinking we were members of the government. I put the car in the garage and went back to my room. I would tell Jerry he could deduct money from my salary to pay to have the car fixed.

That night, after dinner, I decided to pay my bill. I went to the cashier's desk and the woman again took my American Express checks. As she finished figuring out the exchange, she looked up at me.

"Is no good Titograd," she said. "You go back United States."

I was dumbfounded. "You speak English!" I said. "Why didn't you say something? I was so desperate for help."

"You a baby," she replied. "Go home where you belong." She turned back to her figures.

Jerry arrived the next day and was wonderful about the car. Fortunately, we didn't need it for any more photographs and Jerry had been told to just get rid of it. He would do that in Rome where we were going before returning to the States.

40

Rome

I was in Rome, but this time not just overnight. Jerry didn't mind my staying on for a few days to sightsee, though he had to get back to edit all his film. He gave me the money for the fare back to New York so I could find a boat when I was ready to go home.

"Stay for a week if you want," he said. "New York is dead now. Nothing's going on."

It was the middle of summer and my chances of getting acting jobs were pretty slim. I felt I owed it to myself to have my first vacation since I had arrived in New York 11 years ago. I got Jerry and all the equipment to the plane and I was free. I'd gotten a room at the *d'Angleterre* again and, if I were careful, I could afford to stay for at least a week. I made a list of everything I wanted to see. Billy Nichols had given me a small guide to Rome, and I went through it carefully.

It was late in the afternoon before I was back from the airport, too late to go to the museums or any of the indoor sights. I had heard that the place to have a drink at cocktail time was the Via Veneto, so I got a cab that let me out in front of the Excelsior Hotel. There were tables with umbrellas on the sidewalk climbing up the hill, and I found an empty one and sat down. A water immediately appeared and I ordered a Negroni. It had become my favorite drink. I'd seen it listed in the guide book as a popular drink in Rome though I had no idea what was in it. It tasted delicious and I sat sipping it and watching the crowds of people. It reminded me of the *passigiatta* in Titograd: beautiful women getting out of cars and joining friends at the tables, and some beautiful women who just walked up and down the street who I figured were available. There were also young men, well dressed but obviously also available. It was like a bazaar but it looked like flesh was the only thing for sale.

I thought of Alessandro and my night with him. Of course, nothing had happened between us, but that had made the experience even sweeter. Maybe he would turn up. He must visit Rome often. But somehow, I knew that I would not see him again. I had a belief that you met people during your life who could influence you if you let them. I had thought over and over of why Alessandro affected me so much in the few hours we were together. I came to the conclusion that he was a signpost: he showed me that there were men in the world who could be all the things that Eleanor used to talk about. They could not only be attractive, but partners intellectually and spiritually. They could help me achieve the equality that two people must have for a lifetime together. Alessandro was a Prince. Our worlds were not compatible. If we had consummated what was in the air that night, there would have been no future. The lesson I learned was that someday I might find the person to complete my half of the apple of life.

Suddenly, walking toward me I saw Dick Camp, an actor friend from New York. "Dickie," I shouted," is that you?" He rushed over and I stood up and we embraced.

"What are you doing here?" he said.

"Just loving Rome," I replied. "What are you doing here?"

"I live here," he said, "and I work here. I'm just on my way to work now."

"Can you have a drink?"

"I don't have time now, but I'll sit with you for a minute."

He sat down and I told him quickly why I was in Europe. He explained that he'd grown tired of waiting for the phone to ring with an acting job so he'd come to Rome, where he'd always dreamed of visiting, and gotten a job dubbing Italian films into English. He had found an apartment and was having the time of his life.

"I'm on my way to dub a film now," Dickie said. "But I'm having a few friends in to dinner at 8:30. You come too." He wrote his address down for me and dashed off.

The taxi from the hotel took me to the Veneto again, now teaming with the activity of the night traffic, and then up the hill past a small pyramid and into a residential part of Rome. The streets were treelined, quiet, and the apartment buildings were modern and well-kept. I went up in the elevator of Dickie's building to find that his apartment was spacious and attractive. Dickie greeted me warmly and introduced me to a few young men who were his guests. One was from Australia, one a friend from New York and several Italians who seemed like business men. The atmosphere was jolly, mixed with Italian and English banter and, for dinner, a huge pot of pasta Dickie had cooked. There was also plenty of Italian wine that helped the laughter along. At one point I told Dickie how much I loved Rome and would have liked to have lived there myself.

"I'll give you some advice. Stay here" Dickie said. "I'll bet you could get work dubbing. It's not a fortune, but it's enough to live on and I've got an extra bedroom. You can share the rent and I cook, so you won't have to pay as much for restaurants all the time." The more wine I drank, Dickie's fantastic idea seemed extremely sensible.

The next day Dickie took me in hand and I met Gisella, a handsome, middle-aged redhead who was the head of the dubbing business. She did some tests with me and I learned, within an hour, to sync my English words to the Italian actor's lips. It was a fun game and I was having a ball.

"Can you start tomorrow?" Gisella said in perfect but accented English. "I have a new film I want to start."

It took me only a second to say yes. That afternoon, I left the expensive hotel, made a deal that was a pittance next to what I was paying with Dickie, and moved into his place that afternoon. I began one of the pleasantest times of my life. I had no trouble syncing the films and I felt so free with them, I was able to act as I spoke, creating the actor's emotions instead of just using the staid sound that so many dubbed films have. Gisella was constantly excited and complimentary about my work. Dickie said she was after me but I paid no attention to it. She used me film after film.

The days flew by with a 9:00 to 5:00 schedule, and I only had a chance to sample Rome when I was too tired at the end of the day. Dickie had many friends so he was often out on the town, but I enjoyed the quiet of my room, reading a lot about where I was. I kept making plans for the day trip to go to Hadrian's Villa, but always a job came up and I rushed to the studio. I did eventually get to the villa, but I checked in with my agent on the phone as I was waiting to go in. She told me to get right back to the city – I had an audition she had arranged for a film with an American role. I rushed right back to Rome, I didn't get the part, and I never did see Hadrian's Villa.

Jerry had been fine about my working in Rome. We had always had an agreement that my acting career took precedence. As far as Mary was concerned, I had given up trying to contact her. I had read that she had been given the leading role in *Tea and Sympathy*, opposite Tony Perkins, after Deborah Kerr withdrew. It was a big story, "the understudy becomes the leading lady." I had sent her a telegram to wish her well.

I continued my love affair with Rome. Just going to work in the morning, stopping to have a cool fruit drink, a cappuccino and a sugary pastry at a sidewalk stand under a colonnade of trees that shaded the hot sun, was a treat. Wherever I went, I passed a magnificent antiquity – modern buildings built around fragments of amphitheaters and ancient ruins. History was built into everyone's daily life. The past was here today as well as it would be in the future. There was no forgetting the beauty of Rome's art – it was everywhere.

Yet one day I woke up and thought, I left home to be an actor, not a dubber. I had finished work on a movie the day before. I found a ship and left for New York, but not before I put another coin in the Trevi Fountain.

41

The first thing I did, when I had unpacked and paid a few bills that were overdue, was to call Billy Nichols. I wanted to thank him for my fantastic dinner in France. He was home and suggested that I come over for a drink and tell him all about the trip. It was always a joy to go to Billy's apartment just up from the Morosco Theatre. It was like an oasis of culture and calm in the middle of the frantic din of Times Square. I loved seeing the mysterious objects squeezed between his extensive book collection: a fragment of marble from Herculaneum, a small oil painting of Venice done by a friend, tiny figures of gods from Southeast Asia.

Billy had an eye for beauty that he used, while combing flea markets, and on his travels around the world. He didn't stint, however, and if something beautiful was expensive and he had to have it, he paid the price. I enjoyed his treasures almost as much as he did. He let me examine them closely, touch them, hold them and hear about their provenance.

We hugged for a moment and then I sat down while Billy got me a glass of chardonnay. I recounted every course of the Grand Vefour dinner and told him about the rest of the trip. He laughed with me about Titograd. But when I thanked him again for giving me the present of feeling like a privileged, rich person for an evening in Paris, Billy stopped me.

"I'm going to give you an even better present," he said.

"You've given me enough," I interrupted.

"No," he replied. "This is a gift that will keep on giving, and I insist that you accept it." I wondered what it was. He immediately said, "I'm going to pay for a consultation with my analyst. He can't treat you because we're friends, but he'll recommend the right doctor for you."

"Billy, we've gone through this before," I said, "I can't possibly afford analysis and besides, I'm perfectly fine."

"I'm going to level with you," he said. "If I weren't fond of you and wished you well, I would not have gotten into this. You need help. You're getting fewer and fewer acting jobs –"

I stopped him, "That's because Hollywood is taking over television."

"I don't care what the reason is," he said, "but the fact is you're barely getting along. And more important than that, you're not a kid anymore, and you still haven't decided whether you want girls or boys. You're charming and everybody adores you, but you're getting older. If you don't get some guidance now, it will be too late. I care too much about you to see you become a lonely old, out of work actor."

I was stunned. Was this really what Billy thought would happen to me? How awful. I wasn't in any trouble and I thought I was doing pretty well. I thought back to something I had told Billy before I went to Europe. I had been offered a small part in a television drama. It wasn't even a part, just the voice of a radio announcer. I wouldn't even be seen. I needed the money and, if there was anything I could do with ease, it was radio announcing. I didn't even have to go to rehearsals, just be there the day of the show. There was a run-thru before the dress rehearsal. I stood in a sound booth, the script in my hand, ready to read a couple of paragraphs. My cue came and I panicked. I couldn't open my mouth. The director stopped the rehearsal and came over to me. He was terribly nice and assumed, because I hadn't had to be at rehearsals, that I hadn't been given the proper script. He got me a new one and I read the lines, but not very well. After the dress rehearsal, when I was a little better, the director came over to me.

"Are you alright?" he asked.

"Oh sure," I replied. "I just needed to go through it once."

"OK," he said.

I was terrified when it came to my moment on the actual show. It was as if I were about to play Hamlet and I'd forgotten all his lines. Somehow, I got through it, but I was so shaken. It was just reading a few lines – I'd done it for hundreds of hours in Boston and New York. I told Billy about it because he was in analysis and I thought he could help me. Of course he couldn't, and I put it out of my mind.

"Billy," I said, "is this because I told you about that TV job of the radio announcer?"

"That's just one of a series of things."

I knew Billy was a real friend and that it wasn't easy for him to talk to me this way. We had never gotten into serious matters. He was always just fun and games. But he had broached the subject of analysis with me before and I had always pushed it away. I couldn't help feeling that what he was saying was somewhat the truth.

"Billy," I said, "thank you for your concern. You may be right, but I can't possibly afford it."

"You'll see," he said, "I quadrupled the money I was making after a year in analysis. There's something about having to pay for it yourself that makes you earn more."

"But you're paying for me –"

He cut me off. "Only for a consultation, then you're on your own. And by the way, you make the decision to continue after you talk to my doctor. No one else does. You can just call it quits."

Billy's doctor was surprisingly fat. He had some trouble getting out of his soft leather armchair to shake my hand. It put me off for a moment, but his warmth and welcoming mien quickly made me feel at ease. We began to chat like old friends. He made it clear that this was not an analytic session – just a probe to uncover information about me that would determine the kind of doctor I should have. I explained that I wasn't sure I wanted a doctor and I had little money. He smiled, both his cheeks getting even bigger, and said why didn't we wait before deciding anything. He kept reminding me of S.Z. Sakall, the wonderful character actor in the movies whose cheeks wiggled when he shook his head. He was called "Cuddles" and I smiled thinking what it would be like to call your analyst "Cuddles."

He interrupted my thoughts, "Why don't you tell me about your friends and your lovers, if you've had any."

I thought, *what the hell, why not? Billy had paid him to listen.* I started out with Louis, then Cass, Eleanor and Mary. I even threw in Jacqueline. Before I knew it, I was talking about my acting career that seemed to be stalled. At one point, tears came to my eyes and he handed me a Kleenex. I felt as if there was a mass of something in my chest that was longing to get out but, it just couldn't escape.

"We have to stop," the doctor said. "but I think you would be very much helped by working with an analyst."

"I've already been with one for several years," I said.

"Some people need to be with a doctor for many years," he said. "I don't think that's true of you, but I know it would help you have a more successful life. There is a very good man who is not a medical doctor. He is a psychologist rather than a psychiatrist. He is very good and I think I can get him to see you at $15 a visit. You could start with once a week and keep adding sessions as you can afford them. I would gladly tell you if you didn't need help. You do, and you will succeed at it. Your emotions are just waiting to burst out and lead you to a better life."

***

What an ugly room, I thought as I sat waiting for my new doctor. I looked at the pale green walls, the amateurishly drawn prints of Sacre Coeur and the Arc de Triumph in their cheap rococo frames, and the pair of red Chinese lamps on the matching green lacquer tables. 'How can anyone with this kind of taste help me?' I wondered. Then I smiled to myself. *I'm not exactly here to find an interior decorator, but I guess I do have to redecorate my own interior. That's a pretty smart remark. After all, it's what analysts do. I think I'll tell the doctor that.* Then I realized I was just being flippant. My spirits fell lower and lower the longer I waited. Seven years had passed since I had first been in analysis and I was no happier now than I had been then.

The inner door opened and the doctor appeared. I was glad to see that he was fairly young, probably in his mid-forties, and he was handsome and robust as well. "Come in," he said and he led me into a dark room. Since I was unfamiliar with it, I didn't know which way to go. As I turned, I almost bumped into the doctor who then motioned me to a chair. "Why don't you just talk?" he said after we were settled. I suddenly felt the way I had when I'd been in pain and gone to a physician. The minute I saw him, the pain lessened. I knew I was in good hands. I felt that he would take care of me and everything would be all right. Somehow this doctor had the same aura.

I started by saying brightly that it would be my birthday in a few days. I would be 29. Then my mood suddenly changed. I talked about my failures: my lack of money, my successes that were minor, my personal life – I had been with Eleanor for a year, Mary for three and neither of them had worked out. Then there were the men, but they were also not lasting relationships. I wanted to give up smoking. I was always worried about my health. I had a problem as an actor: I never felt I was moving freely onstage. I always sensed that I was a little stiff as if I were hiding something. Why did I have to hide what I felt? And then there were my parents: my father's excessive care of himself and my mother's sentimental Cinderella dreams that she'd handed down to me. And finally, I described my difficulty on the television show as the radio announcer. Why had I created such an obstacle to acting in a small role? The doctor sat quietly, listening, but not saying a word. I thought I'd better tell him I'd been in analysis before. "Why was I released if I still had all these problems?" I asked him.

The doctor put down a book he was making notes in. He said in a calm reassuring voice, "An analysis is like two people setting out on a long voyage, the patient and the analyst. They may, at times, come close to islands that seem dangerous so they veer away from them and go to happier places. When they're able to, they return to the hazardous islands to find out what is on the islands and what it was that frightened them away. Eventually, they discover at the end of the voyage, the world or really themselves – the patient. What he truly is. It may be that when you were in analysis before, you insisted on steering clear of the terrifying islands. The doctor couldn't get you to alter your course and explore them. In that case, there was nothing to do but to let you go."

"I won't do that this time," I protested, "but will you, at least tell me just what analysis is all about. My last experience, I could never get any answers. The analyst would always say 'why do you think you asked that' whenever I asked a question."

The doctor smiled at me and said, "There are three steps in analysis: One – free association, or not only discovering what you are thinking, but what surrounds the thoughts – the thoughts, so to speak, on the periphery of the mind – things you think of often but reject because they don't relate to the subject at hand; Two – synthesis, or relating what we find out through free association and dreams; and Three – reality, once the sores have been discovered, the reasons for them, how they developed emotionally, and this information is then applied to the present moment, every day, the patient must then face the reality of the outside world beyond the analytic room."

I sat for a few minutes trying to take it all in. I was managing to pay for two sessions a week, but at that rate I'd never get to the bottom of all this. Maybe, if I really did begin to make more money, as Billy said I would, I could increase the number of sessions. It sure looked like a long tunnel to get to the end of.

"Would you like to talk of something else?" The doctor asked. "We still have a little more time."

"I don't think so," I said. "I did bring a dream unless it's too early to talk about dreams."

"It's never too early to talk about anything," the doctor responded. "Why don't you tell me about the dream."

"I wrote it down," I said.

"Fine, then read it to me."

I took the crumpled piece of paper out of my pants pocket and read:

I died and found myself under the ocean, diving way down where no one had ever been. I came to two huge doors made of gold, like the doors on the Duomo in Florence. The doors were closed, but I knew when they were opened, I would go through to paradise. As I waited for them to open, I examined them more closely. There were reliefs, many of them, beautifully sculpted. As I looked at them, I realized they were all parts of my life from childhood – highlights – good things and bad things. They were all there for anyone to see, or maybe just for me to see. They were images that conjured up a whole story that pieced together made up a life.

I waited as the doctor made some notes in his book. I could hear the sound of children playing in the park across the way. It reminded me of lying in bed after I'd been in the hospital as a child. I had heard the same sounds of children playing and I longed to be out of my room, outside with everyone else. Maybe one day I would be.

The doctor brought me back to the present. "This is a lovely dream to begin our journey," he said. "I'll see you on Friday."

42

I was back in Jerry's office paying bills, ordering supplies, filing and occasionally going out on a job with him. I worked until 1:00 and then I'd go a couple of blocks down Central Park West to the YMCA where I would lift weights to follow my quest of being a jock. A hunky body had become a necessity for actors. Marlon Brando had erased the sensitive image that some male stars made popular in the thirties and forties, when he appeared in his torn shirt in *A Streetcar Named Desire*.

Actors could still be somewhat poetic, but muscles were in. I huffed and puffed and started to look like I could "blow the house down." The same guys were at the gym most of the time and we all encouraged each other: "Come on, do five more, you can make it; come on, only three more – you did it; you're looking great!" It was a tough but fun hour or so and then I 'd go home. I now went twice a week at 8:30 in the morning to the analyst. On those days, I had to be up so early that, after my workout, I went home and slept for an hour. There were still classes with Sandy Meisner, but they were late in the afternoon. Everything, except the doctor, was pushed to the side if I got a play or a television, and I did get one of them a few weeks before Christmas.

Clarence Derwent was a Broadway figure, mainly because he had established the Derwent Award. It was given to the most promising young actor and actress each year. Derwent was an actor of the old school, born in England in the 1880's. He had a few small roles in plays, but he was a bit of a ham. That, and his juicy British accent limited his work, but he seemed to have money from some other source. He had always longed to play Shylock in *The Merchant of Venice* and he finally decided to bankroll his own production. He hired a theater and got Iza Itkin to direct. She had directed me in *The Infernal Machine* and *Angel Street* so it was no surprise when she asked me to play Bassanio. I would be opposite Lesley Woods as Portia. She had been Jocasta when I was Oedipus. It was to be a limited engagement meaning that no one thought it would draw audiences, but maybe enough friends for a few weeks.

Rehearsals were pleasant enough and Mr. Derwent acted in a style I had only heard on recordings of 19th century actors. Iza didn't help much because she wasn't able to bring him into the 20th century. As a result, none of us knew what style to use to keep Clarence from looking ridiculous. It seemed that in my role, I had to keep coming on stage with several of my buddies, for no apparent reason. There was no indication in the text where we were coming from or what we were doing there. We couldn't find any motivation. We resorted to "enter laughing" – a cliche in Shakespearean productions. I never knew what we were laughing at but we had to get onstage somehow. The costume designer suggested that, since Shylock was dark and Bassanio was of a different faith, I should be blond. I wasn't about to have my hair stripped for a couple of weeks work. So they used a blond spray on my hair every night. It looked like shellac and gave me, I thought, a phony look.

Between Clarence's singing the lines, Lesley's slightly pouty lips as she did "The quality of mercy" speech, my fake hair and the actors constantly laughing for no reason that the audience could see, *The Merchant of Venice* was not a high point of the New York season. At least I was able to act again, a little later, in an excellent production when I did *The Story of Mary Surratt* on television. I was one of the followers of John Wilkes Booth in his plot to kill Lincoln. It, unlike *Merchant,* was a success.

There were two gifts of the new year. The Theater Guild, one of the top producing companies in the theater, was building a huge Shakespeare theater in Stratford, Connecticut. In order to assemble a company to be in the new theater, they opened a workshop in New

York to train actors to become more familiar with the technique of acting in Shakespeare's plays. I was chosen to be one of the actors, from an audition, and after several months of courses, we would all audition again to see if we could be in the actual company. I was excited by the whole project, and I went to the first session with high hopes.

As I walked through the door of a huge rehearsal space with about 30 folding chairs set up, I got my second gift: I saw Mary. I knew her play had closed, but I hadn't run into her at Joe Allen's, where actors hung out, or the Five Oaks Restaurant in the Village, a place we had often gone to when we were together. I had missed Mary, and a part of my life had been taken away when she stopped seeing me. Despite my proclivity for sex with men, I had genuinely loved Mary and had thought we would stay together forever. I looked at her across the room and saw that she was looking at me as well. When she didn't turn away, I felt myself being pulled toward her.

When I stood in front of her the first thing that came out of my mouth was, "You look beautiful."

"Thank you," she said. I didn't know if she was saying it as if I were a fan praising her appearance or what.

"This is silly," I said, "are we going to go on avoiding each other, or can we, at least, be friends again?"

"Which would you prefer?" she asked without a trace of warmth or even recognition.

"You sound like my first analyst who always answered my question with a question."

"You have a second analyst?" Mary replied.

"Yes," I said, "and I'm deep into it, twice a week, but I'm about to go on to three. I know I gave you a bad time, but I'm really making progress. I'd like to see you again. I've missed you a lot. Are you with someone?" I said with some trepidation.

"No," she replied.

As we both stood without saying anything for a moment, we were suddenly surrounded by the activity and noise of dozens of actors arriving and plunking themselves down on the noisy wooden chairs. I saw that Mary's cheeks were getting flushed. Her skin was very white and it only got that way when emotion was taking hold of her, usually when sex was in the offing.

"I have to sit down," she said almost in a whisper.

"May I sit with you?" I asked.

I could barely hear her say "Yes."

The class was called to order and a young man from The Theater Guild welcomed us all and introduced our first speaker, a famous British character actress named Cathleen Nesbitt. She was very beautiful, around 70, with a cloud of gray hair, wonderful heavy-lidded eyes and meticulous speech. She told us that her acting teacher, when she was young, had trained her to concentrate on the consonants, not the vowels. That must have been the reason for the perfect clipped sound of the words as she uttered them. I could feel the admiration, this refined, elegant woman, created among the actors. I could see, in her, what Mary would be like when she was old. Miss Nesbitt spoke briefly of her long career and even about the poet Rupert Brook who had been in love with her. But then she got down to the business of the day – what could she tell us about acting in Shakespeare.

"What I do," she said, "is to take a speech, like Juliet's famous speech on the balcony, and write it down on a piece of paper. Then I get a box of crayons. I choose a color to go under every line. For example, let's say I underline 'Romeo, Romeo, wherefore art thou, Romeo?' with a blue crayon because Juliet is blue at not being with Romeo. The next line she is demanding when she says, 'Deny thy father and refuse your name,' So I underline that with a red crayon. And so on through the whole speech. When I've finished, I look at the paper. 'Oh,' I say, 'there's too much blue, not enough red and no green at all.' So I go back until all the colors are pretty much equal. Then, vocally I can match the colors and I won't be monotonous."

I looked at Mary and we almost broke each other up. It was so ridiculous, so totally opposed to the acting we were doing now. Our technique was based on the truth of taking something imaginary and making it real, using our own emotions and our own life experience.

I whispered to Mary, "That's almost like Estelle Winwood. She told me she created her role in *Madwoman* on a piano, playing different notes for each line, so all the lines have different melodies when she speaks them. It's crazy."

Though we were seated separately, I could almost feel Mary's body against mine and I sensed that she was having the same experience. "Want to go to the Five Oaks after class?" I asked her.

"I have to go back to the apartment first," she answered. "But I can meet you there at 7:00."

43

"Julius Caesar"

It was finally the opening night of the Shakespeare Theater in Connecticut, but nothing was ready. The building wasn't quite finished, the acoustics weren't fully adjusted, and there was something wrong with the drainage on the floor where the dressing rooms were. We all had long cloaks that we scooped up, like brides carrying their trains, to try and keep them out of the puddles of muddy water, but they still got wet. We'd had weeks of rehearsals, but technically we were still unprepared. The stage was always being worked on, either when they were installing the lighting or erecting the complicated platforms that would become part of the scenery. Most of the time we rehearsed in a huge room without even the props we would need to use. The day before the opening, there wasn't even time for a full dress rehearsal. We kept stopping to fix the lighting, or to find a prop, or a stool that someone had to sit on, that was missing.

The audience was filing in to an attractive, finished auditorium while backstage was pandemonium. Most of us played several roles in *Julius Caesar*, the opening play, so we were busy checking out our different costumes, making up, trying to keep our costume dry on our way to and from the john and hoping to avoid the movie star who was playing Cassius, Jack Palance, and his pregnant wife Ginny who were fighting as usual. Fortunately, he was not being aggressive toward her which we sometimes had to witness. He'd been a 6'4" boxer and his temper was monumental, so we were all afraid to interfere. It did create a pall on the already gloomy unfinished cement basement where we all had to spend so much time.

I was glad Mary wasn't going to see what I was sure would be less than great. She had gotten her first movie in Hollywood opposite Bing Crosby. We had grown even closer together and she kept saying she didn't want to leave me. Of course, she couldn't give up such an opportunity and besides, I had already accepted the Stratford offer. We'd make it up when she returned. We didn't speak of it, but I think my going back into analysis made her think I would eventually lose any desire for men. I thought so too, but when I told the analyst Mary and I were together again, he didn't shout for joy. He acted as if I had just said the rain outside had stopped. He had no reaction whatsoever. *All right*, I thought, *Just you wait. I'll show you how I've changed!*

The actors had all been told that many important theater people had come up from New York to celebrate the opening of the new theater., Lawrence Langner, the head of The Theater Guild, and Lincoln Kirstein, a philanthropist, had both spearheaded the project and their friends, the cream of New York cultural life, were all coming. The Mayor of Stratford England had flown over along with a coterie of Shakespeare aficionados. The governor was supposed to come with the big politicos of Connecticut. Because the cast also included more movie stars like Raymond Massey – James Dean's father in *East of Eden*; Hurd

Hatfied – the star of *The Picture of Dorian Gray*; and Roddy McDowell – the boy in *How Green Was My Valley*; the press was out in force. It was like a Broadway opening with people running up and down the aisles greeting friends.

Since I was in the opening scene as one of the Tribunes, I was onstage waiting for the curtain to go up. I could hear the din of what sounded like a full house. As I went over my speech in my head, I tried not to think of how the great comedian Imogene Coca, who'd become a friend, had grabbed my script one day and read my opening speech hilariously. It was supposed to be an angry warning to the crowd. I worked myself into a lather so I could really bawl them out. I paced up and down in my magnificent black Elizabethan costume until the stage manager waved me to get into position. The curtain went up to the applause that the set usually got at the opening of a play. Our scene went well and I went back to my dressing room to change clothes for my next role, Cinna the Poet.

As I got ready, the actors I got dressed with came down from playing their scenes. They reported that the audience was just sitting there as if they were in a stupor. I wasn't too surprised. The director, who had been brought over from the Old Vic, had been disappointingly old-fashioned, and just told the actors where to stand and when to move. It was like Marla Forbes, in my first job in summer stock, reading the directions out of a Samuel French copy of the play. The result was a stodgy uninteresting version of a play most people had been subjected to either in high school or in seeing second rate touring productions.

When I was dressed, I went up with some of the actors to hear the speeches that were going to be made in the intermission. The best one was the Mayor of Stratford, England. We couldn't see him because he was on the other side of the curtain, but we heard him say, as he faced the audience, "I wish all of you could be where I am now and see what I'm seeing – that's where the real show is tonight." I'm sure he meant the construction of the theater, but we had to laugh. It sounded like his was telling how bad he thought the show was.

It was getting to be time for my scene. The role had been made famous by Norman Lloyd in the Orson Welles production. It only lasted for a few minutes. Cinna was a poet with the same name as one of the conspirators. When men from the mob heard my name Cinna, they didn't believe that I was the poet and killed me. I hated my costume. It was all pink and green and made me look like a kid going to a costume party on Valentine's Day. I wasn't a star who could have insisted the costume be changed, so I just put up with it. But I was sure it presented the wrong picture of the character.

The scene went perfectly. I was appropriately hysterical and literally bruised when I was forced down, trampled upon and left for dead. There was a solid applause and I went back to my dressing room to get ready for my last role as Brutus' soldier who will help him to die at the end of the play. Several of my roommates had watched my scene from the wings and followed me down, telling me how moving it was. I was quite shaken by it and relaxed in front of my makeup place and slowly started to change clothes. I demurred as they praised me and said I felt I could have been better.

I was stripped down to my jockey shorts when I heard a scream: "Shayne, Shayne, where are you? You're on!" I jumped up and started to run but I stopped short. I was practically in the nude. How could I go onstage? I grabbed a robe and ran up to the stage. The scene I should have been in was just starting. Brutus was to tell two soldiers to sleep near him in his tent. He then would go to sleep, have a dream about Caesar, who he had killed, and wake up the soldiers to ask if they had seen anything. I stood mesmerized in the wings watching what I was sure was a terrible accident about to happen. Raymond Massey was an older man. He had not grown up in The Method where an actor's eyes were glued to the other actor's eyes so that they could get signals from each other. Massey often didn't look at the other actors at all for fear they would distract him.

As he summoned the two soldiers, he said. "Both of you, sleep in my tent." I wasn't there and the other soldier was a walk-on from the town who had no lines. He walked in alone and lay down on the floor. Massey didn't notice that one soldier was missing. He went to bed, had his dream, got up, terrified, woke the soldiers who again he didn't realize were only one, and said, "Did you see anything?" The poor walk-on didn't have any lines so he just stood there. Then Massey turned to the space where I was supposed to be and said, "Did you see anything." He waited for an answer and when nothing happened, he turned and went over to a stool and sat down. This was the worst moment of all. The stool broke and Massey tumbled to the floor as the blackout signaled the end of the scene.

I apologized vociferously to the stage manager, but he said it wasn't my fault. Since we never had a dress rehearsal it was impossible to gauge how long we had between our roles to change costumes. He said it was the management's fault for not giving us the time to be ready for the opening. I went back, finished putting on the soldier's uniform and returned to play the scene where Brutus asks me to help him commit suicide. When I stood begging Massey not to die, I was really asking him to forgive me for ruining his scene. Tears came to my eyes and then he ran upon my sword and died.

After the curtain calls, Massey came over to me. I thought he was going to attack me, but instead he said, "You were so wonderful in that last scene. I was so moved at the way you looked at me – you really played the whole scene for me. Thank you."

Massey never did know what happened in that scene. In addition to not always looking at the other actor, he also must not always have read reviews. One critic said, the next day, that he was drunk.

44

With Fritz Weaver in "The Tempest"

The second play of the Stratford season fared better than *Julius Caesar. The Tempest* was a comedy and, by the time it opened, the theater was in much better shape. This time I was playing Sebastian, one of a pair of villains. The brilliant actor Fritz Weaver played the other one. In the play, we had been shipwrecked on an island in the West Indies. I had the idea that my character would hate the tropics as well as the heat. I found a fake palm frond, among the things that had been left over when they built the set, and I used it to fan myself constantly. Looking back, I'm surprised that Fritz didn't knock it out of my hand. It must have seemed like Martita Hunt or Estelle Winwood waving a handkerchief or fiddling with beads to get the audience's attention. Fritz was too good an actor to let it bother him, and he must have known I was trying to flesh out my character, not do a stunt.

Stratford was a small city with nothing much to do after we finished a show. We formed a small group of friends who met in one or another of our rooms, mostly in rooming houses, and drank and ate something we got from a delicatessen. One of the gang was Leora Dana, who I had played opposite in *Madwoman*. She'd been making movies but had a hiatus and wanted to try her hand at Shakespeare.

We all soon discovered that Leora was on the road to being an alcoholic. As she got drunk, she would become amorous. She would try to make love to anyone who was on her left side, when she was sitting on a sofa. It didn't matter if it was a man or a woman, but it was never anyone on her right side. When we realized this, we all made a beeline to sit on her right side and to keep any newcomer from sitting on her left. Leora had recently married the actor Kurt Kazner, so we protected her from doing something she wouldn't even remember the next day. When she was sober, she was not only a fascinating actress, but tremendously appealing and great fun.

Leora's husband arrived to spend some time with her on one of the hottest days in July on record. Kurt was tall, overweight and hardly a matinee idol, but he was a wonderful character actor with all the charm of his native Austria. I had known him since his Broadway debut in *The Happy Time* when he played a slightly tipsy, lovable uncle. It catapulted him to Hollywood and movie after movie. He was an odd choice for Leora to have made. They seemed so totally unsuited to each other – he, blustering and outgoing and she, shy and withdrawn. Leora did tell me, however, that Kurt had given her a trip as a wedding present but he wouldn't tell her where they were going. He just told her what clothes to take, and to update her passport. Not until they were in the plane, holding a glass of champagne, did she find out their destination. The flight attendant announced the time they would be landing in Vienna. I thought it was the most romantic gift imaginable, and I understood how Kurt had won her.

Kurt was much older than I was, but whenever we met, he was very friendly. He always found something to tease me about, but it was always done in good humor. Several days after Kurt arrived, I saw him driving Leora's convertible as I was walking to a brush-up rehearsal at the theater. I was surprised when he pulled up and parked beside me.

He didn't wait to even say hello before he started what I was sure would be one of his teasing games.

"You won't believe where we're going on Sunday," he said. It was our one day off. I knew he was up to something, but I was determined not to let him get to me.

"Oh," I replied. "you must be going in to New York to enjoy the empty city and all the heat."

"Not funny," Kurt said. "No, we're going to Oyster Bay to see the two most important men in motion pictures – Arthur Loew Senior and Nick Schenck. I'm sure you've never even heard of them."

"As a matter of fact," I said, "I haven't. What movies have they been in?"

"Don't be stupid," Kurt replied with a slight shake of his head, "Arthur Loew just took over the presidency of MGM from Nick Schenck and now Nick's the chairman. They practically control Hollywood. I'm taking Leora over to meet them."

"Oh," I said, "that's great."

So many times I'd listened to Kurt and Leora talk about being in movies and the money and prestige it had brought them. They knew I'd been offered a stock contract at Universal by a movie scout who saw me in summer stick, but that I had turned it down. I opted instead to be a serious actor. I'd actually been sorry ever since. The movie actors often got the best parts on Broadway. I figured Kurt was up to something, but the thought of two movie moguls made me let down my guard.

"Leora and I know how much you'd like to be in movies," Kurt went on, "so we thought we could take you with us and introduce you to them both. Unfortunately, Arthur Loew's son who's picking us up – by the way, he's a big movie producer himself – said there just wasn't enough room on the yacht. We wanted it to be a big surprise, but it just didn't work out."

I was in shock. Suddenly any thought of Kurt putting me on went out of my head. "Kurt," I said, "I'd take up so little space on the boat."

"I told him that," Kurt interrupted, "but he seemed to want just Leora and me. I couldn't get him to change his mind. I'm sorry. It would have been a great opportunity for you. Anyway, I wanted to tell you that we tried."

"Well, thanks," I said trying not to look like one of the neediest cases in The New York Times Christmas issue. "That was very nice of you." We said we'd see each other later and Kurt zoomed off, leaving me with the feeling that I'd just discovered that I was one number off from winning the billion-dollar jackpot.

I wondered if Kurt was making it all up just to tease me. Who were these tycoons he was talking about? I decided to go to the library and find out if they were for real. I couldn't believe what I read about them. This Arthur Loew, who Kurt had mentioned, was the son of Marcus Loew who had practically created Hollywood. He had immigrated to the United States with his brother when they were kids. They worked hard at a variety of jobs and saved their money and invested it, until they had enough to start acquiring nickelodeons and eventually theaters. Marcus decided he would have to fill his theaters, so he began acquiring small production companies. He finally bought MGM, the home of Clark Gable, Katharine Hepburn, Judy Garland, and practically every big star in the movies.

The Loew's chain of theaters became the most important in the country. Along the way, Marcus got to know and trust Nick Schenck. When Marcus died suddenly, it was discovered that he left the business in Nick's hands.

Nick stayed in New York where the money was, but he kept a tight fist on the production schedules of the MGM movies. He was, at MGM's height, the eighth richest man in the United States. Arthur Loew, Marcus's son, was close behind him and now had taken on the reins as Schenck was getting older and wanted to do less. They both continued to live in mansions on the north shore of Long Island, where Kurt had said that he and Leora were going to visit them.

For the next few days, I buried my pride and begged Leora and Kurt to somehow get Arthur Loew Junior to take me along on his yacht. I was so convinced that if the movie moguls could just see me, they'd realize that I had the potential to be a star. Kurt kept repeating that he had asked Arthur several more times but the answer was, "He's sailing the boat by himself, and he just can't take anyone else." I gave up.

Saturday, the day before Kurt and Leora were to go to Oyster Bay, Kurt walked Leora to the theater for the matinee and came into my dressing room. "I've had an idea," he said, "we can't take you on the trip tomorrow, but why don't you come down to the dock to see us off. That way you'll at least meet Arthur Junior. He's making a lot of movies now, and I think it might do you good just to meet him."

"Gee thanks, Kurt," I said, "it would be fun for me just to see the two of you take off. Just tell be where to go."

"It's very early in the morning," Kurt replied, "but be sure to dress up to make a good impression."

The next day was beautiful, sunny and hot but with a cooling breeze that made it seem more like June than July. I dressed very carefully and managed to get my hair to stay in place for a change. I had listened to what Kurt had said and tried to look as good as I could, as if I were going for an interview at the studio. I didn't have any illusions, though. I figured, at best, it would be a very quick meeting.

I found the right number on the pier and, although it was just 10:00, Kurt and Leora were already on the boat that looked more like a big sailboat than a yacht. They waved at me wildly as I approached and I was able to step right onto the boat and hug them both. I saw a good-looking man, in his early thirties, with dark circles under his eyes, at the other end of the boat. He was undoing ropes.

"Arthur," Kurt yelled, "this is Alan."

Arthur shouted hello, but he didn't even look in my direction. I figured he'd come over to us when he was finished. The three of us talked for a few minutes about last night's show of *The Tempest* that Kurt had seen for the first time. I was delighted that my constant fanning with the palm frond had made him laugh. I noticed Arthur go down below and suddenly I heard the sound of a motor starting. Arthur's head appeared, from an opening in the deck, like a jack-in-the box.

He shouted, "Alan will have to get off now. We're ready to go." Then he disappeared again. "I'm so sorry,' Kurt said as he and Leora steered me over to get back onto the pier, "I thought you'd have some time with Arthur, but the guy who usually helps him is sick, so he's short-handed."

"Oh, that's OK," I said, covering as much as I could my disappointment.

"At least he knows your name now," Kurt said.

"It was fun to just come and see you off," I replied putting a good face on it. I kissed Leora on the cheek and stepped onto the pier. The motor got louder and the boat started to heave. I held up my hand to be ready to wave them goodbye.

Suddenly Kurt grabbed my hand and yanked me on board as the boat left the pier. I opened my mouth instinctively and yelled, "Wait!"

"You idiot," Kurt said, "of course you're coming with us."

It had all been one of Kurt's practical jokes, games that he was constantly thinking up. He had played his hand brilliantly. I was suckered in from the beginning. The three of us laughed and giggled as Kurt recounted all the details of his triumph. I couldn't stop thanking Kurt and Leora. What luck. I was going to meet the two moguls after all.

The day was getting hotter so the three of us sat under a shaded section of the boat to escape the sun. Arthur was busy steering so I never got to talk to him, but my thoughts were all on Arthur Loew Senior and Nick Schenck. I was actually going to meet them. Kurt said we were going first to the Loew house for lunch, and then we'd pay our respects to Mr. Schenck before returning to Stratford. We were on our way to Glen Cove and Pembroke, the 30-room mansion that Arthur Senior owned.

When we arrived, there were two men waiting to help us dock and a car to take us to the house that was quite a distance away. We passed endless formal gardens and finally arrived at a mansion that looked like one of the great English houses I'd seen in books. There were columns and pools and fountains. It was breathtaking. Waiting in front of the huge entrance was Arthur's father, pleasant looking in his late fifties but already balding. He embraced his son, and shook hands with Kurt, Leora and me. He then took us inside to give us a tour of the house. I was stunned: grottos, caves, a shooting gallery, an indoor tennis court as well as an indoor mosaic lined swimming pool. He only showed us part of the estate or we'd have been there all day.

We went to lunch in a huge dining room filled with flowers and plants. There was an enormous table where the father and son sat together at one end and the three of us at the other. They talked together in low tones that we couldn't quite hear. They didn't ignore us purposely. It just seemed like they had things to talk about that couldn't wait.

Kurt had told me that Mrs. Loew would not be joining us. She was Loew's third wife and Kurt had heard that she and her husband had spent 20 years having dinner together although they never spoke to each other. There were endless courses served by several waiters and then we got up to return to the boat. There wasn't really a chance for me to impress Mr. Loew with my potential for being a movie star, but he was very pleasant to me and said how nice it was to meet me. At least, I thought, he might remember my name if it came up at a casting session. So maybe it wasn't a total loss.

The trip to Sands Point, where Nick Schenck lived, took about a half hour. We crossed what looked like a bay and then went around wooded land that was surrounded on three sides by the water. We passed enormous estates and finally pulled up at a huge dock. The house looked as staggeringly impressive as Arthur Loew's had. But this time there was no tour. A servant took us right to an Olympic-sized outdoor pool with a shaded terrace, a row of cabanas, and at least a dozen small white tables, each one with four folding chairs. Some of the tables were covered with dirty dishes as if a small party had just taken place. Sitting all alone in the blazing sun, at one of the tables, was a little old man in his seventies reading the Sunday *New York Times*.

He looked up as he heard us approaching and smiled as he said with a Russian accent, "Hello, Arthur. I've been vaiting for you." Arthur quickly introduced us to Mr. Schenck for, no surprise to us, that's who it was.

"Please forgive us," Arthur said, "we have some private things to go over, and then I have to go in and call the coast." He turned to Kurt and Leora, "Why don't you sit over there in the shade and rest." Then he turned to me. "Alan, feel free to use the pool." He had lent me one of his bathing suits on the way over. "You can use any of the cabanas to change." He sat down with Mr. Schenck and Leora, Kurt and I walked over to the far side of the pool.

I suddenly had a brainstorm. I had been working hard at the gym and was in rather good shape. I would strip down, put on the swimsuit and swim in the pool. I would show the old man how ready I was to be in the movies. I changed quickly and then stepped out to the side of the pool nearest the two men's table. I stretched for a minute or two, showing as many muscles as I could summon up, and then I dove into the water. I became a younger, more vital Ricardo Montalban, swimming in a movie with Esther Williams. I had had a swimming teacher who kept telling me to smile when I swam to make it look effortless.

I smiled incessantly and swam back and forth like a champion. I would look at the men as I came up to breathe, but they didn't seem to be even looking in my direction. I did notice Arthur get up and leave and the old man hide behind his newspaper again. Finally, I gave up and climbed out of the pool. As I stood drying off with one of the towels stacked on a table, I saw Schenck put down his paper beside the dirty dishes on his table and get up with some difficulty.

He looked around toward Leora and Kurt and said, "Vell, I tink I'll clean up."

My mother had always trained me to help clear the table at relative's dinners, and I saw my opportunity at last to make an impression on the old man. I threw down my towel and walked over to him, my tanned body shining, still wet from the pool. I was every movie idol in the history of film.

"Can I help you?" I asked in my deepest baritone.

Mr. Schenck seemed stopped in his tracks. He turned and looked at me for the first time. He examined my face and then my body from top to bottom. He didn't speak for a moment and then he said, "You a barber?"

I was speechless as he continued to look me over. Then he turned away as if he'd decided I wasn't a barber and went into the house. As soon as he disappeared, Kurt and Leora let go of the laughter they'd been holding back. They screamed, "You a barber?" And I found myself laughing too. I never blamed Leora for telling everyone the story. It was too good to keep quiet. For the next month, until the season was over, actors would come up to me and say, "You a barber?"

So much for my Hollywood dreams.

45

Fall was particularly beautiful. New York was at its best and Mary and I were the happiest we had been. Mary's movie hadn't done much for her career. Hollywood seemed to have taken away all her special quality. They made her up like everybody else and succeeded in making her look like everybody else. She seemed rather staid in the movie and not terribly appealing. Part of the problem was playing the role of Bing Crosby's ex-wife. His girlfriend in the movie, played by Inger Stevens, had the sexier and more appealing part. Mary's acting, as always, was impeccable and she got good reviews, but the studios weren't clamoring for her.

Mary didn't care. Her heart was in New York where she was now considered one of the leading young actresses. I was feeling good about the Stratford experience and felt I was becoming known as a talented actor. I immediately got the lead in a staged reading of Dos Passos' *U.S.A.* for Lucille Lortel at her well-known White Barn Theater. I felt it was just a matter of time before I found a Broadway play.

I had saved money from the summer and I was back at work in Jerry's office. I had also begun to take photographs myself on the European trip with Jerry. One of them, a wheat field partially buried in the fog, won me a prize in a contest of a Pentax camera. I started to take pictures of actors for a fee. So for once, I wasn't as worried about money. My analysis continued with good days and bad ones. It looked like it was not going to be over for some time.

Mary and Gaby had become friends. Gaby was going with a successful songwriter, Jerry Leiber, who had written "Hound Dog" as well as many other hits. We double-dated occasionally. Sometimes we'd drive out to the country in Jerry's car and stay at an inn. We got along well and laughed at Gaby's antics that never stopped surprising us. Jerry thought Gaby was like Lady Brett in *The Sun Also Rises*. Gaby certainly had the charism and beauty that men went after, but her humor and take on life were unique. Her father was a well-known art dealer and Gaby had inherited his love of art. Her best friend was Helen Frankenthaler who became an important artist. Jerry and Gaby were an odd couple, but they finally married and managed to stay together for many years.

My parents had told me, in a phone conversation, that they were going to spend a couple of days on Cape Cod. Mary's mother, who they had never met, had moved to a cottage in Chatham near where they were going to stay. I said to Mary, "Why don't we stay with your mother when my parents are there? We can have a drink together and they can finally meet." Mary thought it was a great idea. My parents had met Mary and liked her enormously, as everyone did, but they didn't know Mary's mother. I knew she wasn't too keen about me, but she knew we were getting serious and there wasn't much she could do about it.

The weekend came for the event. Mary and I flew down and hired a car at the airport in Hyannis. Mary's mother had bought a Cape Cod cottage and, since her husband's death, had lived in it full time. It was charming, if a bit cliché: flowered wallpaper, lamps made out of old lanterns, rag rugs on the wooden floors and even a figure of a sea captain as a door knocker.

She'd bought a cake and made sandwiches for a late tea. The sherry bottle was waiting on a silver platter with the makings of martinis. The weather was cold but clear, and I had lit a fire in the living room. Mary's mother fussed over everything, pulling the draperies to the right spot so you could see what was left of the summer garden and picking a few dead petals off the roses she'd gotten at the market.

The doorbell rang and my parents arrived bringing a chill in with them. I didn't think the older people would become friends. I just hoped they would get along. Mary's mother was very welcoming and my parents shed their overcoats. My mother kissed Mary on the cheek, and Mary gave her a hug. We all went into the living room and sat around the fire. Everyone opted for sherry so I poured it. We were about to toast before the first sip when I stopped everybody.

"I just want to say something first," I said. I pulled out a small box I'd been concealing in my pants pocket. I held it out to Mary and got down on one knee in front of her. "Mary," I said, "will you marry me?"

Mary made a sound like a gasp and then put one hand under her breasts as if she were holding herself together. Then she let out a breath, took the box and slowly unwrapped it. She discovered a ring she had loved that we had seen in a jewelry store when we were window shopping. She set the box down on the coffee table, took the ring out and cupped it in her clasped hands.

She brought the hands to her lips and said, starting to cry, "Yes, I will."

I put my arms around her and looked straight into her eyes. "I love you," I said. I could hear the two women sniffling into their handkerchiefs.

46

With Mary

I had no idea that my mother had been holding her breath, hoping I would marry Mary. Now the flood gates were open and mother was sailing through life on a boat called "Fame." Her daughter-in-law to be had not only played the lead in a successful Broadway play, but she had also been in a movie opposite Bing Crosby. The telephone lines were sizzling in Brookline, Massachusetts as Mother lorded it over the women who had always treated her like a poor relation.

Looking back, I think Mary had the success my mother dreamed of having when she studied to be an opera singer. Now she had a small piece of Mary's success and she set about exploiting it. Engagement announcements were sent out, and she arranged parties for Mary, who happily agreed to take the train from New York to Back Bay where my father would pick her up. I, fortunately, got a job in an Omnibus TV show about the Constitution, so I was able to avoid most of the ladies' lunches.

Mary got presents of everything she didn't need, from monogramed hand towels to his and hers napkin rings. I did go up for one dinner my rich uncle and aunt gave. They had always looked down on my parents and me, but celebrity had taken hold of them too. Mary told me later that my uncle had put a not too subtle make on her. "I would like to show you some of the buildings I have designed," he said. She replied, charmingly, that she would have loved it, but she had to get back to New York. Several years later my aunt discovered my uncle had had a mistress most of the time they'd been married. She threw him out of the house and got all the money. So much for my relatives.

My parents and I were suddenly, much against my will, reconciled. I'd kept in touch with them all these years, but we hadn't been very close. Now Mary seemed to envision a happy family, for all of us, that I had left home to escape. My claustrophobic nightmares of suburban life came back, but I put them out of my head. I told myself that Mary and I would be different – we would be a theater couple with friends in the arts and politics, nothing like the suburban street with the kids on bicycles that had haunted me when I was with Eleanor. Mary acted as if she enjoyed the bridge parties and teas, but she was a superb actress. I knew that she couldn't possibly like that kind of dreary life. Did she really think my father's insurance salesman jokes were funny? She laughed her head off. I decided not to bring it up with her.

Spring was approaching, and it was as if all the jobs had dried up. The phone never rang with an audition or an availability for a television show. I finally did get a call from my teacher and friend Bobby Lewis who was producing and directing a new play and asked me to audition. It was called *Mister Johnson* and was about a Nigerian native and a British officer who have a wonderful friendship that ends tragically. Bobby told me later he was really having me audition for the understudy since an actor had already been hired in England. He wanted to have Cheryl Crawford, his co-producer, see me, and she approved of my being hired. She was one of the founders of the Group Theater and a monumental figure on Broadway. It was a feather in my cap that she now had seen me act.

I remembered an anecdote about her that I had heard. Several people were waiting outside her office to see her when the costume designer Miles White came out, shut the door, and fanned the air in front of his face with his hand. "Oh," he groaned, "the cigar smoke."

Bobby knew I needed work so they also offered me the job of assistant stage manager. I could make a little extra money. I hadn't worked as a stage manager since the USO, and I had never understudied in a play. It was a cut below what I thought I should be doing, but I thanked Bobby and said, "When do I start?" Though Mary and I would often go dutch, I needed more money now that we were making plans together.

I was made even happier that I'd taken the job when Gaby called and said she was going to be in *Mister Johnson* with a "delicious" role. She would play the British officer's wife who held on to her British demeanor even though she was in the middle of Africa. There was a hilarious scene where Gaby, dressed as if she were going to tea at the Ritz and holding a pretty umbrella to shade her from the sun, went to call on the native's wife, played by Josephine Premice, who was dressed in practically nothing. One of the high points was when the native woman said she wouldn't let her husband near her because she was pregnant and it would "spoil me milk." It was the perfect East meets West con- trast and, when the play opened, the two women played it to the hilt. If only the rest of the play had been as entertaining. It made a political statement that only a few wanted to hear. It closed in a few weeks.

Again, it was too late in the season to find any meaningful work in summer stock. The good roles were in plays with big stars that toured the leading summer theaters, but they were already filled. So I was back working for Jerry and struggling through analysis, except for the "crazy" month of August when all the doctors were on vacation or seeing their own analysts. Mary and I played house, cooked, went to Coney Island, had rather dreary times with her mother in Chatham and saw friends.

Billy Nichols had bought a rather grand apartment overlooking Central Park and gave lively parties for jazz musicians that we went to. It was 2:00 or 3:00 in the morning before we got home and his parties were still going on. Mary's friends were a little more staid. They had kids who mustn't be wakened. Most of them were actors or directors, but the laughs weren't as loud or as often as at Billy's and Gaby's and at my other friends' homes.

Mary and I seemed to have settled down but, oddly enough, neither one of us brought up the subject of when the wedding would take place. It was as if we were already married and had been for a long time.

47

Over the holidays, Mary had to go to parties without me since I was busy working. Bobby Lewis was directing another play, *The Hidden River*, and again had given me a job. I was understudying and assistant stage-managing as I had in *Mister Johnson*. We weren't going out of town before opening in New York, so I was able to continue with the analyst and still keep an eye on Jerry's office. The play, written by Ruth and Augustus Goetz, was to open the third week in January, so we were rehearsing in December, and after the usual four weeks, there would be previews to judge how an audience reacted to the play. Gaby was in the cast and so was Lili Darvas who I had known when we were together in Maurice Evans' *Hamlet*. It was a totally professional experience. The cast was perfect and everything fit together like a finely tuned clock. Lili and the other two stars, Robert Preston and Dennis King, played off each other beautifully.

The mystery, which was the basis of the play, was who was the collaborator that had killed the woman who owned the chateau's son during the war. Lili was playing the woman and her background made her ideal for the part. Lili had been the famous Austrian director Max Reinhardt's leading lady and a star in Germany and Hungary as well as in the United States. I loved to watch her act. There was a moment in the play when she had to burst into tears. No matter how many times the scene was rehearsed, Lili's tears always flowed at exactly the same time. I kept watching her, trying to find the key to how she was able to do this. Then one day, I saw plainly what I had been missing. Just before she cried out, she hit her foot sharply on the floor. It was her impetus, as if she gunned the motor of her car or jump started the dead battery. We had been nodding acquaintances during *Hamlet,* but now we were becoming good friends.

The sad part of *The Hidden River* was the opening night. Everything was going swimmingly until one of the best scenes where the two old people, Lili and Dennis King, rekindled the love they had once had for each other. King was 60 but seemed somewhat older. He not only forgot his lines but put the few he remembered out of sequence so no one could understand quite what was going on. Lili was beside herself and made stabs at getting Dennis back on track, but it only confused him more. He was playing an invalid so he got by with the audience, but Lili seemed ridiculous. It should have been the high point of the evening and a triumph for Lili, but it just lay there, looking like bad writing and worse acting.

Nevertheless, *The New York Times* review was excellent and all he actors were praised including Dennis and Lili. Still, audiences didn't seem to want to remember World War II and the French resistance. The play closed in three weeks. My second shot of being an understudy, but still not going on in the role I was prepared for.

***

It was June and I was on the way to the analyst. I was feeling rather pleased with myself. I had gotten a job to play the lead in a summer stock tour of *Anastasia* opposite the movie star Dolores del Rio. It was about to start rehearsal and I was set for the summer. But I was especially excited because I'd had a dream that I was sure meant that I was done with my analysis. I couldn't wait to tell the doctor.

I was lying down most of the time in my sessions, but I decided to sit up today since I was sure I was about to leave. "I'd like to start with a dream," I began.

"All right," the doctor said, "when you're ready."

I took a minute to settle myself and began to read. *I dreamed that I went out on the roof adjoining my apartment. It was a very shallow roof, only about four or five feet wide. It was high up and I was afraid, so I scrunched up against the wall as far away from the edge of the roof as I could be. The roof dropped right off – there was no fence or anything to protect you if you got too close. A woman came out onto the roof with a little boy. He was very tiny and dressed impeccably in a dark suit, shirt, and tie. He was a miniature man, very small, but still a boy of about 8. The woman watched as the boy walked right over to the edge of the roof and fell off. I panicked on the inside though I was cool on the outside. I couldn't go near where the boy had fallen off, because I had the feeling in my stomach that I get at extreme heights. But I realized that there was no point in my going near the spot, because the boy was already all the way down at the bottom of the building. So I acted as if I had nothing to do with what was going on.*

I must have leaned forward as I spoke, and now that I had finished, I sat back in the chair and waited for the doctor to speak. "What does the dream mean to you?" he asked. "Or does it mean anything?"

"Yes," I replied, "I think it's the most meaningful dream I've had yet. I'm obviously the little boy and the woman is my mother. She's made me into a buttoned-up figure of a man and controlled me to be what she wanted me to be. But I walked away from her, finally, and I killed the boy she wanted me to be. I got away from her. I am no longer afraid. I'm done with her and her attempts to control me. I'm not living her life anymore. I'm my own person." I waited for the doctor to speak, but when he didn't, I took a breath and said, "I think I'm through with my analysis." The doctor still didn't say anything. I suddenly wished I hadn't given up smoking.

Finally, the doctor stopped writing in his book and looked directly at me. "You remember when you first came to me, you asked me to describe what analysis was. I told you it was a voyage we'd take together, and we would come to some difficult islands that you wouldn't want to explore, so we would turn away from them. But hopefully, you would find the courage to go back and find out what it was that was there that you didn't want to face. This dream has a lot in it that we could take the time to decipher, but since this is our last session before the summer, I will tell you that you have reached an island, and rather than cope with it, you have decided that it is no part of you. You don't have to see what happened to the boy. You've killed him off. The height you're on is too risky so keep away from the edge. Why is the little boy so constricted in his tiny suit? Why isn't he playing with children his own age? Why does his mother want him to be a perfect little man? So many questions in this dream that we hope to find answers for. We're just beginning."

He stood up and put out his hand. "Good luck with your play and I'll see you in a few months."

48

With Dolores del Rio in "Anastasia"

We rehearsed *Anastasia* in New York, although we would be doing the play out of town in the Poconos, Cape Cod, and the Hamptons. I had been hired to play opposite Dolores del Rio although I was much younger than she. When I was born, she was already a star of silent movies and considered the most beautiful woman in Hollywood. The producer and the director suggested I grow a mustache and use a streak of gray in my hair to look older. I did both. Miss del Rio arrived the first day looking phenomenally beautiful. She was warm and totally charming to everyone. She had memorized her entire part along with gestures and emotions to match. As the days went by, neither direction or working with the other actors changed a syllable of what she had decided to do, either by herself or with a coach. It was rather like a performance by an amateur in the Junior League – good enough to get by for a performance when friends were full of food and drink, but to quote Noel Coward, "Don't put your daughter on the stage, Mrs. Worthington."

When it was time to laugh, she laughed. When it was time to cry, she cried. She couldn't have been more cooperative or more unassuming. She arrived on time and worked as long as the director required her to. She kept to herself and was friendly but didn't invite close contacts with anyone. Even when we played our first few theaters, we only saw Dolores (for that was what she asked us to call her) onstage during our scenes with her, or for a moment in the wings to say, "Good evening." We heard that she slept 16 hours a day which may have been responsible for her looking so young. She was in her early fifties, an advanced age at that time but certainly not today.

One early evening in the middle of the tour, the director had summoned the cast to go over a few points he felt we'd been missing. We had evidently gotten too comfortable in our performances. As we sat in the garden behind the theater waiting for him, Dolores appeared in a simple blouse and a full Mexican skirt. She sat down beside me in a chair that happened to be empty. She looked young enough to be a sacrifice in the sacred well at Chichen Itza. As often as I had seen her and worked with her, I was still mesmerized by her beauty. There was a sculptural look to her that made me think of old Mayan ruins and strange rites. She gave me a haunting look that seemed to hint that, perhaps, we could find solutions together to all the mysteries of life. I felt she was encouraging me, at last, to enter some undiscovered country with her. I decided to break through the protective armor that seemed to surround her.

"Dolores," I said, "tell me what you have been doing today."

"You don't want to know," she whispered.

"I do, I do," I insisted.

"Well," she replied in her soft, accented voice, and she took a few moments as if she were weighing some lofty thoughts. "I had the most perfect sleep. I didn't wake up until 5:00 this afternoon. Then I bathed and had my dinner. It was so wonderful: tiny little lamb chops, pink in the middle and slightly charred on the outside, and some pretty little green peas, and a baked potato." She hesitated for a moment, and then said, as if the emotion of what she was about to tell me was almost too much for her, "I had vanilla ice cream for dessert."

She gave me a dazzling smile, as if she had just correctly answered an impossible question on a major test at school. I smiled back, pushing my vision of *Green Mansions* and running through the jungle with Rima the bird girl, out of my head.

The tour was a pleasant respite from looking for work, depositing Jerry's money that poured in from *Sports Illustrated*, *Time*, and *Life*, and always haggling with Mary over whether a restaurant was too expensive or not, and deciding whose apartment we'd use to sleep over. Audiences seemed to enjoy the play, especially the scene when Lili Darvas, as the Dowager Empress, resists accepting Anastasia as the Russian princess.

Lili was amazing and managed to make Dolores look like she was really acting. Lili and I ate most of our meals together and I was fascinated by her stories: of her great love, who she got out of Germany, away from the Nazis, and who finally left her; and her husband, the great writer Ferentz Molnar whose play *Liliom* was turned into the musical *Carousel*. Though they lived separately, Molnar would not let Lili divorce him. He felt as long as they were married, he would never die. They met often for lunch and the arrangement worked well for both of them until, of course, he did die.

Lili and I were sometimes joined at dinner by the actress Clarice Blackburn who was superb in the play as a Russian peasant. When we got to Falmouth, where I had lived as a child, we discovered a very elaborate summer theater compound with a restaurant and a club. The three of us went to dinner there and were entertained by a handsome young man who played the piano and sang. He was in his mid-twenties, sophisticated with great charm and a real talent as a supper club performer. He had a pleasant sound that concentrated on the meaning of the song rather than in showing off his voice. Lili insisted that we buy him a drink and tell him how good he was. His name was Richard Harris and he joined us and turned out to be extremely bright and funny.

"What are you doing here?" Clarice asked.

He laughed, "It was something to do for the summer. I know the owner of the theater and he asked me if I wanted to spend some time on Cape Cod. I thought, why not? I'm a writer and I'll do anything to avoid writing."

As if it were planned, Richard did some songs and came back to sit with us. Then he did some more songs and came back to sit with us again. Before the evening was over, we had all become fast friends. In the days that followed the four of us were constantly together, swimming, taking rides into town and shopping and after the theater, we'd go to the club to listen to Richard. Day after day, we were never apart. I was startled when, toward the end of our second week in Falmouth, Lili held out her hands to show me some Tiffany cufflinks she was going to give Richard.

"Why?" I asked. "That's too much."

"Well, he's been so nice to all of us," she replied.

I had been fighting against my attraction for men all of my life, since I had discovered it at 15. Sometimes I won the battle, but more often than not, I didn't. It had become even harder for me to know whether I was winning or losing. Was I on the road that was taking me in the right direction? Or was I planning to marry Mary as just another adjustment I was making to assuage society? I talked about it constantly in analysis. The doctor never, of course, expressed an opinion, but it was clear that he didn't regard my sexual proclivity as a mental illness or a sickness that was the psychiatric conviction at the time. I pitied married men who had separate sex lives with other men, and I felt sorry for their wives. Was I about to become one of those men myself?

Richard was inevitable. He was very attractive and seemed attracted to me. After the four of us spent time together at the club, why wouldn't Richard drop into my room to say good night? It wasn't anything serious – just a romp. There had been others. I had always discussed them with the doctor, almost as if I were in a confessional. I would feel better after the session, no longer guilty but somehow lacking the booster a few Hail Marys might have given me. Richard was no better or worse than the others, but he was going to play a role in my life that neither of us anticipated.

One night, a director friend of Mary's, who was staying at the Playhouse Inn with his family, came by after the theater to have a drink in my room. We talked show business for an hour. I kept hoping he would leave, knowing that Richard would eventually turn up. The director didn't, but Richard did. I introduced them as if it were normal to have people drop into my room after midnight. The director, sensing something, must have decided to outstay Richard to protect Mary's interests, but Richard didn't budge. Finally, the director left with a good idea of what must have been going on. Unfortunately, the doctor wasn't around to hear my guilt and confusion.

Back in New York, after *Anastasia* finished its tour, Richard and I never saw each other. He had known I was engaged to Mary, and he had told me of his own relationship. We had enjoyed being with each other and neither of us felt like endangering what we called "our real life." But one day it did.

Richard called and said he was in the neighborhood and would like to drop by to say hello. While we were catching up on what each other had been doing, the bell rang. I looked at my watch. I'd lost track of the time. It was 5:00, the time Mary was due. It had to be her who rang the bell. She had always refused a key. I suddenly thought she would have heard about Richard from her director friend, and, if she saw him there, would have thought something was going on between us. I had to keep Mary from seeing Richard, but how? I wasn't going to hide him in a closet. I lived at the top of a four-story brownstone. There was only one narrow staircase. If Richard left now, he'd bump right into Mary coming up the stairs. Then I thought, there are two doors to my apartment, one at each end of the landing. I only used the one that opened into the bedroom. If I took Richard to the one in the living room and told him to wait until he heard me let Mary in at my door, then he could go out his door, cross the landing and go down the stairs with Mary never knowing he was there. It was something out of a French farce, but it might work.

Mary hadn't been feeling well lately and I was not about to upset her, especially since I was now going the straight and narrow. I got everything arranged and rang the buzzer to let Mary in. When I heard her at my door, I opened it and saw, over her shoulder, Richard standing at the other end of the landing. He must have thought he heard my door close. We all looked at each other. Richard, acting as if he had gotten lost, said "Good evening," crossed the landing and went down the stairs as if he didn't know who we were or where he was.

"Who was that?" Mary asked.

"I don't know," I said, "he must be here to see someone in the apartment below and just. walked up too far." Mary looked at me quizzically and then walked in and put her things down. She didn't say anything more about it and we had a pleasant evening. But it wasn't over yet.

Shortly after that, Mary had to have some tests done about a stomach disorder. She went into the hospital for a few days. The doctor wanted her to have a complete rest with no visitors. She asked me not to come to see her, but we could keep in touch through the nurse. I called often for reports and the nurse told me the tests were looking good and Mary was resting well. One time I called and a man answered. I assumed he was a doctor and he took my name and said he'd tell Mary I had called. When she was about to come out of the hospital I mentioned to an actor, we both knew, how happy I would be to see her again. He looked at me and his mouth opened, as if in amazement.

"Are you serious?" he asked.

"What do you mean?" I replied.

"You don't know?"

"Know what?" I said.

"I'm not going to be the one to tell you," he said.

"What are you talking about?" I demanded.

He then proceeded, with some relish, to tell me Mary had been seeing a lot of the actor James Congdon while I was on tour. I knew of him. He was very handsome and successful. I was in shock. How could she not have told me? That must account for her never visiting me during the summer, in any of the nearby theaters. She had said she was always too busy with a television she was doing or an audition that she had to go to. How stupid I'd been.

I telephoned Mary and got her answering machine. I left a long message. I said, "I know about Congdon and I would like to see you, to hear from you, not strangers, what is going on." I ended with, "At least, after five years, if you want to say goodbye, we should be able to do it in person. I promise not to upset you, but I need to at least plead my case or wish you well." It was several days before I heard back from her. It was a brief message on my answering machine that said, "Come to the house Tuesday at 4:00 if that's convenient."

Mary lived alone since Neva had married. The apartment was the same except that a woman let me in. She was in her fifties, a motherly figure who was obviously taking care of Mary. She led me up the stairs and showed me to Mary's room, as if I didn't know where it was. She opened the door and I saw Mary lying on a chaise where we had often made love. A blanket was over her feet though she was completely dressed. She looked wan and half asleep. She didn't say hello or look me in the eyes.

When the woman left us, I said, "Did they find out what was wrong with you?"

She then did look at me and said, "Isn't it funny? After all the tests of every part of me, they concluded I'd had a slight nervous breakdown."

"Oh, Mary, I'm so sorry."

"Don't be," she interrupted, "it's quite over and I'm just in the resting stage."

"I had no idea," I said, "maybe we should talk another day."

"No," she shook he head, "I've been dreading this, but I think it will probably make me feel better."

"I want you to know that I love you," I said.

"I know that and I've loved you," she said, "but I love someone else now."

I sat down on a chair near her. "Was it because a friend told you I was seeing someone and you saw that guy outside my apartment? Nothing was happening between us."

"No, I was injured by then."

"I didn't think you were upset," I said. "We made love that night."

"Yes," she said, "I wanted to see if I had any feeling left for you. I don't."

"But what happened?" I asked. "You were so supportive and so loving. And you knew I was in analysis and fighting my demons."

"Yes," she sighed, "but I couldn't wait any longer. I was exhausted. Suddenly James was there, strong, no longer struggling for the next role, confident, and a rock to lean against. He made me realize that I had an alternative. I didn't have to worry about competing in a game I couldn't win. I could have fought a woman you took up with, but I knew it was impossible for me to fight a man. I just didn't have the physical equipment."

Mary had never talked to me this way and I didn't know how to respond. At last, I got out, "But I was on the way –"

Mary cut in, "I don't mean this in a rude way, but I don't believe you'll ever get where you think you're going. Maybe that's all right. It's a part of you to be with men and that may finally give you the most happiness. We know men who are having great lives together. That may be the best thing for you. I just realized I couldn't marry you and worry each time you were late for dinner or off on a tour. Meeting James made me see the kind of life I wanted and could have. He loves me and wants to take care of me and it's not complicated. I'll always think back to the years we loved each other, but I've got to have a life I can count on. You can't give me that. James can."

Mary married James Congdon within the year and we never saw each other again. I also didn't see Richard, but I did run into him many years later. We decided to have a drink together. He had, by then, written quite a few fascinating travel books. After a second drink, he talked about our being together in Falmouth such a long time ago.

At one point, he smiled sheepishly. "Did you know," he asked, "that I was having sex with Lili Darvas when I wasn't with you?"

I suddenly remembered the expensive cufflinks in Lili's hands. We all had so many secrets. They no longer seemed important.

49

With Lennie Hayton and Lena Horne

I felt like the bottom had fallen out of my life. I guess I hadn't realized how much I had depended on Mary. Suddenly I was bereft, as if someone had died, and I had the awful feeling that it was me. Our friends, for the most part, had been Mary's more than mine. I'd been seeing less of the ones, like Billy Nichols and Gaby, who I'd known for years. I couldn't face sitting alone in a restaurant, and I wasn't much of a cook. I began to lose weight. I smoked a lot.

Bobby Lewis, my director friend, got me back on track. He was doing a musical with Lena Horne and there was a job for me. I would again be the assistant stage manager, understudy the part of an old British Governor, and do a small part as a radio announcer, voice only. It was the best thing that could have happened to me. I was caught up in the excitement of a huge David Merrick production called *Jamaica*.

The entire cast was African American. The only two exceptions were Ricardo Montalban as the lead opposite Lena and the Governor played by Erik Rhodes. The music was by Harold Arlen and the book by Yip Harburg and Fred Saidy. It had been originally fashioned for Harry Belafonte who pulled out, and it then went to Lena. The advance was enormous, but the show was a dud. Lena's charisma and star quality kept it running for a year and a half, but the book was banal and the songs not top-notch Arlen.

The first day of rehearsal, Bobby Lewis read the play which he always did when he was the director. He felt it would keep all the actors from being nervous as they waited only for their entrances and their scenes. Bobby thought that they didn't get a picture of the play as a whole, only the parts they were in. The story was of a Jamaican dressmaker (Lena) in love with a fisherman (Ricardo) who kept putting off their marriage although he loved her. Lena is enticed to go to New York with a big spender but a hurricane gets in the way. Surprise – there is a happy ending. A high school student could have done better.

Bobby read the whole play as we all listened and at the end, there were tears in Bobby's eyes. The only thing, I thought, that could possibly have brought on the tears was the prospect of having to direct such a banal mess. The amazing thing was the people involved were some of the most honored and successful creative artists in the theater.

Rehearsals went well enough. The main excitement came from the brilliant choreographer from the movies, Jack Cole, who whipped the amazing dancers into a frenzy. They were all talented and beautiful, including the magnificent young Alvin Ailey. I watched the pros like Lena, Josephine Premice, and Ossie Davis as they worked out the numbers that would hold the show together. Bobby Lewis had been in the Group Theater and was a master at The Method. He constantly gave directions to Lena out of the Stanislavski handbook.

Lena and I had become friendly and she begged me for help. She didn't understand Bobby's directions about actions and motivations. She began to doubt that she could act at all. I convinced her to be herself as much as she could. The audience was coming to see her and the story was so simple. "You love him, but when he does the wrong thing, you just bawl him out, get even with him. Just like you do with Lennie" (her husband). Somehow, comparing the play to her own life made it easier for her, and she grew more confident. I wasn't going behind Bobby's back and I never spoke against anything he was doing. I just gave her a baby version of how to act in what was, after all, a fairytale.

The opening night was all Lena's, though Josephine Premice stopped the show with a song about leaving the atom alone. The dances were stunning. All of us felt good because even if the notices were only fair, they'd be great for Lena who sang up a storm and brought all her night club savvy to Broadway. Afterwards there was the usual celebration and the reviews were, as expected, all about how great Lena was.

The weeks and months that followed were pretty much the same for me: I had the analyst early in the morning three times a week, Jerry's office every morning but Saturday and Sunday until 1:00, working out at the gym, and then home to clean the apartment, shop for food, try to get some reading in, have dinner and then to the theater by 7:30 to be ready to check that everybody was signing in. I had to knock on every door at half hour and again for 15 minutes and finally places. Matinee days were, of course, different. As time passed, I began to run the show myself. It meant giving all the light cues through my microphone, counting sometimes to 50 as the lights dimmed or grew bright, and alerting all the stagehands for set changes. It was complicated, and I was at the stage manager's desk for the entire show watching out for any problem that might arise.

The fun of the evening was visiting with Lena before the show. She often asked me to come into her dressing room and chat as her maid put her hair in rollers and then brushed it out. Lena had a light, slightly yellow complexion, with a lot of freckles, that she covered up with a dark makeup. She put the base on meticulously. As she did, she would talk about her day and ask me about mine and sometimes she'd gossip about people we knew in common.

Lennie Hayton, her husband, who was a star on his own, having been nominated for six Oscars for musical scores and won two, often brought her to the theater and he was always smiling as he did no matter what Lena asked him to do for her. Lennie looked like a Southern colonel with a white beard and mustache. Lena called him "Daddy," and he always came back at the end of every show with a drink ready for Lena when she came off from the curtain call. The three of us became friends. Lennie insisted I have a suit fitted by his tailor that I could ill afford, but it made me look rather grand.

Lena had people at her apartment almost every week after the Saturday night performance. She didn't have to work the next day so she could stay up late and drink. She didn't drink that heavily, but she loved sweet-tasting combinations of liquors that Lennie concocted for her. I was at many of the parties in her rambling West End home, and she made me feel as welcome as Hazel Scott (the pianist) or Billy Strayhorn (the composer of "Lush Life") or the talented couple Flossie Klotz (the costume designer) and Ruth Mitchell (renowned production stage manager) or any of her other friends.

I did manage to do one very important television program while I was in *Jamaica*. Omnibus TV, the most prestigious show on television, shot on Sunday so I was able to make rehearsals during the week – they worked around me during my Wednesday and Saturday matinees – and I did have all day Sunday off for the dress rehearsal and the actual shooting. Joseph Welch was doing a program on *American Trial By Jury*. I was to play a man who had committed a crime for which his lawyers were pleading insanity – a plea that was seldom used in a court trial.

Joseph Welch was a staunch New Englander (though he was born in Iowa) who uttered the famous words to Senator Joseph McCarthy, "Have you no sense of decency?" that started the end of McCarthyism. My part was extremely complicated. I had paresis of the brain that had affected my mental functions. I was also physically impaired. It was arranged for me to see an ophthalmologist an hour before the show who would put drops in my eyes to enlarge the pupils for closeups.

I researched the disease and came up with a character who was barely there. I was in a world of my own that had little to do with where I was or what I was doing. One of the questions I was asked, when I was being examined, was what my favorite color was. My answer was, as if it were the only color there was, "Black." It turned out to be a chilling moment and I got incredible reactions for my performance from all the people connected with the show.

The jury voted my character not guilty by reason of insanity. Robert Saudek, the creator of Omnibus and the producer, told me some time later that it was "totally unfair" that I hadn't gotten the best actor award at the Emmys. I did get a great review in *Variety* and endless praise from so many people. But the best part of the whole experience was acting again and working on such a complex role. It was the most exciting acting time I'd had since *Justice* and *The Marble Faun*.

50

Some months after *Jamaica* opened, Erik Rhodes, who played the old British governor, gave his notice. The part was small and Erik had been a well-known supporting player in many movies. He said he was bored, but I think he felt the role was a come down. When I heard he was leaving, I immediately asked if I could audition for the replacement. Everybody thought I was crazy, but they said, why not? I used my almost-perfect British accent and squashed my features into an old man's face that seemed to be squinting at the world.

The Merrick office was famous for finding ways to save money, so they jumped at the chance to use me for just a few dollars more a week, instead of finding a new actor who would cost them much more. It meant that I now got to the theater earlier, made-up like an old man with lines and hollows under my eyes and put on the governor's shorts and shirt. I then went about my stage-managing duties, announcing the time at each dressing room door and running the show. I kept my eye on the book for all the cues and was ready to help anyone who forgot their lines. I stayed in costume and makeup until the end of the show when I brought the curtain up and down for the curtain calls. If the production stage manager was running the show, I got to be in the curtain call, but only then. I didn't care. I loved being busy. I had to be there all evening so why not fill the time with more work, and my meager salary did get a little larger.

Toward the end of the first winter with the show, I heard of another possibility. Ricardo Montalban had an understudy who was one of the singers. As the show became even more of a hit, Lena worried that the understudy didn't look old enough to play opposite her if anything happened to Ricardo. The management was looking for a replacement. I immediately asked if I could audition for it. They said no, I couldn't possibly be right to play a native fisherman.

True, I wasn't dark but neither was Ricardo, and I had a scoop nose, but so did one of the dancers. I mentioned it to Lena who thought it was a great idea and insisted that I be given an audition. Of course, I knew every note and word that came out of Ricardo's mouth, since I was in the wings at every performance. I also had watched all of his movements. My audition was a finished performance that surprised the powers that be and I got the job. Another $15 a week and I would also be at an afternoon rehearsal every Tuesday with the other understudies.

***

It was spring and 8:00 in the morning, and I was having my usual Wednesday session with the doctor. The smell of flowers and grass cuttings wafted through the open window. I had walked through Central Park from Fifth Avenue, and I had seen my magnolia tree in full blossom. I had stopped to look at it as I had for so many springs on my way to the doctor's. How many years have I been in analysis? I couldn't even remember. The blossoming tree had become a symbol to me. *One day*, I thought, *my life will flower like this tree.* I had hurried to the session to get on with it. Maybe today will be the breakthrough I'd been waiting for.

When I was with the analyst, I reached into my pants pocket and pulled out a piece of paper. I had had a dream the night before and had written it down so I wouldn't forget it. I began reading.

I was the lead in a play. My role was the long, lost son of royalty. The audience knew that I was an impostor, but the King and Queen believed that I was their son because the Prime Minister had told them so. My father, the King, loved bric-a-brac, but I had taken it all out of the living room. He thought the room was bare without it, so I told him I would put it all back, which made him very happy. I got my mother, the Queen, to help me and we took things out of a closet, among them, three figurines. These were my favorites. They're Romeo and Juliet and the third is the Nurse.

"No," my mother said, "the Nurse is old and this is a young girl."

I looked and she was right. The figurine came to life and began to kiss my hand which I had given her with a royal gesture.

"You are not the Prince," the figurine said.

"But he must be," the Queen said, "the Prime Minister said so."

At that moment, the King walked in and said to me, "Stay where you are."

He had known all along that I was an impostor. There was a sinister smile on his face as he raised a shotgun to my head. That was to be the end of the play, and although all of us stood frozen, the curtain did not come down.

I folded the paper and put it back in my pocket. I lit a cigarette.

"What do you think the dream means?" the doctor asked.

I inhaled several times and blew the smoke out as I wondered. "I think it has something to do with my fantasies of being adopted when I was a child," I said.

"What do you mean?" the doctor probed.

"I always thought that I was adopted. I know most kids do, but I thought I was of royal birth. I wanted so much not to belong to my parents. I looked in the baby book that my mother kept, with the changing height and weight measurements as I grew, and locks of my hair. I thought that they could have had the newspaper announcements of my birth, which were in the book, printed up afterwards, and even forged the birth certificate –"

"I don't think that's what it is," the doctor interrupted. "In the dream, your parents were only interested in things, like the bric-a-brac, and it was only when you gave them things, or did things for them, that they cared for you."

"You're right," I said. "I just remembered that I spoke with my mother last Sunday on the phone and she said, 'Is anything new?' I felt awful because there was nothing to tell her."

"You see," the doctor said, "you have to give her things, even news."

"Yes," I said, "but I'm just playing a small part in *Jamaica*, understudying Ricardo and stage-managing. Still, it doesn't seem like enough."

"Enough for who?" the doctor interjected. "Are these things for you or for your mother? Because if you're doing them for her, it may never be enough." I sat, quietly trying to absorb what he had said. "There's something else," the doctor continued. "You've talked so much about not feeling completely free on the stage, that you seem somewhat restricted in your movements. Isn't it interesting that in the dream, your father tells you to stay where you are and you are frozen, waiting for the curtain?"

"You mean," I said excitedly, "that my father is the reason I'm not free?"

"I don't think we can say that yet," the doctor answered. "There's a lot more we have to discover."

I sat for a moment staring past the doctor into the sunbeams his smoke had accentuated. "Do you think there is a trauma in my childhood that is the key to all of this?" I asked.

"What do you mean?" the doctor said.

"Well, you know I told you about that man forcing my brother and me to have sex when I was a child."

"If you mean, was there one incident that made you the way you are today, I don't think so. It would have made it very simple for us, but I'm afraid it's much more complicated than that."

"Don't you think that childhood is important?"

"Of course," the doctor said, "everything is important, but the process is not just picking out a time –" The phone rang, making me jump almost imperceptibly. I was brought back to the office from far away. I was annoyed when the phone rang during a session, but the doctor had explained he had to answer it in case it was an emergency with one of his other patients.

"I'm sorry, Alan," he said as he picked up the phone. "Hello?" There was a pause while I waited, eager to continue. "It's for you, Alan," he said. I reached over and took the phone from him. I had given the doctor's number to no one except the theater in case of an emergency.

"Hello?"

"Alan," a voice I didn't recognize said. "This is Jack in the Merrick office. We've just had a call from Ricardo Montalban's doctor. Ricardo is sick and you're going to have to go on at the matinee."

I rubbed my tongue under my front teeth. "Will there be time to rehearse with Lena?" I asked.

"We can't reach her, but she's always at the theater by 1:30 so you can go over some things with her then. I know you'll be fine."

I hung up and started to shake. "What is it, Alan?" the doctor asked.

"I have to go on for the star today, opposite Lena Horne. I won't even have a rehearsal!"

"But that's wonderful. You've rehearsed the role, haven't you?"

"Yes," I replied, I couldn't stop shaking, "but never with Lena – just in understudy rehearsals."

"Do you know the lines?"

"I think so, but all those songs, I've never sung with the orchestra." I started to fold my hands and rub my fingers against each other.

"Alan," the doctor said, "you wanted very much to get this understudy, didn't you?"

"Yes."

"As I remember, they didn't want to let you audition, yet you pursued it until you proved you could do the role. You've said that everyone was enthusiastic about your performance in the understudy rehearsals."

"Yes, that's true."

"You're very talented, Alan, and I know you can do this. Why don't you, for once, do something just for yourself, not for your parents or anyone else, just for yourself? Wouldn't it be wonderful to sing opposite Line Horne in a big musical on Broadway? Think of the fun.

You've always wanted it and now it's within your reach. You can have a wonderful time and it's all yours."

I realized I had stopped shaking. I took a deep breath and smiled at the doctor. "Thank you," I said. "I'll be fine."

My eyes smarted, but there were no tears that had usually come all my life when someone praised me. For just one moment I hesitated and wanted to be back where it was safe. I got up and pulled back my shoulders. "I'll see you on Friday," I said and walked out the door.

51

Koli in "Jamaica"

I rushed up the four flights of stairs to my apartment. I'd have to hurry to shave and shower. I had awakened late, so I had just jumped out of bed and gone to the doctor. I opened the door and slipped the metal rod away from the back of it. I'd been robbed twice in the past couple of months, and I was hoping this new preventive would work. I tore off my coat, my jeans, and my shirt, threw them on the unmade bed and went into the kitchen where I shaved in the only sink – the narrow bathroom didn't have room for one.

I suddenly thought I'd better put on the record of *Jamaica* and go over the songs as it played. I began with the opening number, "Savannah," that I would have to sing. I knew it perfectly, and as I shaved and showered; I sang along with the rest of Ricardo's songs. I knew them all so I stopped worrying about that part of it. Doing the scenes with Lena was the problem, but I hoped we could rehearse them before the matinee. I kept going over and over Ricardo's scenes in my head as I drove to the theater in a taxi (I had decided to splurge since it was getting so late.) I seemed to remember every word and movement. I began to feel more confident.

At the theater, since none of the singers and dancers had arrived, everything was dark and quiet. There was almost an atmosphere of gloom. Charlie, the production stage manager, was waiting for me. He told me Lena was not there yet so he took me up to Ricardo's dressing room. I stopped for a moment in front of the door. It was white with slats that made it look like a shuttered door in the West Indies. Ricardo's name was painted in black letters above the doorknob. At the top of the door was a huge gold star marking it as the star dressing room. *It's about to be mine*, I thought. I took a deep breath and felt a shiver of panic. I stopped it. *I mustn't think about it now.* I opened the door to find Ricardo's dresser standing there, smiling, waiting to help me.

Since the show was about dark-skinned natives, I had to use body makeup that the dresser had begun to apply as soon as I stripped to my jockey shorts. I hadn't thought, in my rush, what I would wear under Ricardo's skimpy fisherman clothes, since my jockey shorts would show through. Luckily, the dresser had a newly laundered jockstrap with Montalban printed across the band. As I put it on, I thought *not only am I in the star's dressing room, I'm even wearing his jockstrap.*

Although I was in very good shape, I wasn't the movie star hunk that Ricardo was. My hair had been dyed black in case I ever had to go on, and I used Ricardo's dark pancake makeup and some eyeliner. There wasn't much I could do to look like the rest of the cast, but then Ricardo didn't look much like them either. I certainly couldn't do anything to disguise my long scoop nose, but there was too much else to worry about. I started to look through the script to check the words I would have to speak, but I quickly closed it. Either I knew the lines or I didn't. It was too late to worry about it.

When I was dressed in the fisherman costume that fit perfectly, I asked the dresser to find out if Lena had arrived yet. He went down to her stage floor dressing room and returned to tell me that she was there, but her maid was doing her hair so she wasn't ready yet. It was getting close to matinee time, and I realized we wouldn't be able to go through any of the scenes we had together. The stage manager came back to get me and take me down to the stage. He thought I'd better rehearse with the stagehands the moment when Lena would have to push me over-board from a boat. I would have to fall out and be caught by the men who would be hiding out of sight. I was so staggered by the enormity of what I was going to have to do in the next few hours, that I got up in the boat and just let myself fall without any fear. The men caught me with no trouble at all.

I hung around the stage waiting for Lena. I could hear the noise of the audience coming in. Some of the singers and dancers wandered by. Most of them ignored the fact that I was standing there in costume and makeup. Only one or two whispered, "Good luck." I realized that they must be resenting my playing the role rather than the other under-study who was one of them. I had thought since they all liked me so much when I was the governor and the stage manager, that they would be pleased for me. But I now realized that the other understudy was family and I just wasn't. But Lena had chosen me so there was nothing I could do.

I walked around the stage marking out places where I would have to play scenes. Even the people I was most friendly with avoided me. I had been on the stage playing the old governor, and I had watched everything, but now it looked totally different. I was covered with dark makeup from head to foot, I was wearing a string vest that exposed my arms and chest (the dresser had outlined my pectorals to make them more prominent that he said he had done for Ricardo) and a pair of tattered pants that barely covered the rest of me. I was suddenly a stranger in a strange land, and I obviously wasn't going to get any help from the natives.

Lena appeared looking incredibly beautiful as always. The stage was still dark except for the work lights. She walked over to me, dressed in her opening costume. "Hello, Koli," she said and I could feel a strong emotion welling up in me. She had used the name of the character I was about to play. It was the nicest thing she could have done to reassure me. "There's no time to run scenes," she said, "but you know everything so well – you'll be fine."

"Lena," I said, "there's just one thing. You have to let me kiss you."

I knew I was about to do love scenes with Lena Horne, and although we were friends, we were about to break a barrier that had to be broken, or I couldn't play the role. She nodded her head, and I kissed her on the lips with the same passion that I would feel when we did the love scenes. She then went up the stairs to the little house on the set from which she made her first entrance. I watched her go and suddenly saw that she was more nervous than I was.

The orchestra was tuning up and the dancers and singers took their positions without a look in my direction. I went upstage right and did some push-ups that I was used to seeing Ricardo do before his entrance. I then got into a mock fishing boat that would be pushed all the way downstage as soon as the curtain went up. I waited for the overture to begin and then I heard an announcement over the loud speaker. The stage manager's voice was loud and clear.

"At this afternoon's performance, the part of Koli, usually played by Ricardo Montalban, will be played by Alan Shayne."

There was a great groan from the audience that must have been heard in Newark. I felt as if I had been physically slapped. The orchestra quickly began the overture to keep people from leaving the theater. I took a deep breath. *OK,* I thought, *they don't want me, but fuck them, they're going to get me, and, somehow, they're going to like me. I'm going to be a big star and this is going to be a snap.* I pushed out my chest, pulled back my shoulders and decided to have the time of my life.

The overture ended, the curtain went up, the music started again and I heard my cue. I sang the first few lines of the opening song from offstage. Then the boat was pushed by the stagehands and I went sailing down to the footlights. I stepped out of the boat and sang "Savannah," begging Lena, as Savannah, to come out of her little house to be with me. I wish I could say that I went out there and came back a star, like in the movies. I didn't. But the show went very well. I never forgot a line or a lyric. I invented a few dance steps that Jack Cole, the choreographer, would have winced at.

The audience didn't know the difference. They seemed perfectly happy with me after the shock of not getting the movie star they'd paid for. People said later that I'd performed as if the part had always been mine, that I looked great and had loads of charm, but I didn't kid myself. I could pretend for a couple of hours that I was a star, but it was over once the curtain came down. I did get a terrific hand from the audience at my solo curtain call, but the cast only applauded me perfunctorily when we were behind the curtain.

They did, however, give an ovation to the other understudy for Ricardo, who also covered me, and had gone on in my role of the governor. I only allowed it to be a momentary hurt. I had to play again that night, and I wasn't going to allow it to get me down. Lena was sweet and complimentary, but I realized she was brooding about the groans that greeted Ricardo's absence. She took it personally that she wasn't enough for the audience by herself, when, of course, she was the one everyone came to see.

I was as high as I could be. What was really a herculean task for an actor who wasn't a great singer or a great dancer, I had managed to do. Unfortunately, since I had to perform that night as well as the rest of the week, I ended up wrecking my voice. I had to be sent to a doctor, called by people in the know as "Doctor Feelgood." He gave me an injection that made me feel wonderful, and I did the show singing like a bird.

Only years later did it occur to me that I had been given drugs. I did discover, however, that in order to do the show each time, as the audience groaned when my name was announced, that I still had to psych myself into believing I was a star or I couldn't get through the show. It made me behave, for a short time, like an important, rather imperious person. It had never been a part of my DNA. Fortunately, for me and my friends, it only lasted until a short time after the show, and then I was myself again.

52

With Lena Horne in "Jamaica"

I stood in the wings waiting for the curtain call, the perspiration streaming down my darkly stained body. The July heat was eliminated by the huge theater air conditioners, but the physical activity of singing and dancing drained me, even though by now, I had played Ricardo's role many times. The performance had gone off without a hitch. I had never made a mistake in a lyric or a piece of business since the first time I had done the role several months before, when I had surprised everyone.

Looking back, I remembered how I had gone to pieces when the call came in the analyst's office that I would have to play the star role at the matinee. I had only applied for the understudy to get a little more money. Ricardo was such a jock. I never thought he'd get sick and I'd have to go on for him. The doctor gave me the courage to do it. Analysis had really helped so much. There were so many indications that my whole drive toward performing was related to my mother's dream of being on the stage. She had wanted so much to be a star when she was young. I had almost laughed when I heard her distinctive cough, just as I opened my mouth to sing my first number. She had come down from Boston to see the matinee. Little by little however, with the doctor's help, I was managing to push the specter of her off the stage and take it all for myself.

I saw that it was time for my bow, so I lifted up my head and ran on the stage, smiling at the enthusiastic audience. They applauded warmly and then thunderously when Lena Horne appeared. She looked at me affectionately, and when the curtain went down, she said, "It was very good today." Several of the actors came over and slapped me on the back. The cast had finally decided to accept me substituting for Ricardo, after resenting my not being at all right to be one of the natives on the island. Ricardo was no more right than I was, but he was a star. I think they had finally realized I was keeping the curtain up. If I weren't there, there wouldn't be a show. Ricardo's dresser came onto the stage and put a terrycloth robe around me and we walked together to the dressing room.

I was standing on a box, naked, except for some jockey shorts I had pulled on over the jockstrap I had to wear in the show. My dresser was repairing my body makeup so I would be ready for the evening performance. My mother came in, reached up to kiss me on the cheek, said how wonderful I'd been and sat down in the arm chair. There was a knock on the door and the dresser opened it and let in an actor I'd worked with on a television show. Another man accompanied him.

I have replayed this scene so many times in my mind. It is only when a moment changes your whole life that you keep going back to it. Did I know at the time how important it was? Of course not. I do remember I was stunned by the man who was with my actor friend. He was about my age and phenomenally handsome. He was the same height as I was (though standing on my box I towered over everyone) with a mass of thick, black hair that fell across his forehead, almost hitting his startling brown eyes. His eyes looked both aggressive and hurt at the same time. He had a big, curved nose that, together with his other features, made him an arresting presence like a young, intense movie star, or a French, avant-garde writer. His skin was deeply tanned from, I guessed, lying on the beach in the July sun, but there was no sign of vanity about him. He was wearing a seersucker jacket, a pair of gray pants, a tie, and a white shirt (people dressed for the theater in those days) but nothing to call attention to himself.

I was able to study every aspect of him since I was looking into a mirrored wall and could see him in back of me. All of this was taking place as my actor friend praised my performance profusely. I barely heard him. I just kept looking at his companion. "This is a friend of mine from California, Norman Sunshine," the actor said.

I tried not to show too much interest. "How do you do," I said formally, but I panicked that the man was not from New York and I'd never see him again.

"I thought you were very good," he said, but his face was unsmiling, as if there were more serious things in the world to talk about.

"Thank you," I said as I turned back to my dresser who was applying more dark makeup to my body. "When are you going back to California?" I asked him, trying to act as if I were just making polite conversation.

"I'm not," he answered. "I live here."

The actor interrupted, "Norman is an artist."

I nodded as if it were of little interest to me. Now that I knew he lived in New York, I saw a greater obstacle. Was Norman – now he had a name in my mind – having a relationship with the actor? I didn't really know the actor that well. He only played bit parts, but his family had money. He had a wife and four children. I knew he also went to bed with men, and I immediately assumed he was sleeping with this guy.

My mother had settled into her chair after I introduced her and had begun to babble about shopping for some gloves and having trouble finding them.

"I just went in one store and out the other," she told the dresser. I smiled at the two men who had noticed her gaffe. She had started to use malapropisms in the last few years that amused people. I had once heard her singing, "Oh my darling serpentine." I was never quite sure that she wasn't doing it deliberately.

"We have to be going," the actor said, "but I'm so glad I had tickets for today. I got so excited when I heard your name announced. You were terrific."

I thought *I've got to make them stay, at least long enough to give Norman the right impression.* He seemed so totally uninterested in me. But here I was, practically in the nude with my dresser patting every part of my body with makeup. And I'm making everything worse by still having the star personality that gets me through the show. It must seem fake to someone like Norman. This guy must think I'm a horse's ass carrying on like this. I wanted to say to him, "Look, this isn't me. I'm a really decent person." He seemed so serious and sensitive and shy. I wanted to get through to him, but I couldn't in front of his lover, and my mother being there didn't help.

"You don't have to rush," I said. "I don't go out between shows. I just take a nap. Maybe you'd like a drink."

"We have to get to dinner," Norman said. I was afraid I'd sounded too eager so I resumed my star facade.

"Thank you so much for coming back," I said graciously. I turned to Norman, "Very nice to meet you." I watched the two of them walk through the door.

"Who were they?" my mother asked as soon as they were out of earshot.

"Just an actor I worked with," I replied, "and a friend of his."

"The head usher was so nice to me," she gushed. "When I told him who I was, he took me all the way down to the fourth row and sat me right on the aisle. There was the loveliest woman next to me. She said what a good job you were doing—"

I wasn't listening. I was going over and over in my head everything I'd said and done in the past few minutes. *I must have behaved like an idiot,* I thought. *I'm sure it seemed like I was showing off standing around in the nude having my body made up. Why didn't I put on a robe? Maybe I wanted him to look at me. But he couldn't have been less interested. Anyway, I'll never see him again – unless I can get his phone number. But I can't ask for it. They may be involved.* It was as if Norman's going had left me with a physical loss. *There's no way I'll ever run into him in this damn city.*

A week later, as I was rushing up the stairs from the subway on my way to work, there was Norman at the top of the landing. It was like a movie. The sun was setting behind him and he was backlit by its rays. For a moment I thought it was someone who looked like him, but there was the same dark hair tumbling down toward his eyebrows, the same intense look of being a million miles away, as if he were thinking of something important that couldn't be shared with the world. He was carrying a huge art portfolio.

"Hello," I said. He looked at me, squinting his eyes slightly as if he was trying to remember who I was. "We met in my dressing room," I said.

"Oh yes," he replied, "I didn't recognize you."

I wanted to say, "you mean with my clothes on?" but he seemed so humorless that I didn't. People were going up and down the stairs and we seemed to be in the way.

"Well, I'd better be going," he said. "I did enjoy your show. See you around."

And he was gone.

53

Norman

It was almost as if Norman and I were the only two people in New York. We couldn't stop bumping into each other. Norman was always lugging his heavy portfolio, and I was usually rushing from the analyst to the photographer's office or from the gym to the theater. We still never said more than "hello" and often not even that. A nod maybe or a slight wave, but never even a smile. That was Norman's fault. He was so preoccupied that I was afraid to show the interest that was keeping me up at night. I made all sorts of plans of what I would say the next time I saw him, but I chickened out when I encountered that withdrawn look that seemed to say to everyone, "Leave me alone."

One day, I walked out on the balcony area of the gym, where the weights were, to see Norman lying on a bench doing a chest press. He was breathtakingly attractive which made it even more difficult that he didn't even notice me. I went through my workout and saw Norman leaving. I had the same feeling I'd had when he'd left my dressing room, like something terribly important was being taken away from me. After I'd showered and dressed, I went down to the lunch counter in the Y to grab something to eat. Norman was sitting all alone and there was an empty seat beside him. I thought, *what the hell, I might as well try one more time.*

I was amazed that he actually began to talk to me. Norman was still smarting from his meetings with his parents, who were in town from California trying to make him go home, to be in his father's furniture business. I think he was anxious to tell anyone about it, and I turned out to be the lucky one. He also complained that he had to draw a shirt ad and every model he knew was busy. That was my cue.

"What about me?" I said. "I'm free until this evening when I have to be at the theater. Can I help?"

Norman thought a minute and then said, "We can give it a try."

Norman had an apartment on Jane Street in the Village, around the corner from the furnished room house I had lived in when I first came to New York. It was in the front of the building on the level of the sidewalk so people were able to look in as they walked by. Norman had painted the windows white so that light could go through, but no one could look in any longer. It gave the rooms a subdued, grayish feeling that was quite depressing. He had gathered furniture from the Salvation Army, pieces that today would be worth a lot of money but at the time, they seemed heavy and unwieldy. It was unbearably hot, and I had to stand with a shirt pinned tightly to my body.

Norman sat on an artist's stool with a board propped in front of him. The paper he drew on was tacked to the board. I thought he would look at me with some kind of interest or acknowledgment, but his face was dark and brooding. He scowled and kept throwing each drawing on the floor before it was finished. He put down the board and walked over to me.

I thought he was going to say something to me, but instead, he adjusted one of the clothespins in the back that was holding the shirt tight to my body. He was totally preoccupied and I realized I was going through all this for nothing. I wanted to cry out, "Look at me. Don't look at the shirt. Look at me."

Finally, he said, "I can't draw you," as if I had been doing something wrong.

"Should I change anything I'm doing?" I asked. "Do you want me to stand differently?"

"No," he said, "just go. I'll somehow do it from scrap. It's not your fault, I just can't draw you. I'll write you a check."

I was shocked. "I came here to help you," I said. "I didn't come for money."

"I'm sorry," he sighed, "I didn't mean to offend you. I'm just so pressed." I was really angry. I dressed quickly. I had to get out of there. "Can I have your phone number," he said holding out a pen and a piece of paper, "I'd like to call you."

I quickly wrote it down without even looking at him and walked out the door. I heard him yell "Thanks," but I didn't even look back.

Norman phoned me the next morning to say how sorry he was that he'd been unpleasant when I had been so nice to pose for him. He said he'd just been so desperate to meet his deadline that he couldn't think of anything else. He said he'd been up all night and finally gotten a drawing that the company accepted. "I want to make it up to you," he said. "Can you come to dinner?"

I had been on the verge of giving up my pursuit of him. I didn't want to be a masochist, and he seemed like nothing but trouble. On the other hand, I'd never felt this way about anyone before, man or woman, so I said "Yes" and we settled on a date. I wish I could say that the evening was wonderful, but it was almost as bad as the time I posed for him. He had decided to cook dinner, though he made it clear he didn't know much about cooking. He told me that he'd had an inspiration.

Since he was an artist, he would make a dinner that looked like an artist's palette. Everything would be a different color. He rushed around his apartment as I sat waiting. We didn't even have a chance to talk since he was so busy. I just sat and drank wine until Norman appeared from the kitchen with two plates heaped with different colored vegetables and a reddish looking meat dish. The dinner should have been painted, not eaten. I did my best but I couldn't disguise my inability to do more than sample a few things. Norman didn't seem to enjoy it any more than I did. He was glum, so I took off right after he'd cleared the still full dishes from the table. It just wasn't working out.

I let a few days go by, but I found I was thinking of nothing else but Norman. I'd reached a point in the analysis where I felt really open to having a relationship with someone. I wasn't satisfied with the fly-by-night sex I had been having from time to time. I was healthy and strong, so sex was as much a part of my life as hearing my heartbeat or having to feed my body every day. But I wanted more. I was 32 and I didn't want to look forward to a life alone. I thought often of what Mary had said, that perhaps I would be happier with a man rather than a woman. I had thought I loved Mary, but there was a certain relief when she left me. I felt a twinge when I saw in the paper that she had married. But even when I was with her, I was more attracted to the men I came into contact with than the women.

My earliest sexual memories were of men. Even as a child, they had begun to fill my dreams, both asleep and awake. I couldn't ask my parents any questions about what I was going through – they were horrified if anyone uttered the word "sex" – so I had to find the answers to my yearnings somewhere else. I searched through books at the library, but all I could find was historical gossip about Oscar Wilde doing obscene things with stable boys, and obscure references to South Sea natives and puberty rites. I glanced furtively at *Strength* and *Health* magazines in the local bookstores. They gave me an erotic charge as I glanced at the glossy pictures of musclemen, but not until the bookseller's head was turned away.

As I grew older, I grew increasingly aware that my desire was not only not normal, but if I allowed it to continue, it would bring me shame as a constant companion. The time I spent with Louis wasn't love. It was like two buddies going through school together. And with Cass, we were two mismatched jigsaw puzzle pieces that could never have been made to fit together. But Norman was different. We were from similar backgrounds, we were enough of the same age that I was sure we shared movies and books that we had both grown up with, and we were both artists. The more I thought about it, the more I thought I couldn't let him go out of my life without a fight.

"OK," I said on the phone when I'd gotten the courage to call Norman again, "You've given me the artist's dinner, now you're going to have the actor's dinner."

"When I didn't hear from you," Norman replied, "I was sure you'd died of ptomaine poisoning."

Oh my God, he does have a sense of humor, I thought. "The thing that saved me was that I'm color blind so I thankfully never knew what I was eating."

"Well, you'll be happy to know I've decided not to open a restaurant." We both laughed and settled on a date for him to come to my apartment.

My dinner was much more successful. I wasn't a cook either, but I had torn out a recipe from *The New York Times* that was a Hawaiian concoction with meat and pineapple and rice. It was something you might have gotten by the pool at a party in the suburbs. It was easy to make and strangely tasty or maybe that was because of the good bottle of wine I had opted to serve with it. We had a great time. I'd prepared everything so I could spend all the time with Norman. He looked fantastic, and he was bright and funny and perfect.

We ate in my small dining room with candles spreading a soft light over the old, cracked walls and the linoleum floor. I kept pouring wine into Norman's glass as I got increasingly amorous. Finally, I couldn't resist it any longer and I started to make love to him. He pushed me away gently, but I wasn't to be denied. I had wanted him so badly now for such a long time. I was used to people popping into bed after just saying "Hello."

He kept saying things like, "This is too soon – let's wait until we know each other better" – but I wouldn't listen and finally he gave up and went through with it. It was awful. We ended up on the hard floor, awkward, uncomfortable, and both feeling, I was sure, like we never wanted to see each other again. Norman straightened himself out, thanked me for dinner, and got out the door as quickly as I had after the multi-colored dinner.

54

I thought the botched sex between Norman and me was the end of any possible relationship we could have had. I tried to put him out of my mind. I even pretended he'd gone back to California so it would be impossible for me to see him any longer. I thought I was on the way to forgetting him when the phone rang. I ran to get it. If only it were Norman – and it was.

There was no "Hello" or small talk, just Norman's voice saying he would like to see me. He wanted to come to my apartment later that day. We set a time and he hung up. I got terribly upset. I figured he just wanted to tell me that he didn't want to continue to see me. But why did he have to tell me to my face? Why not just disappear from my life? *No*, I thought, *Norman isn't someone who believes in loose ends. He'll have to get his feelings out in the open so he can say "goodbye" properly.* I hung around waiting for the time to pass when he would arrive, going back and forth over possible scenarios of what the visit would be like. I was wrong about all of them.

Norman arrived, looking even more serious than usual. I asked him to sit down and as soon as we were both seated, he began. "I really like you," he said, "and I want to go on seeing you. But I have to get one thing straight: we are not going to have sex. I want to get to know you and see how I feel. I can't do that if we're huffing and puffing all the time. I want us to go slow and find out how we really feel about each other."

"Then you don't find me attractive," I couldn't help saying.

"Of course I do," Norman said, "but there are lots of attractive people in the world. I want to find out who you really are, and whether you're the only one I want to be with."

"But you've had sex with other people – did you always put them through a test period?"

"Of course not," he said, "I knew they were not going to be a part of my life so it was meaningless."

"Norman," I said, "I'm in love with you. I want to know every part of you, but I'm a healthy male in the prime of life. I have to have sex, and if you deny me, I'll have to have it with someone else."

"Do whatever you have to do," he said. "Look, this wasn't easy for me to talk about," he went on, "but I have a sense that you are important to me, and I don't want to spoil it."

"OK," I said. "We'll try it your way."

We went to the movies. We went to the Met and saw the new exhibits. We looked longingly at the rooms Bloomingdale's had created. We sopped up the sun on the dock in the East River. We wandered along Fifth Avenue looking in the windows and we checked out the new books at Doubleday's. We had dinner together whenever we could and sometimes late supper after the theater. Always, the moment we were finished, Norman would leave me. He wouldn't come back to my apartment. It drove me mad. I decided to take the attitude of our just being friends, and I would have sex with other people. I told him that was the way I was going to behave. He didn't seem to care. He just kept saying, "I have to see how I feel."

One day, infuriated, I did pick someone up, but I realized it was not the answer. I just had to wait for Norman so we continued the way we were going. Norman seemed to want to be with me and I certainly wanted to be with him. I was still in *Jamaica* eight times a week, and at the photographer's office in the morning, and between the analysis and the gym to keep fit in case I had to go on for Ricardo, I had little free time. Norman was busy doing his fashion drawings as well as illustrations for magazines, so, between the two of us, it was hard to get together. And yet, every free moment we were with each other. I introduced Norman to Billy Nichols and a new friend, Neil Hartley, who was the production head at the David Merrick office. I think they were stunned.

Not only was Norman startlingly handsome, but he was extremely erudite. He talked endlessly of *The Sound and the Fury* and other literary works that he had studied in college. Billy and Neil just stared at him as he talked, their mouths slightly open with startled expressions on their faces. I had told them I was in love and that it was forever. They never said anything against Norman nor did they encourage me. But they must have known that it was a *fait accompli* even though I had told them we weren't making love or even necking once in a\while. Yet we continued to be together as much as we could.

55

Norman and I sat at a table, our heads resting against the old brick wall in P.J. Clarke's restaurant. It was crowded, but it was as if we were all alone. We only saw each other, and we ate without looking at our food. Months had gone by, and we had been like students taking a course in love: exploring each other, testing, probing, comparing, soaring to moments of exhilaration and even moments of disappointment and despair. Norman would still not allow any physical contact between us. I knew he was right. *Sex is all too easy and everybody takes it for granted*, I thought. I had finally come to agree with him that not having sex would force us to really find out if we did love each other. And it seemed to be doing the job. I loved Norman even more.

For the first time in my life, I was pursuing someone instead of waiting to be pursued. In the past, I'd played it safe and waited until I knew someone cared for me. That way I could never get hurt. This time, I held back nothing. I had never felt so totally myself with anyone. Now I didn't have to be careful of anything I said. I no longer watched myself to be sure I wasn't doing the wrong thing. Norman and I were equals. We weren't the same, nor would we ever be, but neither one of us would dominate the other or be subservient to the other. And we wouldn't play games at each other's expense. Funny, I kept thinking of Eleanor and her demand for equality in love and here I was, finding it with Norman.

We had discovered that we were the same in so many ways. Our families had similar backgrounds. We both loved nature, literature, and music. We wanted to travel, and we wanted to live in the country one day. Even our differences made us exciting to each other. We both were working hard. I was still at the theater every night but Sunday and the photographer's office in the mornings, and Norman was doing his fashion illustration in the daytime and his serious painting in the evening. Yet we rushed together whenever we had a free moment.

A waiter put two Scotch sours on the table. I was talking about my analysis and Norman interrupted me. He had started to see an analyst. "I hope we're not using analysis as an excuse," he said, "for rationalizing ourselves into safe, unimaginative lives. We may get to be good, ordinary, moral people, but will we lose the eccentricity that made us become artists? I know we have to search within, but we mustn't live out our lives just trying to accomplish something. What's the point of working harder, identifying more with the fantasies of work and less with the realities of ourselves? Right now, money is our motivating force. We know better than that."

He lit a cigarette as I waited for him to continue. "Let's leave it all," he said. "We can have a garden, paint a painting, write a story. We can do it all. We can feel more, love more, if we take the plunge and get out of this pointless money-oriented existence we cling to." He blew out some smoke and then looked at me, waiting for my reaction.

"It sounds great," I replied, "but what are we going to do for money? I'm just getting on my feet after all these years of struggling."

"We don't need much," he said. "I've figured it all out: Italy for six months, then India. We must see and talk to the spirit that seems to have influenced all of Western civilization. Then we go to Greece to see creative beauty at its most cerebral. After that, we'll search for a place to live and work, and grow younger, not grayer."

"Oh," I said, "if only it could be."

"It can," Norman insisted.

I put my hand over my mouth as I thought of what to say next. "It will be," I said, "but we have to prepare for it. I grew up in the Depression. I remember what it was like to get the cans of food the government doled out to my father as he stood forever waiting in line. Each can had a different label: veal, lamb, beef, yet they all tasted exactly the same. And the clothes they gave us – I can still feel that scratchy wool sweater that made my skin itch. I won't be poor again, and I won't allow you to be either. You'll see, the time will come when we can do everything."

Norman sat silently, obviously disappointed that I had burst his bubble of expectation. I felt terrible at having been the voice of reason, but I had to be honest and there was no way we could set out for Shangri la yet. I wanted to bring back the euphoria that we had shared earlier. I reached into my pocket and took out a piece of paper. I handed it to Norman. "I wrote you a poem," I said. He sipped his drink as he read it in the dim, smoke-filled light.

WINDOW SHOPPING
You asked if I were cold -
my coat was open.
I looked at you,
your coat was closed around your neck.
Your hands were warm in gloves.
I didn't need a coat or gloves,
I was so warm.

In front of each store window on the street
you asked if I liked this or that.
I didn't care.
I didn't care about the windows on the street.
You were so pleased,
So pleased with colors, textures, everything.
You were so happy.

You took in all the world.
I took in only you.
You were the world.
Not the shops, or the people, or the buses or the cars,

Not the skating rink or the Christmas tree,
Not the travel posters or the house of glass.
You -
Walking along seeing everything – happy.
Me -
Walking along seeing you – happy.

Norman looked up at me. "Let's get out of here," he said.

We paid the bill and walked out onto Third Avenue. Norman led me toward 52nd Street where we turned and walked to Second Avenue. I watched our breaths steam as we covered the few steps that led to my building. We seemed to move together up the four flights of stairs. Neither of us spoke as I closed the door of my apartment Our search was over, but the adventure had just begun.

56

The secretary's voice was impersonal yet somehow pompous. "I'm, calling for Mr. Michael Shurtleff," she said with a slight British accent. "He would like to see you at 2:30 tomorrow afternoon at the David Merrick office. Is this convenient?"

My heart skipped a beat, maybe several beats. Michael Shurtleff was the most important casting director on the East Coast. He did all of David Merrick's shows, and I had never been able to get in to see him. Now, he was asking to see me. It must be about a part in a show. *Oh my god*, I thought, *at last. He must have seen me go on for Ricardo in* Jamaica. All sorts of thoughts kept racing through my head as I managed to say I would be there tomorrow, without letting out whoops of joy.

I hung up the phone. I lit a cigarette and sat down on the bed. Why didn't I ask her what it was about? But that's silly. She's the secretary, how would she know? He could have come by the theater to see me, but I guess that's not done. *Jamaica* had finally closed after a year and a half run, but I'd been given another job in a Merrick show, *Irma La Douce*. I was just the assistant stage manager, no acting in this one, but the office had told me they would try to keep me always working.

Was it possible that Shurtleff was going to offer me just another stage manager job in a different show? No, that couldn't be it. He only handled the actors in a show, not the production people. I wondered what the new shows were. I had heard of some but, of course, I had no idea of what was in the planning stage – Shurtleff would know all the inside stuff.

How should I dress? In a good suit or maybe just a pair of pants, a shirt and a sweater. But how could I know what to do when I had no idea of the part? Will he be offering me a job, or maybe it's just to meet with a director. But the secretary would have said the appointment was with Shurtleff and somebody else, and she didn't. Could he have seen me in *Ernest In Love*? Maybe that's what got him interested. I had received good reviews playing a snobby butler in the musical version of Oscar Wilde's *The Importance of Being Ernest*. The maid and I sang a delightful number about making love that was a showstopper. But that was a few months ago. Wouldn't I have heard from him sooner? No, he must have seen me in *Jamaica*. I'd heard he went to everything, and he'd have had to see *Jamaica* since it was a Merrick show. I was stymied.

I decided to wear a suit the next day. If Shurtleff had called me in for a special appointment, it must be for a leading role so I thought I should look dignified. All I kept thinking was 17 years of doing any job I could find and at last I would be getting a good part in a new play that would make all the difference in the world for my career. I tried not to pin my hopes too high, but it had to be good. There was no other reason for Shurtleff to see me. I had wanted to ask some of the actors at *Irma La Douce*, the night before, if they knew of any of the new shows that were starting to cast, but I was afraid they'd discover I was up for something and try to get an appointment themselves. The best thing was to keep quiet. Actors were competitive.

I arrived at the Merrick office exactly on time. I didn't want to seem too eager. I was told that Mr. Shurtleff was delayed at a lunch meeting, but he would be there soon. I took a deep breath and sat down near the receptionist and tried to be calm. I had trained myself, when I was anxious waiting for the few minor operations I'd had, to go over the objects in my apartment to take my mind off what was going to happen. I did that now, starting in the living room with the desk that looked like a small piano and the swivel chair that an accountant must have sat on in the 19th century. I had worked myself over to the furniture under the windows overlooking Second Avenue, when I heard the clicking of heels on the polished wood floor, almost like the sound of a flamenco dancer. I looked up to see a short man with scant hair the color of rotting oranges, a paper white round face, dressed in a tight-fitting tan suit.

"Hello, Alan," he said, "I'm Michael. I'm sorry I'm late."

"Oh, that's all right," I said. "It's nice to meet you."

"Let's go into my office," he said, and I followed him.

The office was small, lined with files and, on his desk, papers, cards, and scripts, everything arranged with impeccable neatness. He took off his jacket, hung it on an old-fashioned clothes tree, waved me to a chair on the other side of the desk, and sat down. He glanced at some messages in front of him, put them into a neat little pile, and then looked up at me.

"You're a very talented actor, Alan," he said, "but you'll never be a star." I felt like I'd been kicked in the stomach. I just looked at him. I couldn't speak. "I've seen you act many times and you're always good, sometimes very good," he said, "but you'll never make it big."

I wanted to hit him, but I tried to compose myself. What was he talking about? I had to say something, but I knew I should be careful. I worked on Merrick shows and I couldn't afford to alienate one of the biggest executives in the organization. There was also a prissiness about him that I sensed could be dangerous when he was crossed.

"I don't understand what that has to do with you asking me to come to see you. I know you're a great judge of talent and you can pick out the actors who will succeed, but I hope you're wrong about me."

"I'm just about to tell you why I sent for you," he said, sitting up straighter to show he was in command. "I think you'll always work. Everyone likes you and you'll get jobs understudying stars, being a stage manager and finally you'll get small character parts that don't amount to much, You'll get older and never have enough money to do more than have a beer with your actor friends who are in the same boat as you. You'll sit at Joe Allen's and criticize the actors who have made it." I was feeling so put down. I wanted to just get up and leave, but he went on. "None of what I'm saying is an insult, Alan. I just think you deserve so much more. I'm going to offer you something that will change all that for the better. I want you to be my assistant."

"Doing what?" I said without even thinking.

"You'll be a casting director. You'll make good money, go to every show, have an expense account for the best restaurants and even be able to take someone with you. It's a gateway to wonderful possibilities, jobs in the future that will make you even more money and give you prestige." He stopped and smiled at me.

"I'm an actor," I said. "I don't know anything about casting."

"But you do," he disagreed. "You have talent so you can recognize it in others. Everything else is just keeping track of all the actors, what they have done. You go to the theater constantly, find new actors, and see the ones you do know stretch themselves in ways you didn't suspect. The whole bookkeeping aspect of casting I can teach you." He again smiled at me, but this time like a lawyer who was pleased with his summation. I thought I'd better be grateful for a moment and then I could get out of there.

"You're very nice to think of me," I said, "but you may be wrong about me not being a star. It's really just a question of getting the right part, and so far, I just haven't been lucky."

"Alan," he said gently, "I've followed your career for years. I saw you play opposite Lena in *Jamaica*. You were amazing to be able to do that. You acted well, you sang nicely and you looked really good, but the star quality wasn't there. Sure, you weren't perfect casting for the part, but the star spark was missing. The audience thought you were fine, but they didn't go out of the theater whistling Alan Shayne. How many women waited at the stage door? Don't tell me. How many fan letters did you get? Don't tell me that either. Stardom is a gift from the gods. All the studying and practicing backs it up, but if it's not in you to begin with, it never will be. I've seen a lot of stars, and actors who become stars, and there is always an aura about them, as if a spotlight is on them all the time. You can't take your eyes off them. You don't have that gift. I think you'd be a great success in casting and have a happy life. Otherwise, I wouldn't take the time to say things that I'm sure you don't want to hear."

He stood up so I did too. "Think about it," he said. "I need someone immediately so I can't wait more than a few days, but I hope you will come and work with me. If you say yes, we'll work out the salary and everything else." He stuck out his hand which I shook. It was clammy and unpleasant, completing a picture of a man I didn't want to spend a lot of time with.

"Thank you." I replied and walked out the door.

I was furious. How could that little, obnoxious priss tell me what my future would be? How dare he play god and decide I wasn't going to be a star? I kept remembering every word he had spoken. I plowed through the crowds past Shubert Alley and crossed Times Square. I was automatically walking east without even noticing where I was going. So Shurtleff did see me in *Jamaica,* but he didn't even have the courtesy to come back to congratulate me. He was with the Merrick office – he should have.

If he had come backstage to my dressing room, he might have seen me behaving like a star and changed his mind. There was something about being in the star dressing room that made me different when I was there. But Shurtleff was too smart. He would have known I didn't belong there. I had just been given the temporary use of it.

I started to think about all the times I had played for Ricardo; how I had pumped myself up to be a star when I heard the audience groan because they weren't getting the real star. How I would hype myself by saying "I'm going to be great." But I knew even then I was good, not great, and I certainly wasn't a star. It just didn't happen for me. I never admitted it to anyone else but I could tell, looking out at the full house as I sang, that they were watching me but they weren't watching a star.

I suddenly felt that my balloon was being burst and I was the one who was sticking a pin in it, not Shurtleff. He had brought it out into the open, but I had known it for a long time. I had starred in early television shows, but I was never picked up for movies or for the lead in a Broadway show. I had roles in Shakespeare with stars, but I never got a great part. I played leading roles off-Broadway, but I never got ecstatic reviews. I began to go over my whole career, trying to look at it honestly without the old fantasy of "one day it will happen." I'd been in New York for 17 years and I had finally found my métier – stage-managing and understudying. How awful. It took this little man to rub my face in it. That one great role I had waited for will probably never come my way. But if it does, someone else will get it.

I found myself in front of my apartment building. I had walked all across town without even noticing where I was going. My mind was teeming with memories, defeats, so-so reviews, disappointments. I walked up the four flights of stairs and unlocked my door. I'd been living there for years, and struggling, at times, to pay the $50-a-month rent. Now I shared it with Norman, but having him there had made me notice that there really was no bathroom, just doors that closed off a space that had a tub with a makeshift shower and a toilet – no sink to wash and no real privacy for either of us.

Was this the way we were always going to live? I remembered that Shurtleff had said I would end up with small character roles. I had occasionally gotten unemployment insurance when I was out of work. I would see old actors in line, their faces gray with disappointment. I vowed I would never end up like that, but was I, without realizing it, already on the same path?

I went into the living room with its overpowering noise of traffic from Second Avenue. The sofa and chairs were still the same fake stage furniture, uncomfortable to sit on for any length of time. Is this what I want for Norman and me? I promised him we'd travel and one day live in the country. Not at this rate. I lit a cigarette and looked out the window at the trucks. When I was a child, we could see four gas stations from our apartment and hear the traffic. Was I any better off now?

I sat down on the wood sofa that was camouflaged with a thin layer of cotton covered with a patterned material. There was something else. Analysis. I kept going back, no matter how I tried to avoid it, to the discovery that so much of my impetus to be a star had come out my mother's ambitions, not mine. Did that mean that I could leave acting and not miss it because it wasn't what I wanted? Then what did I want now for the rest of my life? Some kind or creative work, but not necessarily acting, and a good life. Being able to share with Norman the beauty of living, travel, literature, music, art and an environment free of money worries that I'd never experienced. I tried to clear my head as much as I could.

The writing on the wall was that Shurtleff was offering me all the things I longed for. I couldn't wait for Norman to return to get his reaction to all of this. My one worry now was how would Norman take to my leaving acting. I knew he was proud of my talent. How would he react to me being a casting director?

The first thing Norman said, after I described the meeting with Shurtleff in detail and all the reasons to consider his offer, was, "But you've described someone you don't like. How could you work with him?"

"I thought about that," I said. "We'd be doing things by ourselves, such as going to different theaters and not seeing the same actors. I guess we'd be together as we actually cast something and, of course, he'd have to train me. But if the money is right, as he has assured me it would be, and you and I can have a better life together. I can learn to put up with him. Imagine, now we only get to see each other after I get home from the theater at 11:30 at night. If I accept this, we'd have dinner together in really good places, and then you'd come with me to the theater. We'd be with each other so much more. I would, of course, give up my job with the photographer, and not have to take pictures of actors for extra money. All my energy would go into one thing, and I know I could make a success of it."

"My worry," Norman said, "is that you'll miss acting. Won't you be upset when you see a role you wish you were playing?"

"I don't think so," I replied. "I don't look back. When something's over in my life, it's over. I think with the analysis, anyway, as I saw my real motives for being an actor, I grew less and less enamored of it. And I love you. I want to spend my life with you – a happy life full of achievement and beauty. I know now I won't get that life for us through acting. Why don't I try another way? I can always go back to acting."

"I think you're wonderful and brave," Norman said. "I'm with you all the way."

I called the next morning and accepted the job. I never acted again.

Epilogue

I was deep in a dream. I was trying to persuade a young man that he was wasting his time being with me. "You should be with people your own age. Why do you want to be with me? I'm much too old for you." I didn't want to hurt the boy, but I wanted desperately to be free from him. The boy protested and wouldn't let me go. I struggled with him and pushed him away to discover I was pushing away a blanket and a sheet. I focused on a pewter chandelier that brought me back to where I was, the Ritz Hotel in Boston.

I heard Norman shaving in the bathroom. He had been considerate, as usual, in letting me sleep. He knew the day was difficult for me. I thought of the dream. It was many years since my analysis had ended, but I still wanted to figure it out, if I could. What was the dream telling me? My subconscious was sending me a message if I could just decode it. Who was the boy? I asked myself. And then I remembered why we were in Boston, and that it was here, where I thought I could get rid of the boy.

I lay still in the bed thinking *I don't have to go. It's as simple as that. Norman and I can find a little French restaurant on Beacon Hill and have a great lunch.* But I knew I had to be there and I dreaded it. I thought, *This is the time to exorcise the boy in the dream, the boy I was. If he's anywhere, he'll be there today.*

The entrance to the Boston Museum had been changed since I'd gone there as a kid, but I automatically slowed down as I saw the statue of the Native American shooting at the sky. I drove around the corner to let Norman out. I went over the plan with him again. "If I'm not here by 2:30," I said, "just take a taxi to the Marriott. Do you have the paper with the instructions on how to get there?"

Norman felt in his pocket. "Yes," he said.

"I'm sure I won't want to stay long," I said. "There are just a couple of people I want to see."

"Stay as long as you want to," he replied. "It may be better than you think. I can always sit in the lobby and read the paper."

"Anyway," I said, "if I don't pick you up at the museum at 2:30, I'll see you in the Marriott lobby at 3:00."

"That's fine," he said. He turned back to me after he shut the door. "You look very handsome," he said and then he walked away.

I made a turn on Huntington Avenue and headed the Mercedes back to Copley Square, so I could get on the Massachusetts Turnpike. The day had a chill in the air, but I had put the top down to enjoy the fall colors. The car was the only symbol I had kept from my Hollywood days. Warner Brothers had given me a new Mercedes every year of the ten I had been President of Television. This was the last one and I brought it with me when I came back east. It seemed a fitting way for the "prodigal son" to come back home.

The colors were almost overpowering. I drove through flaming rows of trees on either side of me. The profusion of yellows, reds, and oranges made me feel as if I were driving through the middle of the Red Sea after the waters had been parted. The concierge at the Ritz had given me exact instructions, and after a stoplight and a right turn, I saw the Marriott Hotel. It was an enormous pile without any character. What a contrast from the old-world look of the Ritz. I thought that most modern buildings were instantly forgettable and about as lasting as a Chinese meal.

Every space seemed to be filled in the huge parking lot. I had to drive around until I could find one that I could squeeze into without scraping the car. As I walked toward the entrance, I saw an old couple going in. Could they be part of the group? Are we that old? I wondered. As I opened the door into the marble lobby, I saw the sign:

Reunion Class of 1942 – 1992
Brookline High School

There must have been a couple of hundred people milling about in front of a very long table. I walked over to see three women of what I thought of as my grandmother's age when she died. They were seated in back of signs with letters of the alphabet. I found the S's and wrote my name on a sheet of paper. The woman looked at it.

"I'm Jean Schwartz," she said, "do you remember me?"

I stared at a huge pin she was wearing with a picture of a girl of 17 and her name underneath. I tried desperately to remember back through the years and I could vaguely see the girl in the picture sitting in biology class. The old woman sitting in front of me had no connection to the girl on the pin. Suddenly, I did get a picture in my memory of the girl. She had a huge bust that she had shown off in different colored angora sweaters.

I said, "Of course I remember you," but I didn't say why. We shook hands and she gave me a large white pin with my picture at 16 and "Alan Shayne" printed below it. I was shocked at the young boy looking out at me as he posed for his high school graduation portrait. He looked like such a baby with his wavy hair, full lips pulled into a slight smile, and his brown eyes that seemed to say *help me. I'm afraid of growing up.*

Once I had attached the pin, several people said a quick hello and moved on. As they had approached me, they had taken a quick look at the picture on my pin, and then greeted me as if they had known me all along. I realized I'd have to do the same thing, so I went in search of the people I hoped to see, by examining everyone's pin.

"Oh, I had such a crush on you," a tiny gray-haired woman stopped me after a surreptitious look at my pin.

A carefully coiffed and made-up woman next to her said, "We used to go dancing, but I bet he doesn't remember. I just loved that *Bourne Identity* show with Richard Chamberlain," she said. "We thought you'd win the Emmy."

I said, "Thank you, and I do remember you."

It was Roberta and I used to take her to parties when my girlfriend Nancy couldn't go. Roberta rattled on about Palm Beach and a cabana at The Breakers, and her husband, who was retired, but still on several boards. She was obviously a decent woman who had raised a family and had a good life.

"Have you seen Elaine?" she asked.

"No, I've been looking for her," I replied.

"She's right there," she pointed across the room.

I followed her finger to a blond, fleshy woman who looked at me with a similar lack of recognition. I walked over to her thinking of the once slender, dark haired girl with ivory skin who we all thought would be a movie star. She looked quickly at my pin.

"I would have known you anywhere," she said with the same fake mid-Atlantic accent she had glommed onto for a role in the senior play. "You wouldn't have recognized me because I'm now a blond and I've had two husbands – they wore me out."

"You look great," I lied. I couldn't help remembering how self-centered she was. One of her girlfriends, who had come backstage to see me once, had told me that a few minutes after Elaine's first child was born, she had called her to gossip and never even mentioned that she was in the hospital and had just given birth.

"If you're ever in D.C., I'm in the book under 'Elaine Stafford.' I'm very in with the political people so I give a lot of parties. It might amuse you."

"Thank you," I said.

"By the way, I just saw Bunny," Elaine said. "She's in the other room in a red Chanel." She turned back to the people she'd been talking to.

I wandered away thinking Elaine hadn't changed a bit. She hadn't even asked me how I was or what I'd been doing. No interest in anyone but herself. I suddenly recognized the guy who'd been the best student in the class. He seemed to be the head of the whole operation with a sheaf of papers that he kept referring to. I went over to him.

"I'm Alan Shayne," I said.

"I know who you are," he said as if I were the new sheriff come into town who wasn't welcome. Why? I wondered and then it was clear. He went on, "I know how successful you've been." added.

I thought I'd better say something nice to him, but I didn't know anything about his life. "What have you been doing?"

"I'm a chemical engineer, but I'm retired now."

"Is Jack Dreyfuss here?" I asked.

He seemed taken aback. "He's dead," he answered.

"No," I said. "When?"

"Some years ago."

"But what happened?"

"I think it was cancer," he said. "There were a lot of write-ups in the paper because he was a leading doctor, but I don't remember what they said the cause was. Look, I'm sorry, I have some work to do." He turned away.

I couldn't believe Jack was dead. He'd been my idol in high school: he was an "A" student, voted handsomest, best liked, most likely to succeed, and president for three years. I'd skipped second grade so I was a year younger than Jack and he always indulged me in, what he must have known, was my hero worship. He even once invited me to his apartment to see miniatures he had made of the British royal jewels. I was so awed to be with him alone that I could hardly speak. I left as soon as I could. Now he was dead. A man walked by whose name I recognized. I was sure he would know about Jack. I stopped him.

"I just heard Jack Dreyfuss is dead," I said. "Do you know what happened?" He looked at me with an odd expression on his face.

"AIDS," he said and walked away.

Oh my God, I thought, *that day at his house, I wonder if he–*

"Alan," a woman screamed and I felt myself being grabbed from the back, hugged and kissed. I knew without looking around that it was Bunny.

As she held me, she whispered in my ear, "I don't give a fuck about the rest of these people. I just came hoping to see you."

I pulled her around and saw the girl who'd been my closest friend in grammar school, high school, and even Sunday School. Now her face was twice the size it used to be and her little body was like a full toothpaste tube. I kissed her on both cheeks.

"You look wonderful," I said and I meant it.

"I haven't done any plastic surgery, if that's what you're thinking, though everybody I know has," she said. "Did you see Elaine?" We both laughed, Bunny didn't have a line on her face. "Just good genes," she went on and then she started on me. "I want you to know we've followed very step of your career. That's my husband over there with the bald head and the glasses. He's a dear."

"We've watched every one of those sitcoms you did like *Alice* and Bert loved the car stuff in *The Dukes of Hazard*. We even go back to *The House without A Christmas Tree* that we watch with the kids every Christmas. The class should give you an award."

"Don't be silly, Bunny," I said. "For what?"

"For getting out of here and making a life. I read that piece about you and your partner in the *Times* years ago. You've been brave and true and I love your books. These fools here don't even know what you've gone through, but I can guess. I think you're great. Now come and meet Bert."

Bert turned out to be as genuine and welcoming as Bunny. I heard about their wonderful children and the tragedy of the one they lost. The crowd was sweeping us into a room where tables were set up for lunch. An orchestra began to play "In The Mood" and a few old people did halfhearted jitterbug steps. I kissed Bunny.

"It's just been wonderful to see you," I said. "you're a wonderful friend."

I slipped away. There was no reason to stay in a room with the others. They would never be people I would want to know. Let the young boy stay with them and try to get them to notice him. The older Alan finally knew better. I took off the pin with my picture as a young boy and put it in my pocket. Jack was gone. All the young people on the pins were gone. We had to deal with what we were now. The past was past.

It was 1:30 when I got to the museum, too early for Norman to be outside, so I parked the car and went in. There was an endless line waiting for tickets, and I realized I would never find Norman in the maze of galleries, so I went into the bookshop and looked through pictures and artifacts for sale. I kept checking the time. What if I missed Norman and had to go back to the Marriott to find him? Every few minutes I went to the front of the museum, but I knew he wouldn't be there.

At 2:20 I walked out into the main lobby and there, with his back to me, looking out the front door, was Norman. I saw his hair, turning gray, a little too long in the back, curling over his Irish tweed jacket. His corduroys were wrinkled, and beside him on the floor was a shopping bag with, what I knew, were newly purchased art books. *He looks like the fine artist he has become*, I thought.

"Norman," I said, and my eyes welled up when he turned and smiled at me.

"Did you find what you were looking for?" he asked.

"Yes," I answered, "I found you."

CPSIA information can be obtained
at www.ICGtesting.com
Printed in the USA
LVHW060326070623
749043LV00016B/300/J

9 781950 544387